THE WORLD OF HASIDISM

THE WORLD OF HASIDISM

by

HARRY M. RABINOWICZ

HARTMORE HOUSE – HARTFORD

First published in Great Britain 1970
by Vallentine, Mitchell & Co. Ltd.,
18 Cursitor Street, London E.C.4

SBN: 87677-005-7

Library of Congress Catalogue Card No: 79-113413

Manufactured in Great Britain

Contents

Illustrations

*To the Revered Memory of
Michael (1882–1960)
son of Aaron Jacob Caplin*

Preface

In the mid-eighteenth century Eastern Europe gave birth to the greatest revivalist movement in Jewish history. This was Hasidism, the cataclysmic force that wiped away the narrow intellectualism that had estranged the Jewish masses from their heritage. Hasidism was not a new form of Judaism but a renewal of Judaism. It focused upon sublimely simple principles—the joy of living, love of God and man, service to God and man, genuineness and dedication. In the Hasidic perspective the man in the market place could draw as near to his Father in Heaven as the scholar in his study. Mystically, almost miraculously, Hasidism brought comfort, courage, and a form of other-worldly ecstasy to these suffering step-children of humanity. For Hasidism is more than a collection of ideals and noble purposes. It is a way of life, a civilisation, a culture with a message that transcends the barriers of time and place.

Like drowning men, the Jews of Eastern Europe clutched at this rejuvenated Judaism. From the Ukraine the movement spread across the border to Poland, Hungary and Rumania. As the flames of Jewish life were extinguished in Nazi Europe, sparks flew even further and the fires began to burn with a new brilliance in Israel and the United States. Great men arose, *Zaddikim*, who by precept and by practice led the people in the paths of the Torah, helped them to live full and satisfying lives on earth, and to reach for a world beyond this world. In the past two centuries Hasidic Jewry has produced more outstanding leaders than in any other period since the Talmudic era.

Hasidic philosophy has added a new dimension to daily life, and some three thousand works of Hasidic literature have enriched the minds of men. This literature still awaits its bibliographer. Historiography has never been a Hasidic pursuit. With very few exceptions, its chroniclers were not Hasidim. The Yivo Institute in New York is carefully collecting material, but there is nowhere a centre specifically

9

devoted to Hasidic research. In recent years, however, the meteoric movement that flashed with such dazzling brilliance across the Jewish firmament has attracted the attention of theologians, philosophers and historians. Many writings have appeared, ranging from analytical studies to table talk. Yet there are few books in English that give a concise account of the movement as a whole, particularly during the last century. In this respect, "The World of Hasidism" breaks new ground. This book is based on my "Guide to Hasidism", published in 1960. It has been rewritten and expanded and new chapters have been added. I offer it as an introduction to Hasidism, as a tribute to my own parents, and to the memory of the Hasidim who perished in the Nazi Holocaust.

It remains for me to acknowledge my thanks to Mr. J. L. Singer, M.B.E., Mr. A. J. Gleiser and the Rev. Dr. Julian G. Jacobs, M.A., for helpful comments and suggestions. I am indebted to Mr. M. Janovitch, Mr. J. Newman, Mr. A. Epstein and Mr. Arthur C. Lichtig for many of the illustrations. I gladly take the opportunity also of thanking the Memorial Foundation for Jewish Culture, New York for its fellowship grant. I want to express my deep and warm gratitude to my sisters, Miriam and Rachel, for their unstinting help and constant encouragement.

H.R.

London, July, 1969.

Chapter 1

"Here Dwelleth the Lord"

The history of the Jews in Poland can be traced continuously, period by period, for over a thousand years. Jews had begun to settle there before Christianity had found general acceptance in Eastern Europe, and so closely did the Jews associate themselves with their new homeland that its name was etymologically interpreted in Hebrew either as *Poilin* ("Here shall ye dwell"), or *Polaniah* ("Here dwelleth the Lord").

Poland stretched from Smolensk beyond the Dnieper, in the East, almost to the Oder, in the West; from the Duchy of Courland on the Baltic, in the North, to the Dniester, in the South. From all directions —from the South and from the East, from the land of the *Khazars* (Crimea), but most of all from the West, Jewish emigrants flowed in ceaseless streams towards Poland and Lithuania. Many factors were responsible for these mass migrations: the First Crusade of 1096 had brought death and desolation to the ancient communities which flourished on the Rhine and the Moselle; the Black Death (1248–1351), for which the Jews were the inevitable scapegoats; the expulsion from France in 1394; the terror of the fanatical fourteenth century Flagellants; vexatious discriminatory legislation and repeated massacres. The hysterical cry: "Kill a Jew and save a soul!" echoed and re-echoed throughout a blood-splashed Europe.

Just as, centuries later, Turkey was to play host to the Spanish and Portuguese exiles, so Poland welcomed these fugitives from Germany. The Mongol invasions of 1237 devastated large areas, and Boleslaw the Pious, Prince of the Duchy of Great Poland (1247–79) was among the many East European rulers who received the newcomers with warmth. Under the Magdeburg Law they were even granted special privileges. Indeed some of these Eastern European rulers were centuries ahead of their times in tolerance and ecumenism. "The Russians may pray according to their usage, the Poles according to theirs," declared Grand Duke Gedymin (1316–41) of Lithuania, "and we Lithuanians shall worship according to our own custom. For have we not all one God?"[1]

In Poland the aristocracy, which formed about eight per cent of the population, paid virtually no taxes and enjoyed many financial dispensations. They were, for instance, exempt from the payment of import and export duties. The peasants, on the other hand, were enslaved and subject to feudal jurisdiction, which up to 1768 gave their masters the right to inflict the death penalty. The serf either tended his lord's land or else paid dues in the form of produce. Poland needed middle-class administrators to develop its industry and commerce, and the nobility needed financiers. The Jews were well-equipped to play these diversified roles.

With practical measures Poland made her new and much-needed citizens feel at home. As early as 1264, Boleslaw the Pious granted the Jews inviolability of person and property. These rights were confirmed by almost all the Polish kings and became part of the country's Common Law. Jews were free to travel wherever they wished. They were exempted from the jurisdiction of the Common Courts and were empowered to settle among themselves disputes in which both the plaintiff and the defendant were Jews. It is no wonder that Rabbi Moses Isserles (1525–72) lauded in lyrical terms the hospitality of the new-found homeland: "Had not the Lord appointed this land as a refuge, the fate of Israel would indeed have been unbearable. By the grace of God, both the King and the nobles are favourably disposed towards us. In this country there is no fierce hatred as there is in Germany."[2]

By 1570 some three hundred thousand Jews had settled in Poland, residing in one hundred and sixty localities and forming the second largest Jewish community in the world (the largest being in Turkey). At a time when Polish sovereignty extended from the Baltic to the Black Sea, the Jews were quick to recognise the country's economic potential. Whilst in other lands they were restricted mainly to money-lending and to petty trading, Jews here were able to participate in all branches of industrial endeavour. They imported from the East and exported to the West. They were silversmiths, tailors, printers, bakers, metal workers and innkeepers. They managed estates, collected tolls and customs and even distilled liquor. A third of the Jewish population became artisans of diverse kinds. Jewish guilds were established in more than fifty places.

Allied to these opportunities was an almost unparalleled degree of religious freedom, and Polish Jewry became the most elaborately organised Jewish community in Europe. On August 13, 1551, Sigismund II, who reigned from 1548 to 1572, laid the foundation of Jewish autonomy, and not since the days of the Patriarchs and the Exilarchs of Palestine and Babylon had Diaspora Jews been able to enjoy so full a measure of self-government. Every community had its own *Kahal* ("Town Council") which regulated every phase of life from the cradle to the grave: from the assessment and collection of taxes to the supervision of schools; from the maintenance of cemeteries to the selection of a *Shtadlan* ("Intercessor"), who mediated between the Jews and the King or nobles.

Above the local *Kahal*, rose a complex structure of supervisory organisations. The *Kahals* were responsible to district councils (*Gellilot*). The *Gellilot* in their turn were subject to the provincial councils (*Medinot*) and finally the *Medinot* were under the jurisdiction of the supreme governing body, "The Council of the Four Lands". This *Vaad Arba Aratzot* (or *Congressus Judaicus*), embraced Little Poland (including Cracow and Lublin), Great Poland (Congress Poland), Volhynia (Ostrog and Kremnitz), Red Russia (Eastern Galicia) and, for a while, Lithuania (Brest and Grodno). In 1623, a separate body was formed, called "The Council of the Principal Communities of the Province of Lithuania."

Functioning on a parliamentary level, the Council acted as the State's agent for Jewish taxation. It dealt with questions of industry and commerce, regulated the elections of the *Kahals* and approved the school curricula. "The representatives of the Council of the Four Lands," remarked historian Nathan Neta Hannover,[3] "remind one of the *Sanhedrin*, which in ancient days assembled in the Chamber of Hewn Stones (*Lishkat Hagazit*) in the Temple." Backed by the power and the resources of the State, the Rabbinate was almost as powerful as it had been in the days of Hillel and Shammai.

The Minutes (*Pinkas*—volumes)[4] published by Simon Dubnow and Israel Halpern throw much light on the diversity of rabbinic activities in sixteenth, and seventeenth-century Poland. However, while they dealt knowledgeably with political and financial matters, the rabbis concentrated primarily upon maintaining high moral and ethical standards.

A wide assortment of far-reaching edicts issued from the Rabbinate. Overly lavish celebrations and extravagances in dress were effectively curbed through a series of what amounted to sumptuary laws. "One is permitted to wear only two rings on a weekday, four on the Sabbath and six on festivals." Fraudulent business dealings, with Jew or Gentile, were severely punished and a bankrupt was subject to stringent penalties: he was imprisoned for a whole year and not appointed to any office for religious work. "If he already holds such office he is to be deposed and he shall not be called up to the Reading of the Law for a whole year or until he repays all his notes to his creditors."[5]

This elaborate "State within a State" was the ideal setting for intensive Torah education. *Torah is di beste sechorah* ("Torah is the best merchandise") runs the old adage which was the *credo* of the Polish Jew. The sixteenth century was the golden age of Polish Jewry, no less splendid than the golden age (900–1200) of Spanish Jewry, or the Talmudic period in Babylon.

"In no country," records Nathan Hannover, with justifiable pride, "was the study of the Torah so widespread among the Jews as in the kingdom of Poland. Every Jewish community maintained a *Yeshiva*, paying its principal a large salary to enable him to conduct the institution without financial worry and to devote himself entirely to the pursuit of learning. . . . The (poor) boys obtained their food either from the charity fund or from the public kitchen . . . A community of fifty families would support no fewer than thirty of these young men and boys, one family supplying board for one college student and his two pupils, the former sitting at the family table like one of the sons . . . There was scarcely a Jewish house in the whole kingdom of Poland where the Torah was not studied, and where either the head of the family, or his son, or his son-in-law, or the *Yeshiva* student boarding with him, was not an expert in Jewish learning."[6]

This Torah-centred life paid rich dividends. Polish Jewry brought forth a galaxy of savants, who charted new approaches to the fathomless "sea of the Talmud" and to the elucidation of the Codes. The *Haggaot* ("Glosses") of Rabbi Moses Isserles to Rabbi Joseph Caro's *Shulhan Arukh* ("Prepared Table") became textbooks for Ashkenazi Jewry. Scholars from Italy, Germany and the Holy Land sought guidance from Isserles and deferred to his judgements. Like many others, the youngest son of Manasseh ben Israel (1604–57) left his native Holland for Poland, "to pour water on the hands and to sit at the feet of the great ones of the Second Palestine."

It was in Poland that Yiddish grew to rich maturity. The medieval Germanic dialect (Middle German) of the Central Rhine region was transplanted and transformed, absorbing Hebraic and Slavic elements in the course of time. This friendly and familiar amalgam of many languages became known as Yiddish, mother tongue of successive generations, a unique form of Esperanto, second only to Hebrew in its influence on the Jewish masses of Eastern Europe and on the Diaspora at large.

The Jewish community paid dearly for its privileges. Every Jew paid capitation tax of one Polish gulden per head, as well as income tax. In addition, he paid a "purchase tax" on most of the commodities of daily life, including meat, needles, and liquor. Jews also contributed a substantial amount towards national defence.[7]

In the seventeenth century, the Jews were paying annual taxes amounting to one hundred thousand gulden, and by 1717, they were contributing two hundred and twenty thousand gulden a year. Yet, despite this heavy taxation, there was still some truth in the saying that Poland was "heaven for the nobleman, purgatory for the citizen, hell for the peasant and paradise for the Jew."

Lamentably brief was the duration of the golden epoch. In the seventeenth century, the Ukrainian steppes, that enormous stretch of prairie by the Dnieper and its tributaries, came under Polish sovereignty. The Polish nobility cruelly exploited and virtually enslaved the Ukrainian peasants. Their burdens were many and their rights nonexistent. All kinds of abuses were practised without redress, and the landlords farmed out their territories to agents who wrenched exorbitant rents from the hapless peasantry.

Inevitably, Polish oppression of the Ukraine culminated in catastrophe. The climax came under the leadership of a peasant called Bogdan Zinov Chmielnicki (1593–1657), who had been wronged by an arrogant Polish overlord. Encouraged by their priests, an unholy alliance of Tartars, Cossacks and peasants wreaked venomous vengeance, "with fire and sword", on the defenceless Jews, whom they regarded as the agents and allies of their oppressors. Hell was unleashed and a reign of terror began for the "heretical Pole and unbelieving Jew." In the battle of Kniazhey Biarak on May 6, 1648, the Polish Army was annihilated. With the death of the Polish King, Wladyslaw, the way was open for Chmielnicki to march unopposed through the Ukraine, White Russia, Lithuania and Poland.

A Russian historian describes the blood-lust of the barbarous hordes:

"Killing was accomplished by barbarous torture—the victims were flayed alive, split asunder, clubbed to death, roasted on coals or scalded with boiling water. Even infants at the breast were not spared. The most terrible cruelty was shown towards the Jews. They were destined to utter annihilation, and the slightest pity shown to them was looked upon as treason. Scrolls of the Law were taken out of the synagogues by the Cossacks, who danced on them in drunken frenzy. Then the Jews were placed upon the Scrolls and butchered without mercy. Thousands of Jewish infants were thrown into wells, or buried alive."[8]

Bestial beyond description were the atrocities committed by the raging Cossacks. The massacres of Nemirov, Tulchin, Zaslav, Ostrog, Narol and Kremenetz added crimson pages to the already overflowing volumes of Jewish martyrology. In Polonnoje alone, ten thousand Jews perished. Among the victims was Samson of Ostropol, the far-famed Cabbalist. In the Ukraine, over one hundred thousand Jews were slain and many communities were all but extinguished. Some seven hundred Jewish communities were sacked between 1648 and 1658. Only one-tenth of the Jewish population survived in the Ukraine.[9] Manasseh ben Israel, petitioning Oliver Cromwell to re-admit the Jews to England in 1655, gives the number of Jewish victims as 180,000.[10] The genocidal devastation of the *Gezerot Tah* ("The Fateful Events of 1648"), as the Chmielnicki massacres were known, ranks with the destruction of the Second Temple as one of the major disasters of Jewish history, to be surpassed only by the Hitler Holocaust of World War II.

As if the cup of suffering was not already brimming, murderous gangs continued to destroy the grievously depleted communities. In the words of Rabbi Moses Rivkes (d. 1671): "Throughout the whole of Lithuania, there then roamed bands of Russians and Cossacks, who devastated the cities and occupied, among other places, Plock, Vitebsk and Minsk. Whenever the Cossacks appeared, in their lust for spoil, they seized all the belongings of the Jews, whom they slaughtered in masses."

For the first time in history, Polish Jewish refugees, later to become a familiar sight, began to make their way to different countries; to Holland, England, Italy, Turkey and even Egypt. All the *Kahals* were in debt. Poverty was widespread, and in 1657 the Jews were threatened with mass expulsion.[11] "Many of the Jews were robbed or killed by our soldiers," recorded Polish King Jan Casimir on March 19, 1658, "and others were despoiled or massacred by foreign troops; many lost their lives under torture. Those who survived cannot find peace in the towns and at the marts. They cannot expect security. Those who sought refuge outside the Polish boundaries are afraid to return. I know that many of the belongings of the Jews who had been plundered by the citizens are still hidden by the pillagers, and the Jews are as yet unable to recover their losses."[12]

The rehabilitation of stricken Jewry was retarded by the Russian and Swedish invasions of Poland (1649–58) and by the revival of the blood libels. Sandomierz (1698–1710), Poznan (1736), and Zaslav (1747) were scenes of murderous rampages. "Just as Poland cannot do without the *Liberum Veto*," it was said, "so the Jews cannot have *matzot* ("unleavened bread") without Christian blood." Jacob Zelig (or Seleg) sought the intervention of Pope Benedict XIV, for "as soon as a dead body is found anywhere, at once the Jews of the neighbouring localities are brought before the Courts and charged with murder for superstitious purposes."[13]

For Poland, a period of endless anarchy and instability began, since the fate of the "elected" monarchy depended entirely on the whims of the capricious *Liberum Veto*, which became an integral part of the Polish constitution early in the seventeenth century. With one phrase: *Nie pozwalam* ("I do not permit it"), a veto that required neither explanation nor justification, any nobleman could not only doom any Bill under discussion, but could also bring about the dissolution of the *Diet*. Of the fifty-five Diets held after 1655, forty-eight produced no legislation. On accession, every monarch signed a pact (*Pacta conventa*) which virtually ensured his complete subordination to the will of the Diet, itself hardly a bulwark of strength and decisiveness. Nor was it in any position to enforce its decisions, for the Polish army numbered no more than sixteen thousand men at the most. "If this is liberty", commented the British envoy, "then the Lord preserve me from it."

Chapter 2

From the Mists of Mysticism

Mysticism virtually defies verbal definition. Perhaps it could be called "the flight of the Alone to the Alone." In essence it represents man's yearning to unravel the Divine mystery. To some, mysticism is synonymous with the occult, with spiritualism, clairvoyance, magic, visions and revelations. To others, it is "experimental wisdom," "knowledge of God through experience," or "the immediate awareness of the relation with God."

The term Cabbalah is found in the work of the philosopher Solomon ibn Gabirol (c. 1021–56) *Tikkun Middot Ha-Nephesh* ("Improvement of the Moral Qualities"). Yet it was not until the fourteenth century that it was generally associated with mysticism. The literal meaning of Cabbalah, which derives from the Hebrew root *Cabbel* ("to receive") is "tradition" or "acceptance". But although the mystical associations of the word Cabbalah are of medieval origin, the mystic tradition goes back to the very origins of Judaism. Not content with pondering the literal meaning of the Scriptures, the Sages delved deeply into *Sisre Torah* ("The Secrets of the Torah"). Every Biblical word was minutely explored, and the Bible provided ample scope for mystical flights. Thus, an intricate folklore was spun around the story of the Creation (*Maaseh Bereshit*) in the first chapter of the Book of Genesis and around the Divine chariot (*Maaseh Merkabah*) in Ezekiel's dream.

Every reference was minutely explored and a whole hierarchy of angelic beings was envisioned. The diligent and devout searchers wove layer upon layer of inspired conjecture around the power and significance of the very name of the Lord, the mighty and mysterious *Shem Hameforash* ("The ineffable Name of God").

Terrifyingly tortuous is the path of the mystic, and repeatedly men are warned to follow a smoother, straighter road. "Seek not things that are too hard for thee," counsels Ben Sira, author of *Ecclesiasticus*[1] "and search not things that are hidden from thee." According to the Mishnah *Maaseh Bereshit* may not be expounded in the presence of two, neither may *Maaseh Merkabah* be expounded in the presence of one who is not a sage and, therefore, incapable of understanding. "Whosoever speculates upon four things, what is above and what is below, what is ahead and what is behind, such a one should never have been born, for he dishonours his Creator."[2]

Warnings did not discourage the passionate pilgrims, and many embarked on the perilous passage towards the Great Unknown. Not all the voyagers could navigate the strange and stormy seas, and relatively few arrived safely at their destination. The Talmud records the fate of four celebrated scholars. "Four men entered the Garden (*Pardes, i.e.* Paradise) Ben Azzai, Ben Zoma, Aher and Rabbi Akiba ... Ben Azzai looked and died. Ben Zoma looked and lost his sense. Aher mutilated the shoots (became an apostate). Only Rabbi Akiba went up unhurt and went down unhurt."[3]

Among the fabled masters of mysticism were Rabban Johanan ben Zakkai and his disciples, Rabbi Joshua ben Hananiah and Rabbi Jose; Rabbi Phinehas ben Yair and Rabbi Nehuniah ben Hakaneh. Many legends sprang up around the mystics. Rabbi Oshaiah and Rabbi Haninah ben Dosa, we are told, created a three-year-old calf,[4] and Rabbi Joshua ben Levi transformed cucumbers and pumpkins into deer and fawns.[5]

Although some authorities were opposed to the mystical speculations, others regarded them as an integral element of Judaism. "On Judgement Day," declared Rabbi Ishmael, "the Great Judge will ask each scholar: 'My son, since you have studied the Talmud, why have you not also studied the *Merkabah* and perceived My splendour?'"[6]

"The Cabbalists received their tradition from the Prophets," affirmed the eighteenth-century Rabbi Jonathan Eibeschütz (1696–1764).[7] For post-Biblical literature is rich in mystical concepts. Around these concepts an intricate symbolism was evolved by Philo (c. 20 B.C.E. to 40 C.E.), the philosopher who aimed at blending the Hellenistic and Jewish cultures. The Philonic concept of *Logos* (the Greek for "word", "speech" or "reason") sought to bridge the gap between the transcendent God and the world.

Hebrew has many synonyms for mysticism and its practitioners: among them are *Hokhmah Nistarah* ("Hidden Wisdom"), *Raze Torah* ("Secrets of the Torah"), *Yorde Merkabah* ("Riders of the Chariot"), *Yod'e Hen* ("Knowers of Grace"), *Ba'ale Ha-Sod* ("Bearers of the

Secret") *Dorshe Reshumot* ("Searchers of Scriptures"), *Hakhme Ha-Tushiah* ("Students of profound knowledge"), *Yodim* ("Gnostics"), *Anshe Maaseh* ("Men of Action") and *Baale Abodah* ("Masters of True Worship"). The mystical tradition can be traced from the martyred *Tanna*, Rabbi Akiba (c. 40–135), to the Chief Rabbi of the Holy Land, Abraham Yitzhak Kook (1865–1935). Moreover Cabbalah has a library of nearly three thousand printed works and an equal number of manuscripts in private and public collections.

Cabbalah is divided into Contemplative or Theoretical Cabbalah (*Cabbalah Iyunit*) and Practical Cabbalah (*Cabbalah Maasiyit*). Theoretical Cabbalah concerns itself with the nature of God and the cosmos and with the tenets of dogma and ethics. God is the *En Soph* ("The Infinite"), "The Endless", "The most hidden of all Hidden", "The Boundless" and "The Transcendent".

How does one relate God, who is perfection, to the world, which is manifestly imperfect? The answer takes us back to the very dawn of Creation. For the world was created by emanations *Sephirot* (from the Hebrew word meaning either "to count", "brilliancy", or "luminary"). These emanations or agencies are *Keter* ("Crown"), *Hokhmah* ("Wisdom"), *Binah* ("Understanding"), *Hesed* ("Lovingkindness"), *Geburah* ("Power"), *Tipheret* ("Beauty"), *Netzah* ("Victory"), *Hod* ("Majesty"), *Yesod* ("Foundation") and *Malkhut* ("Sovereignty"). When Adam was exiled from Eden, the *Shekhinah* ("Divine Presence") was exiled from the *En Soph*. This explains the evils in the world, and thus the mystics sought to reunite the *En Soph* with the *Shekhinah*.

The Holy Land was the birthplace of Cabbalah, and it was there that a number of studies were written by Talmudists. The *Hekhalot* ("Palaces") literature, as the mystical *Midrashim* written in the early Rabbinic and Geonic periods are known, describes in astonishing detail the halls and palaces, the Household of the Upper World (*Pamelia shel Ma'alah*), the Ministering Angels (*Malakhe Ha-Sharet*), the Angels of Destruction (*Malakhe Habula*), the *Shedim* ("Roving Spirits"), *Ashmodai* (the King of the Demons), *Lilit* (the Demon of the Night) and *Dumah* (the angelic supervisor of the souls of the nether world).

A major work of mysticism is the little book *Sepher Yetzirah* ("Book of Creation") which contains only six small chapters. According to legend it was written by the Patriarch Abraham, but there is reason to believe that it was written in Palestine or Babylonia between the third and sixth centuries of the Common Era. Both Saadia Gaon of Sura (882–942) and Gaon Elijah of Vilna wrote commentaries on it.

The chief premise of this intriguing treatise is that the world was formed through the "thirty-two ways of wisdom"—the twenty-two letters of the Hebrew alphabet plus the ten *Sephirot*. Other topics are the *Zeruf* (Esoteric alphabetical combinations) the *Gematria* (calculations based on the numerical value of the letters), *Notarikon* (Acrostics) and *Temurah* (changing the meaning of a word by transposing its letters).

According to Eleazar ben Judah of Worms (c. 1160–1238), the author of *Sepher Ha-Rokeah* ("The Book of the Spice Dealer"), it was the ninth century Aaron ben Samuel of Baghdad, who sowed the seeds of mysticism in Italy. His pupil, Moses ben Kalonymos of Lucca, carried his teachings to Germany and, during the twelfth and thirteenth centuries, the *Haside Ashkenaz* ("the pious men of Germany"), made their contributions to Cabbalistic lore: *Sepher Hasidim* ("The Book of the Pious") in which Samuel He-Hasid and Judah He-Hasid of Regensburg (d. 1217) dealt both with the soul's strivings and the body's need for a life of devotion. The book has been described as "a noble commentary on the verse 'Love thy neighbour as thyself' (Lev. xix. 18). Some of its dicta equal the best moral utterances of all ages."[8]

Notable contributions to mysticism were made by the pseudo-Messiah, Abraham ben Samuel Abulafia (1241–after 1291). After failing to convert Pope Nicholas III to Judaism, he journeyed to Sicily, where he proclaimed himself the Messiah. The author of twenty-six works, the majority still in manuscript form, Abulafia propounded a "prophetical Cabbalah" (*Cabbalah Nebuit*) that centred on the mystical significance of the four-lettered Name of God. For he believed that devout contemplation of the Divine Names could produce a state of ecstasy. "They called me heretic and unbeliever," lamented Abulafia, "because I had resolved to worship God in truth."

"I thank God every day that I was not born before the *Zohar* was revealed," said Rabbi Phinehas of Koretz (Korzec), "for it was the *Zohar* which knit my very soul to Judaism." Apart from the Torah, no other book is as highly venerated by the Hasidim as the *Sepher Ha-Zohar*, which became the Bible of the Cabbalist.

The origins of the "Book of Splendour" are obscure. It was discovered in the late thirteenth century by the Spanish Cabbalist, Moses ben Shem Tob de Leon, who attributed authorship to the second century *Tanna*, Simeon ben Yohai. A Midrashic and Cabbalistic commentary on the Pentateuch, the Zohar was written in Aramaic.

Throughout the ages scholars have debated on the authorship of the Zohar. Isaac of Acco, Elijah Delmedigo (1591–1655) and Jacob

Emden, among others, maintain that the Zohar cannot possibly date back to the second century. They cite innumerable anachronisms such as references to the Crusades and to Islam, the use of vowels and accents and linguistic formations. Graetz labelled it a "clumsy forgery" and other scholars detect the work of several hands in this complex composition.

"Every word of the Torah contains many levels of meaning and embodies a sublime mystery. The narratives of the Torah are like outer garments. "Alas for the man," comments Rabbi Simeon ben Yohai, "who regards the Torah merely as a book of tales and profane matters."[9] In this spirit the Zohar strips off the semantic screens and attempts to pierce the very core of every Biblical phrase or letter. Among concepts discussed by the *Zohar* is the transmigration of souls (*Gilgul*): "All souls must undergo transmigrations. . . . Men do not understand the ways of the Holy One. . . . They know not how many transmigrations and hidden trials they have to undergo, nor do they know the number of souls and spirits which enter into the world and which do not return into the palace of the Heavenly King."

After the expulsion of the Jews from Spain in 1492, the Holy Land became the scene of a remarkable Cabbalistic renaissance. High on the slopes of the graceful Galilean hills, looking across to lofty snow-capped Hermon, lies the picturesque townlet of Safed, which, in the sixteenth century, became the home of many celebrated scholars. Here lived the far-famed masters of mysticism, men whose vision added new light and new dimensions to everyday life. By means of self-affliction (*Siguphim*), fasts (*Taaniyot*), ablutions (*Tebilot*) and ardent worship, they strove for a closer communion with God. For them prayer was a means of ascent. For them, every word, every gesture, every act, every thought, was fraught with untold significance. Every blade of grass, every budding flower, every element of nature, was a manifestation of the Creator.

To the mystics, the Sabbath was particularly precious, for it was, in essence, a foretaste of the World to Come. With fervour, with prayer, with love and with song, the Cabbalists welcomed the Seventh Day. It would require a Rembrandt or a Chagall to picture the scene when, on Friday afternoons, the white-robed sages, their faces lit with holy joy, would form a procession through the winding lanes of the little picture-book town, chanting the Psalms and *Lekhah Dodi* ("Come my beloved") as they welcomed the Sabbath bride. Here lived the codifier, Joseph Caro, whose diary, published under the title *Maggid Mesharim* records a mystical midnight revelation. Here lived Moses ben Jacob Cordovero (1522–70), the author of thirty works, among them an exposition of Cabbalistic doctrines known as *Pardes Rimmonim* ("Garden of Pomegranates").

King of the Cabbalists was Isaac Luria Ashkenazi, known as the Ari ("Lion") or "The Holy Lion" (*Ari Ha-Kodosh*) (1534–72). Luria was probably born in Jerusalem and lived for a time in Cairo. He studied under Rabbi Bezalel Ashkenazi (d. 1590), author of *Shittah Mekubbetzet* ("Collected Opinions"), but his spiritual mentor, the mystics believe, was rumoured to be Simeon ben Yohai himself. Luria believed himself to be the Messiah ben Joseph. In a letter to his son, Isaiah Horowitz (1565–1630) writes: "Three supremely great men lived here at the same time—our teacher Rabbi Joseph Caro, Rabbi Moses Cordovero and Rabbi Isaac Luria, of blessed memory. These were veritable angels of the Lord of Hosts. The revered principals of the Academies on High, the sages of the Mishnah and even Elijah of blessed memory appeared to them."[10]

It was the "Holy Lion's" chief disciple, Hayim Vital of Calabria (1543–1620) who, in *Etz Hayim* ("Tree of Life") and *Shaare Kedushah* ("Gates of Holiness"), both formulated and recorded the Lurian doctrines. The cornerstone was the daring concept of *Tzimtzum* ("Withdrawal" or "Contraction"), whereby God withdraws from Himself to Himself in order to leave space for the world to be created. The vacuum (*Halal*) was illumined by a thin light of God. When God's light re-entered this space, it did so by means of the *Ten Sephirot*. However, during the delicate re-entry process the lights (*Orot*) of the *En Soph* were shattered. This is known as "the breaking of the vessels" (*Shevirat Kelim*) or the "Death of the Kings". This explains how God can be both immanent and transcendent. Holy sparks were scattered throughout all creation, and the Divine Light was trapped by *Kelipot* ("Isolating shells"). Thus the "vessels" and the "shells" are of paramount importance, for they contain minute particles of the *En Soph*. It is the duty and role of man to awaken the dorman sparks, to redeem the lost ones by prayer and by *Tikkun* ("perfecting"). Only when all the Holy Sparks have been released can the Messiah come.

In these uncharted regions Isaac Luria broke new metaphysical ground. He was a brilliantly original thinker, a man of far-ranging imagination, endowed with what we would today call extra-sensory perception. He could sum up a man's inner essence on sight. He believed that every man left his imprint on the world. He believed that man could, if he willed it, turn "evil spirits" into "good spirits". Luria advocated asceticism, fasting, self-mortification and humility. Every night, a man should say: "Lord of the Universe, I forgive all who have angered and injured me today, whether wittingly or unwittingly, whether in deed or thought. May no man be punished for my sake or because of me."

Glimmer of Hope

Intrinsic to Judaism is belief in the Messiah, who will fulfil the Biblical prophecies and gather together the scattered remnants of the House of Israel. "I believe with perfect faith in the coming of the Messiah," the devout Jew every day declares, "and though he tarry yet will I wait daily for his coming." For this is one of the Thirteen Articles of Faith compiled by Moses Maimonides (1135–1204). And these were the poignant words *Ani Maamin* ("I believe") that the martyrs of the Holocaust sang with death-defying valour as they entered the valley of the shadow of death. For thousands of years, with a fidelity that never faltered and with a yearning that was never stilled, the House of Israel has believed in and has waited for its promised Redeemer.

Like shooting stars, false Messiahs flashed across the skies of Jewish history, so that the flame of Messsianism glowed through the darkness of the endless exile. But in the wake of each falling star came disillusionment, despair and disaster. Rabbinic writings clarified the veiled Messianic allusions in the Bible, the Apocrypha and the Pseudepigrapha. Jewish eschatology envisaged a two-fold Messiah: Messiah ben Joseph, who would subdue *Gog* and *Magog* (the arch-forces of evil) and Messiah ben David, who would establish the kingdom of God on earth and rule over Israel at the end of days. The Jewish Messiah is not a divinity, but a man, an offshoot of the House of David, the long-awaited Prince of Peace, who would inaugurate a golden age of universal brotherhood. Many were the legends woven around the ubiquitous Elijah, precursor of the Messiah, and other dramatis personae of the Apocalyptic vision.

Again and again pretenders arose to raise and then dash the hopes of the people. Akiba, one of Judaism's best-loved Sages, hailed as Messiah Simeon bar Koziba or Bar Kokhba ("Son of the Star") applying to him the verse: "There shall come forth a star out of Jacob and a sceptre shall rise out of Israel" (Numbers xxiv. 17). With the destruction of the Temple and the ruthless sacking of Judea in 70 C.E., Rome thought it had crushed the spirit of revolt. While the whole of the ancient world was cowed, Jews hurled themselves again and again against the massed forces of the Roman Empire. Bar Kokhba led the epic battle that raged for three fearful years (132–135 C.E.). Thousands of Jews were killed and thousands perished as a result of pestilence and famine. "All of Judea," records the historian Dio Cassius, "became almost a desert."

Minor "Messiahs" often appeared on the Jewish scene. Among the more flamboyant ones was David Alroy. Alroy was a twelfth-century native of Kurdistan, who promised to liberate Persian Jews from the yoke of Islam. However, he was murdered by his father-in-law, and his supporters faded away. Another aspirant to the throne of David was David Reubeni, who claimed to be the plenipotentiary of his brother, King Joseph of Chaibar. Reubeni sought the endorsement of the Pope and appealed to Emperor Charles V and King Manuel of Portugal for help against the Turks. Reubeni perished, probably in a Spanish prison. Yet many believed in him and he fired the imagination of Diego Pires (1500–32) who called himself Solomon Molcho and declared that the Messianic era would commence in 1540. Unhappily Molcho did not live to see it; he was burned at the stake by the Inquisition in Mantua, in 1532.

According to Rabbi Israel Baal Shem Tov, even Shabbetai Zevi (1626–76), King of the Pseudo-Messiahs, was endowed with a "holy spark". Jewry was magnetised by his personality and inflamed by his prophetic imagination. Claiming that the Messiah ben Joseph had preceded him in the guise of the Polish Jew Abraham Alman, who was murdered by the Cossacks, Shabbetai Zevi proclaimed himself "Messiah the son of David". Shortly afterwards he was excommunicated by the Smyrna *Beth Din*. Although this was hardly a vote of confidence, his followers were not deterred and his chief aide, Nathan of Gaza, continued to issue Messianic manifestos. "It is difficult to describe the joy with which the reports of Shabbetai Zevi were received in Hamburg," wrote Gluckel of Hameln (1646–1724).[11] "Most of these letters were received by the Sephardim, who thereupon read them to the community assembled in the synagogue . . . Some of them unfortunately, sold everything—house, land and possessions—expecting to be redeemed immediately."

Isaac Primo, secretary to Shabbetai Zevi, issued an edict on behalf of his master, proclaiming that the Fast Day of *Av* had been transformed into a day of rejoicing. "From the first begotten son of God, Shabbetai

Zevi, Messiah and Redeemer of the people of Israel to all the children of Israel, peace. Since ye have been deemed worthy to behold the great day and the fulfilment of God's word by the prophets, your lament and sorrow shall be changed into joy, and your fasting into merriment, for ye shall weep no more . . . because I have appeared."

The marriage of Shabbetai Zevi to Sarah, the Polish orphan whose parents perished in the Chmielnicki massacres, together with the prophecies of Nathan of Gaza and the initial enthusiasm of the Polish Cabbalist, Nehemiah Ha-Kohen, convinced many of the doubters. Moreover the message fell upon eager ears yearning to hear of imminent redemption. "Soon will I avenge you and comfort you even as a mother comforteth her son", Shabbetai Zevi announced to Polish Jewry. "And I will recompense you a hundred-fold for the sufferings you have endured. The day of revenge is at hand and the year of redemption hath arrived."

Believers streamed to the "Castle of Spendour", Shabbetai's residence in Abydos near Constantinople. Yet Shabbetai Zevi preferred a Turkish turban to a martyr's death: he was converted to Islam on September 16, 1666, and for the remaining decade of his life was known as Mahmed "Effendi".

As the volcano subsided, the cinders were scattered far and wide as pygmies tried to tread in the footprints of the giants. Several Shabbetean supporters claimed the messianic mantle, among them Miguel (later Abraham) Cardoso (1630–1706), Mordecai of Eisenstadt (d. 1729), Judah Hasid of Dubno, Hayim Malakh, Nehemiah Hiya Hayum (1650–1726) and Herschel Zoref (1633–1700). In 1700 some fifteen hundred followers of Judah Hasid emigrated to the Holy Land. Nehemiah Hiya Hayum won the support of the *Haham* of London, Solomon Ayllon (1660–1728).

The most notorious of the pseudo-Messiahs was Jacob Leibowitz Frank (1726–91) of Galicia, a one-time clerk and travelling salesman. He joined the Donmeh (Turkish for "Apostates") the Judeo-Moslem sect derived from the followers of Shabbetai Zevi. Later, when he proclaimed himself Messiah, orgies took the place of mystic speculations, and immoral rites were the order of the day. To Bishop Dembowski of Kamenetz-Podolsk, Frank declared in 1757: "The Talmud pretends to be an interpretation of the Bible, but it is full of lies, baseness and opposition to the Torah itself." Ironically enough, Jewry sighed with relief when, in 1759, Jacob Frank and his followers embraced Christianity.

Social Conditions

In Eastern Europe class divisions were clear-cut. The scholars had as little in common with unlettered masses as the Polish nobles had with the peasantry. The scholars lived in a rarefied world of their own, a world of *Tannaim, Amoraim* and *Geonim. Halakhah* sharpened their intellect and the *Aggada* broadened their spiritual horizons.

Primarily, almost exclusively, they focused upon the study of Talmudics and Rabbinics. The philosopher, Joseph Solomon ben Elijah Delmedigo, points out that "the Jews of Poland are opposed to the sciences . . . The Lord hath no delight in the sharpened arrows of the grammarians nor in the measurements of the mathematicians and the calculations of the astronomers."[12] "Talmudic scholarship," records the philosopher Solomon Maimon (1754–1800), "constitutes the principal object of education among us. Wealth, physical beauty, accomplishments of any kind, though appreciated by the people, do not command the same claim on any office and honorary post in the community."[13]

At this time the power of the *Kahal* was weakening. The reins were in the hands of a few wealthy oligarchs, who were indifferent to the wretched plight of the people. In *Yesod Yoseph* ("Foundation of Joseph"), Rabbi Joseph of Dubno describes the late seventeenth-century scene: "The leaders live in luxury and splendour and do not fear the burden of taxes and other communal levies. They impose heavy burdens upon others and lighten their own burdens. They take the lion's share of all honours and distinctions . . . and the congregation of God, the children of Abraham, Isaac and Jacob, are crushed and humiliated, left naked and barefoot by heavy taxes. The tax collectors come to their homes and cruelly extort payment and rob them of all they find. They are left without furniture and without any utensils and without clothing for wife and children. Everything is removed and sold to cover the taxes. The very straw is taken out from the beds of the poor, and they are left in the cold and rain, shivering and crying, each in his corner, husband, wife and children."[14]

The *Yishivnicks* ("country folk") were at the mercy of the squires. "One never sees a smiling peasant in Poland," an adage current at the time, applied equally to the Jews in the Eastern provinces. Most of them were scattered throughout remote hamlets far from the mainstreams of Jewish life.

Social contacts were restricted. The sexes were segregated. Adults prayed separately, children played separately. Child marriages were common. It was not until 1761 that the Lithuanian Council forbade the marriage of boys under thirteen and girls under twelve. Under these circumstances the *Shadkhan*, ("marriage broker") fulfilled a vital role. Although histrionics sometimes prevailed. In vain Jonah Landsofer, a seventeenth-century writer, pleaded: "Whenever you are arranging a marriage between two parties never exaggerate, but always tell the truth."[15] The Hebrew word for *Shadkhan* was taken as an acrostic of the phrase *Sheker dover, kesef notel* ("though speaking falsely, he takes money"). The Polish Council fixed the commission at two and a half per cent of the dowry in a local marriage, and at three per cent if the bride and groom had lived more than forty-five miles apart.

The rabbi in Poland was a salaried official. There was little real communication between him and his congregants. He advised them on ritual matters, but was far removed from the material problems that plagued them. It was rare for the rabbi to preach, except on such key occasions as *Shabbat Ha-Gadol* (the Sabbath before the Passover) and *Shabbat Shuva* (the Sabbath before the Day of Atonement). At such times he usually delivered a *pilpul* ("dialectical discourse") on some abstruse Talmudic passage, or he would attempt to reconcile two conflicting exegetical statements. "They make it their custom to display the subtleties of their learning and their hair-splitting casuistries," complained Rabbi Jacob Joseph of Polnoy. Fellow scholars may have been spellbound, but the masses were unimpressed. "Every one is hungry for power," testified Rabbi Jacob Joseph sadly, "and everyone cries out, 'I want to rule, for I am a scholar'."[16] It was not until much later that the masterly *Maggidim* ("popular preachers") arose, men like Rabbi Jacob Krants, the Dubner *Maggid*, whose discourses stimulated, enlightened and even entertained attentive multitudes.

In the eighteenth century, only a minute minority was privileged to attend a *Yeshiva*. For the great majority, the sole source of instruction was the *Heder* or the *Talmud Torah*, where instructors were not above reproach. Solomon Maimon gives a well-known description. "The school is a small and smoky hut, and the children are scattered, some on benches, some on the bare earth. The master, in a dirty blouse, sits at the table, holding between his knees a bowl in which he grinds tobacco into snuff with a huge pestle like the club of Hercules, whilst at the same time he wields his authority . . . Here the children are imprisoned from morning to night without an hour for themselves, except on Friday and half-holidays and on the New Moon."[17]

Rabbi Jacob Joseph of Polnoy censures the teachers in similar terms. "They find it more profitable to flatter and amuse the parents than to teach the children,"[18] lamented Rabbi Jacob Joseph. So the Torah was a closed book to most of the country folk. Superstition was rife in Podolia and Volhynia, where the massacres were still fresh in the minds of men, bewildered by the smouldering trails of the pseudo-Messiahs. "There is no country," it was said, "where the Jews are as much given to mystical fancies, devil-hunting, talismans and exorcisms of evil spirits as they are in Poland."[19] Some believed in the power of Amulets (*Kamayot*); others believed in magic. Stories of devils and *Dybbukim* ("disembodied spirits of the dead which entered the bodies of the living") were current. "The masses," records Rabbi Moses Isserles, "have taken to the study of the Cabbalah. Students of Cabbalah include simple men who do not know their right hand from their left hand, people who live in darkness and cannot explain the meaning of the weekly portion of the Torah or understand a passage of Rashi."[20]

Rabbi Isaiah Horowitz and Nathan Nata Spira (1584–1633), author of the Cabbalistic work *Megalleh Amukkot* ("Discoverer of the Deep Things"), were the torch bearers of Cabbalah in Eastern Europe. And so highly was Cabbalah esteemed, that Rabbi Joel Serkes declared: "He who denies the truth of the wisdom of Cabbalah is called a heretic." Avidly the people read the ethical book *Kav Ha-Yashar* ("Measure of Righteousness") by Rabbi Zevi Hirsch Kaidanover (1654–1712), with its stories of demons and *gilgulim* ("the wandering souls"). "O man," warns the author, "wert thou to know how many demons thirst for thy blood, thou wouldst abandon thyself entirely, with heart and soul, to Almighty God."

Among the people wandered *Baale Shem* ("Masters of the Name"), itinerant teachers who seemed to perform miracles, healing the sick and driving out *Dybbukim* by means of the Divine Name. Such men were Elijah ben Judah of Chelm (1514–83), Elijah ben Moses Ashkenazi Loans (1555–1636) of Worms, Joel ben Isaac Heilprin of Ostrog (mid-seventeenth century) and Sachiel Loeb Wormser (1768–1846), the Baal Shem of Michalstadt.

The eighteenth century was the age of enlightenment, a period in Western civilisation when traditional concepts concerning the nature of man and society were being scrutinised, challenged and reappraised. The European mind was dominated by man's belief in himself. In a humanistic framework, man divorced the Creation from the Creator and saw himself in control of the Universe. Yet this same era saw the rise of Methodism and Christian pietism as well as Hasidism. The Pietist movement in Germany, led by Count Ludwig von Zinzerdorf (1700–60) was specifically an anti-rationalist reaction, and similar reactions took place in other countries. The Polish Soncinians, Anti-Trinitarians of the sixteenth and seventeenth centuries fought for the simplification of dogma, as well as for social justice. At the same time, the Quakers in England and the Moravians in Central Europe stressed inwardness as the key to faith.

The Jews of Podolia, Volhynia and Moldavia were surrounded by an ocean of hatred, and the sky was overcast by clouds of medieval superstition. They needed a guide to lead them through the maze of misery, to comfort and to strengthen them. In answer to this need, the Baal Shem Tov arose and walked the earth.

Chapter 3

The Master of the Good Name

More legends have been woven around Rabbi Israel Baal Shem Tov, the "Master of the Good Name", than around Moses, father of the Prophets. Just over two hundred years have elapsed since his death, yet he seems to belong to antiquity. Facts and fable are so intertwined that biographers find it difficult to distinguish between them. So it happens that despite the lack of authentic data regarding his parentage and personal life, the picture of the Besht is both colourful and convincing, for we see him clearly through the eyes of his disciples.

Israel was born in 1698 or 1700 in Okopy,[1] a small town near Kamenetz on the borders of Podolia and Moldavia. For a time (1672–1698), Podolia belonged to Turkey; later, under the Treaty of Carlowitz, it was returned to Poland.

Hasidic tradition records that Israel's father, Eliezer, lived in captivity for many years. Yet, throughout his exile, he remained loyal to his father and true to his wife. And so he was rewarded with a son who was destined to "enlighten the eyes of Israel."[2] Another legend gives a different version of Israel's birth: it relates that Eliezer's hospitality was proverbial, and that in the spirit of the Patriarch Abraham he received all men, the destitute, the unlettered and the impious, with the same warmth that he extended to scholars. One day the host's loving kindness was put to the test. In the guise of a mendicant bearing a staff and bundle, the Prophet Elijah appeared at Eliezer's door on the Sabbath day. Although this desecration of the Holy Sabbath must have grieved Eliezer sorely, he did not by word or deed betray his displeasure. On the contrary, he took special care to make his guest feel at home. "Because you did not put a sinner to shame," Elijah assured his kindly host, "you will father a son who will be a light to the House of Israel."[3]

Eliezer died when that beloved son was still very young. He left the little lad few worldly possessions, but Israel was heir to his father's piety and wisdom. From his father he inherited a deep love of nature and genuine concern for his fellow man. "Always remember that the Lord is with you and therefore fear nothing, fear no one" were the dying words of the aged Eliezer. Israel often knew hunger, but he never knew fear and he never felt alone. "And it came to pass, after the death of the Besht's father," records the *Shibbe Ha-Besht*, "that the lad grew up and the Jews of the community dealt kindly with him because his father had been very dear to them. They therefore put him in the charge of a teacher for instruction, and he made rapid progress in his studies. It was a habit of his, however, to study for several days and then to run away from school. Then they would have to search for him and would find him sitting alone in the forest. They ascribed this to the fact that he was an orphan, and that he had no one to look after him and so had to make his own way in the world. They would, therefore, bring him back again to his teacher. And so it happened a number of times; he would run away to the woods in order to be alone until, finally, they lost interest and abandoned the plan of giving him to a teacher. And thus the lad grew up in an unusual manner."[4]

Meanwhile, Israel applied himself secretly to mystical studies, particularly to practical Cabbalah. The writings of Isaac Luria and of Hayim Vital became his vade mecum. Hasidic legend maintains that Israel even had access to the writings of the mysterious Cabbalist, Rabbi Adam, "the identity of whom has eluded all historians."[5]

Outwardly Israel lived an unremarkable life. Since he loved children he became a *behelfer* ("a teacher's assistant") at Horodenka, near Brody, and with kindness he controlled his little charges. No longer were the diminutive scholars dragged or driven to school. Every morning they sang as they followed their lively leader to class. Hasidim say that this daily procession of singing children was as pleasing to the Almighty as the songs of the Levites in the Temple.

Later Israel worked as *Shamash* ("beadle") and *Shohet* ("ritual slaughterer"). But it was as a patient and gentle teacher that he won the affection of the community. They even asked him to settle local disputes, for he was by nature a peacemaker; and it was in the course of an arbitration that he met Rabbi Ephraim Kutover of Brody, who happened to be passing through Horodenka. A shrewd judge of character, Rabbi Ephraim offered the youthful adjudicator his daughter in marriage. Israel readily accepted, with the provision that the betrothal be kept secret and that he be referred to in the betrothal document as "Israel ben Eliezer". But Rabbi Ephraim died before he reached home and the betrothal document baffled the prospective bride, since it contained no clue as to the whereabouts or identity of the bridegroom.

Later, when Israel arrived to claim his bride, the bride's brother, Abraham Gershon, a well-known Cabbalist whom Rabbi Jonathan Eibeschütz called "the pious rabbi,"[6] a member of the Beth Din,[7] was somewhat less than enthusiastic. His prospective brother-in-law seemed uncultured and uncouth. However, he could not persuade his sister to annul the betrothal. "Since our dear father made this arrangement," Hannah insisted, "we need not hesitate about it. Surely this is the will of God."

After the marriage, Rabbi Gershon attempted to "educate" Israel, but his attempts were not very successful. As the friction grew, the newly-wedded couple left Brody. Israel then spent a number of years in seclusion in mystical study and meditation. For him the vast and solitary grandeur of the Carpathian Mountains reflected the power and glory of the Creator. Hasidim relate that Israel's teacher at that time was none other than Ahijah the Shilonite, prophet during the reign of Solomon and teacher of Elijah (I Kings xi. 29). There is no evidence that Israel ever received rabbinical ordination. Nature, however, endowed him with qualities that more than compensated for the lack of formal qualifications. He also acquired a useful knowledge of the healing qualities of various herbs, and people began to come to him for medical advice. By 1736 he was known as Baal Shem Tov ("The Master of the Good Name") or by the abbreviation "Besht".

At first the Besht followed the pattern of the wandering wonder-workers who wrote Kamayot ("Amulets"), exorcised demons, prescribed segulot ("magical healing aids") and healed the sick. But soon he began to chart his own highly individual course. The kindest and most approachable of men, the Besht won the hearts of the poor and the humble. He communicated on equal terms with Dov Baer, the learned Maggid of Mezhirichi, and with the scholarly Jacob Joseph of Polnoy; and he was equally at home with the most ignorant cobbler or farmer.

After a short stay at Tluste (in Eastern Galicia), Rabbi Israel settled in Medzibozh, near Brody, in Podolia, and only occasionally did he visit outlying communities. Now he was able to concentrate on propounding his principles and putting his precepts into practice. In context some of these were little short of revolutionary.

It must be stressed that Cabbalah is a double-edged weapon, dangerous in the hands of charlatans and megalomaniacs, its theories are esoteric and its doctrines complex and obscure. Inevitably, Cabbalah had become the jealously guarded province of an intellectual élite, who revelled in its mind-intoxicating and mind-illuminating profundities. This was the rich inheritance that the Besht wished to share with the masses. He believed that all the children of Israel were entitled to enter the spiritual kingdom, and he threw open wide the heavy gates. For it was not enough that this knowledge should be available. It had to be intelligible. The privilege of the few was to become the prerogative of the many. Just as the "dry bones" in Ezekiel's vision were restored to life, so the Besht fashioned Cabbalistic abstractions into a living reality. Just as codifiers like Maimonides, Joseph Caro and Asher ben Jehiel, systematised the Oral Law into easily accessible compendia, so the "Master of the Good Name" simplified Cabbalah, constructing a road along which all could travel safely.

The fame of the Besht spread far and wide. Even his brother-in-law, formerly so hostile, became a devoted follower. For three years before his departure to the Holy Land, Rabbi Gershon lived in Medzibozh, a close companion of the Besht. For a time he even taught Zevi, Israel's only son. Writing to his brother-in-law in the Holy Land, the Besht makes this startling revelation: "On *Rosh Hashanah* ("The New Year"), 1747, I experienced an uplifting of the soul and I asked the Messiah, 'Let me know, Master, when thou wilt appear on earth', and the reply was: 'This shall be a sign unto thee, when thy teachings shall become known ... when all other men shall have the power of performing the same mysteries as thyself, then shall all the hosts of impurity disappear, and the time of great favour and salvation shall arrive.'"[8]

"I have come into this world," maintained the Besht, "to show man how to live by three precepts: love of God, love of Israel and love of the Torah." According to the Besht, there are no divisions between the sacred and the secular. God is everywhere. "No place is free of Him," and there are no veils between Man and his Creator. A man's soul is a reflection of the *Sephirot* ("Emanations"), and man's every act must reflect the worship of the Creator (*Avodat Ha-Bore*). "I place God before me always" (Psalms xvi. 8) was the principle of the Besht. The *Shekhinah* permeates all four orders: inanimate things, plants and living creatures, as well as man. God revealed himself to Moses in a bush of thorns as proof that His radiance might be glimpsed anywhere and everywhere. For those who have eyes to see, the world is a mirror in which is reflected the glory of God.

The Besht has often been described as a pantheist. However, the pantheism of the Besht had little in common with the pantheism of Benedict Spinoza (1632–77). Spinoza died thirty-two years before the Besht was born and the Besht was probably unaware of his existence. Yet it is interesting to compare their antithetical viewpoints. Spinoza believed in *Deus sive Natura*, the oneness of God and nature. He rejected traditional views of the nature of prophecy, the miracles and the Divine origin of the Torah. To Spinoza, God is immanent. To the Besht, He is both immanent and transcendent. Spinoza sees a world without a purpose. The Besht sees a world created to fulfil His purpose. Spinoza's God dwells in the world. The Besht's world dwells in God. For the Besht God, whom the Sages call *Ha-Makom* ("The Place"), is the place of the world and the world is part of His essence. "Spinoza's world is a world which goes on existing beyond the life which the individual man and woman has lived and beyond the death which the individual man or woman is going to die . . . The Hasidic world is the concept of a world as it is in this moment of a person's life; it is a world ready to be a sacrament, ready to carry out a real act of redemption."[9]

Far from being a casuistic philosopher the Besht was not concerned with speculative metaphysics. He spoke directly to the masses in a language they understood and he taught them what may be called "practical piety". Of course, his teachings were not novel, but his methods were. The anecdote, the parable, the metaphor and the aphorism, took the place of the *pilpul* ("dialectics"), appealing to the heart as well as to the mind. Not since the development of *Aggada* and *Midrashim* had the story been given such importance. To speak of the *Baal Shem Tov* is to speak in stories and legends that glow like sunrays in the darkness.

Though a child of the Cabbalah, the Besht rejected its asceticism. In his eyes, self-mortification was devised by Satan to afflict man both physically and spiritually. "The body must be strong for the worship of the Lord: therefore one must not weaken the body."[10] To his disciple, Rabbi Jacob Joseph of Polnoy, the Besht wrote: "And I received the letter composed by your unsullied hand and saw from its first two lines that Your Excellency believes fasting necessary. This shocked me to my innermost soul. By the counsel of God and His *Shekhinah*, I order you not to expose yourself to such danger, for this path is dark and bitter and leads to depression and melancholy. The glory of God does not dwell where there is sadness, but always where there is joy in performing His *Mitzvah* it prevails. This is well known to you, but I have uttered these teachings many times, as it is known to His Eminence—words which I have taught many times. Let them be upon your heart."[11]

Joy was the keynote of the Besht's philosophy. "Our Father in Heaven hates sadness and rejoices when His children are joyful. And when are his children joyful? When they carry out His Commandments."[12] This immediate, this worldly joy is the true reward, the greatest reward, for the performance of a good deed or the fulfilment of a commandment (*Mitzvah*). Rewards to be received in the World to Come are incidental, for a *Mitzvah* should be performed for its own sake. Tears of joy are permitted and are even desirable. But a man should subdue sadness and raise himself to the higher realms of joy. Should a man err, he is urged not to brood over his transgression, lest he sink further into a morass of melancholy. He should demonstrate the sincerity of his repentance by returning instantly, and with renewed ardour, to the service of God. For the evil impulse (*Yetzer Ha-Ra*) and the good impulse (*Yetzer Ha-Tov*) were created at the same time. God can be served by the evil impulse if the flame is directed towards Him.

The secrets of the upper world were revealed to the Besht he maintained, not because of the intensity of his studies but because of the intensity of his prayers. For man must pour his very essence into every word, into every God-directed thought. Prayer is part of the *Shekhinah*, which may be why the *Shekhinah* itself is called prayer.

But how can a man divest himself of the distracting influences and desires that constantly assail him? Song and dance are potent aids. For a man is like a ladder, his feet are on the ground but his head can reach the heavens.[13] Through *Bittel Hayesh* ("negation of self-existence") man can rise above himself. Even *Mahashavot Zarot* ("Unworthy thoughts") can be harnessed to godly purposes. When Rabbi Israel prayed, it seemed that all Creation listened in awe. His son Zevi related that his father once appeared to him in the shape of a burning mountain. "Why do you appear to me in this form?" enquired Zevi. "In this form I serve the Lord," was the reply. On another occasion, the Besht refused to enter a house of worship. "I cannot go in; the sanctuary is crowded with prayers," declared the Rabbi, standing on the threshold. To his puzzled listeners, he explained: "The prayers had been recited in a lifeless and mechanical manner. They had no wings with which to fly upwards to the higher spheres. Those poor prayers, lifeless, fill every corner of this House of God. So you see, there is no room for me to enter."

Worshipping with spontaneity was more important than worshipping at prescribed times. *Hitlahavut* ("enthusiasm") and ecstasy replaced formalism. The verse "All my bones say, Lord who is like unto thee!" (Ps. xxxv. 10) was taken literally, and when Hasidim communed with their Heavenly Father it seemed as if every rib, every fibre of their being was included.

In every single Israelite Israel perceived a spark, sometimes dormant of holiness. With boundless love and compassion he looked upon his people. Rabbi Israel once told a friend: "I believe that I love the most sinful member of the House of Israel more than you love your only son." For the Besht evil did not exist. "What shall I do with my son, he is so wicked?" asked a despairing father. "Love him all the more," was the characteristic counsel of the Besht.

Wherever he went, the Besht sought the straying lambs, fearful lest a single sheep be lost from the fold. For "God dwelleth with them in the midst of their uncleanliness." Deeply the Besht lamented the apostasy of the Frankists. "I hear the *Shekhinah* grieving and mourning," he once said. Yet he refused to give up the hope of their ultimate return to Judaism. "As long as the limb is attached to the body, there is still hope that it will be healed, but, after the limb is amputated, then everything is lost. Every member of the House of Israel, is a limb of the *Shekhinah*."

"Fire and brimstone" descriptions of hell and its horrors belonged to some of the *Maggidim* ("itinerant preachers"), whose harsh castigations he forthrightly condemned. "Woe unto those," the Besht declared, "who dare to speak evil of Israel. Dost thou not know that every Jew, when he utters even a brief prayer at the close of day, is performing a great work before which the very angels in heaven bow down in homage." Reprimands were not the way of the Besht. "God does not look on the evil side," he explained, "how dare I do so?" God alternates between the "attribute of justice" and the "attribute of mercy." The Besht dispensed only mercy. The Besht was the prototype of the *Zaddikim* who were to play so unique a role in Hasidism. "A helper is needed" explains Martin Buber, "a helper for both body and soul. He can heal both the ailing body and the ailing soul, for we know how one is bound up with the other and his knowledge gives him the power to influence both. It is he who can teach you to conduct your affairs so that your soul remains free, and he can teach you to strengthen your soul, to keep steadfast beneath the blows of destiny... The *Zaddik* must make communication with God easier for his Hasidim, but he cannot take their place ... The *Zaddik* strengthens his Hasid in the hours of doubting, but he does not infiltrate him with truth. He only helps him to conquer and reconquer it for himself... He develops the Hasid's own power for right prayer. He teaches him how to give the words of prayer the right direction, and he joins his own prayer to that of his disciple, and therefore lends him courage, an increase of power-wings,"[14]

Ceaseless strivings for communion with the Creator, constant cleaving to the Divine, are known as *Devekut* and this is the key note of the *Zaddik*'s life. Even seemingly ordinary conversations are conducted in such a way that the *Devekut* is not disrupted. Even when he is performing a *Mitzvah*, his absorption in the actual performance does not lessen his consciousness of its true purpose and ultimate end, the glorification of God. Hasidism believed that the *Zaddik* could bring heaven closer to earth, that his power was unlimited, that he could even abrogate evil decrees.

It is a popular misconception that the Besht disapproved of study. The fact is that he put a different emphasis on study. It was not simply an intellectual exercise. He believed that the Torah, the living words of the Most High, should transform the student. For man "must study the Torah to become a Torah." In the words of the *Mishnah*, it should "Clothe him in meekness and reverence; it fits him to become just, pious, upright and faithful; it keeps him from sin, and brings him near to virtue."[15] *Kavanah* ("sincerity") and *Hitlahavut* ("enthusiasm") were as essential in study as in prayer. Humility was important, too, and the scholar must guard against intellectual pride. Penetrating were the Besht's comments on the Torah and impressive his knowledge of Talmud and Cabbalah. According to legend, Rabbi Israel was one of the three scholars who participated in the public disputation between the Frankists and the rabbis which was held in Kamenetz-Podolsk in 1757. "They shall not take the Torah from us," he exclaimed, "for without it how shall we survive among the nations?" Yet, as we have noted, Rabbi Israel did not spend his boyhood in *Yeshivot* (Talmudical colleges). He was truly self-taught. He did not write learned books; this was the task of his successors, who faithfully recorded the doings and sayings of the great founder of Hasidism. This was a man of true qualities of mind and soul, of profound sensitivity and vision.

Rabbi Israel exercised great influence over his followers. No one could meet him without falling under the spell of his unique personality. His disciples loved him, revered him and all but worshipped him. "If he had lived in the time of the Prophets, he would have become a prophet." Rabbi Leib Sarah's, a contemporary of Rabbi Israel, averred: "If he had lived in the age of the Patriarchs, he would have ranked with them, so that just as one says 'God of Abraham, God of Isaac and God of Jacob,' one would also say 'God of Israel'." Among Rabbi Israel's devoted scholars was Rabbi Meir Margolies (d. 1790). "All secrets were revealed to him," testified Rabbi Meir.

On *Sivan* the seventh[16] (the second day of *Shavuot*), 1760 Rabbi Israel died in the presence of his family and disciples. With joyful anticipation he went to meet his Maker. "I do not lament my fate," he remarked comfortingly to the mournful bystanders. "I know full well that I shall leave through one door and enter through another . . . Let not the foot of pride overtake me." With this verse from the Psalms (xxxvi. 12), he was gathered to his fathers.

"The Praises of the Besht" (*Shibhe Ha-Besht*) was first published in 1815 in Kopyss and Berdichev. These were legends collected by Baer b. Samuel, the son-in-law of the first scribe of the Besht. A collection of the sayings of the Besht, *Keter Shem Tov* ("The Crown of a Good Name") compiled by Aaron ben Zevi Kohen of Opatov, was printed in 1794 in Zolkiew. Important, too, is *Zavaat Ha-Ribash* ("Testament of Rabbi Israel Baal Shem Tov") by Rabbi Isaiah of Janow, which was first published in 1793, and which has since appeared in twenty-six different editions.

In the eighteenth century, when the work of the scientist was demonstrating that the earth is not the centre of the universe but rather a small planet revolving with hosts of other bodies around the sun, the Besht considered that man constituted the centre of the universe. "Once in a thousand years," declared Rabbi Aaron of Karlin (1736–72) "does a soul like that of the Besht descend into the world."

Chapter 4

The Magic Circle

So Hasidism took root, but it was a tender plant. At first the movement was local, confined mainly to Podolia, Volhynia and Galicia. To capture Poland and Lithuania, a new kind of leader was needed, for only a Talmudist could influence the Jewish classicists. Fortunately there were among the sixty-nine disciples that tradition ascribes to the Besht many outstanding Talmudic scholars, bound to their master by unbreakable bonds of love and loyalty.

The only daughter of the Besht, Udel, was the mother of three children: Moses Hayim of Sudlikov (1748–1800), author of *Degel Mahne Ephraim* ("The Banner of the Camp of Ephraim"), a source book of Hasidic lore; Rabbi Barukh of Medzibozh (1757–1811), and Feiga, mother of Rabbi Nahman of Braclaw. The only son of the Besht, Zevi, was of too retiring a disposition to be his father's spiritual heir. But the survival of Hasidism was more important to the Besht than the perpetuation of his own dynasty. Like Moses, his successor was a stranger, not a son, and the "Joshua" of the Besht was Rabbi Dov Baer, *Maggid* of Mezhirichi (Miedzrzecze). Son of a Hebrew teacher, Abraham Dov Baer was born in 1710 in Lukatsch, Volhynia. The boy showed a great aptitude for learning, and he was soon sent to a *Yeshiva* at Lvov, where he studied under Jacob Joshua ben Zevi Hirsch Falk (1680–1756), author of *Pene Yehoshua*, novellae on the Talmud.

Eventually Dov Baer settled in Tulchin, where he became first a teacher and then a preacher—a *Maggid*—in Korzec and Dubno. It was as a *Maggid* that he became renowned, for he was both potent and persuasive. With graphic parables, he illumined abstruse texts, which suddenly became meaningful and relevant. The *Maggid* was, moreover, a diligent student of Cabbalah and adhered rigidly to ascetic Lurian practices that gravely undermined his health.

From the Besht, Dov Baer sought healing for his stricken body and received instead an elixir for his soul. His first visit was brief; but the second visit lasted for six months. "Your interpretations are correct," the Besht told his new disciple, "but they lack inspiration." Dov Baer recognised the truth of the statement. Humbly, thirstily, the Preacher of Dubno crouched at the feet of the Besht to listen and to learn. "He taught me the language of the birds and the trees. He revealed to me the secrets of the Sages and the mystical meaning of many things," recorded Dov Baer with awe. "Once, while we were studying the *Maaseh Merkabah* (the narrative concerning Ezekiel's Divine Chariot), we heard mysterious thunder and perceived flashes of lightning that continued for nearly two hours. I was terrified and I almost fainted."

The Master perceived that Dov Baer would be a suitable successor, and so it came to pass after the death of the Besht that the new leader settled in Mezhirichi. "What can be done?" asked Rabbi Jacob Joseph, submitting to the inevitable, "For since the day the Besht ascended to heaven, the *Shekhinah* has moved from Medzibozh to Mezhirichi and we are forced to bend our heads in obedience."

Failing health restricted Dov Baer's travels and confined him mainly to Mezhirichi, but what he was unable to do in person he achieved through his disciples. His court was the centre of a conclave of remarkable men, who later became the founders of distinguished dynasties. Seldom had so much talent been gathered in so small a town, for the *Maggid*'s court was a college and a spiritual training ground for future Hasidic leaders. From the Ukraine came Levi Isaac of Berdichev, Menahem Mendel of Vitebsk, Nahum of Czernobiel and Zeev Wolf of Zhitomir; from Lithuania came Aaron of Karlin, Shneur Zalman of Liozno and Rabbi Hayim Heikel of Amdur. "In the house of my teacher the holy *Maggid*," said Shneur Zalman, "you drew up holy spirit by the bucketful and miracles lay around under the benches, only no one had the time to pick them up."

Evangelising zeal was never the hallmark of Judaism in medieval times, but as far as fellow Jews were concerned, Hasidism became a "missionary movement." Rabbi Dov Baer's emissaries spread Hasidic fervour to remote villages and far-flung townships throughout Poland and Lithuania. Solomon Maimon testifies to the success of these mystical missions and describes one such encounter: "As I was quite captivated by this description, I begged the stranger to communicate to me some of these Divine teachings. He clapped his hands on his brow, as if he were waiting for inspiration from the Holy Spirit, and turned to me with solemn mien, his arms half bared, which he brought into action somewhat like Corporal Trim, when he was reading the sermon. Then he began as follows: "'Sing unto the Lord a new song; and his praise in the assembly of saints" (Ps. cxlix. 1). Our teachers explained this verse in the following way. The attributes of God as the most perfect Being must surpass by far the attributes of every finite being; and consequently His praise, as the expression of His attributes, must likewise surpass the praise of any such being. Till the present time, the praise of God consisted in ascribing to Him supernatural operations, such as the discovery of what is concealed, the foreseeing of the future and the manifestations of His will. Now, however, the Hasidic rabbis are able to perform such supernatural actions themselves. Accordingly, in this respect, God no longer has pre-eminence over them; and it is therefore necessary to find some new praise which is applicable to God alone.'"[1]

Maimon then describes his own visit to the *Maggid*. "At last I arrived at M . . . and, after having rested from my journey, I went to the house of the Master, under the impression that I should be introduced to him at once. I was told, however, that he could not speak to me at this time, but that I was invited to his table on the Sabbath along with the other strangers who had come to visit him . . . Accordingly, on Sabbath, I went to this solemn meal, and found there a large number of respectable men who had come from various districts. At length, the awe-inspiring Master appeared clothed in white satin. Even his shoes and snuff box were white, this being among the Cabbalists the colour of grace. He greeted every newcomer in turn. After the meal was over, the Master began to sing a melody awesome and inspiring. Then he placed his hand for some time upon his brow, and began to call upon such and such a person of such and such a place. Thus he called upon every newcomer by his own name and the name of his residence, which excited no little astonishment. Each recited, as he was called, some verse of the Holy Scripture. Thereupon the Master began to deliver a sermon for which the verses recited served as a text, so that, although they were disconnected verses taken from different parts of the Holy Scriptures, they were combined with as much skill as if they had been formed as a single whole. What was still more extraordinary, every one of the newcomers believed that he discovered, in that part of the sermon which was founded on this verse, something that had special reference to the facts of his own spiritual life. At this we were, of course, greatly amazed."[2]

For a short time the *Maggid* lived in Annopol, where he died on December 15, 1773, thirteen years after the Besht. "My sons, let there be unity among you," he had exhorted his disciples, "United you will prevail over all." Rabbi Abraham, "the Angel," succeeded his father. There are conflicting figures regarding the number of the *Maggid*'s disciples: estimates range from thirty-nine to three hundred. By this time there were Hasidim in many parts of the country, even in Vilna, the *Mitnagdic* stronghold.

What the Besht had achieved through parables, the *Maggid* achieved through discourse. Like the Besht, he himself did not write books. His discourses were published by his disciple, Rabbi Solomon of Lutsk (d. 1813), in three works: *Maggid Devarav L'Yaakov* ("He declareth his words unto Jacob") or *Lekute Amarim* ("collection of sayings"), *Or Torah* ("Light of the Torah"), on the weekly portions of the Pentateuch, and *Or Ha-Emet* ("Light of Truth"). In these discourses the *Maggid* explained his conception of the Diety, cosmology and the role of the *Zaddik*. If the Besht was the soul of Hasidism, the *Maggid* was its body. He created the Hasidic court. Unlike his master, who is reported to have visited at least fifty localities, the *Maggid* was homebound. Like the Besht, he taught that in every act or thought of man there is the Creator, for no move can be made without His power. There is, therefore, a divine manifestation in all human deeds, even in the evil ones. A man should be self-critical, and even when performing good deeds, he should scrutinise his actions to find out whether they are tinged with ulterior motives. Man can attain communion with God when he endeavours to rise to the upper worlds by raising his thoughts and aspirations. When praying, a man should not pray merely for his own material needs, but should pray that the *Shekhinah* should no longer be in exile.

The *Maggid* developed further the Hasidic concept of the *Zaddik*. He believed that the *Zaddik* could bring heaven and earth closer together, that unlike a cedar, mighty but barren, the *Zaddik* is as a palm tree which produces fruit and fills the air with fragrance, but in every human being there is a trace of Cain as well as of Abel.

Rabbi Jacob Joseph of Polnoy (d. 1782)

While the Besht gave birth to the movement and the *Maggid* developed and organised it, Rabbi Jacob Joseph Katz of Polnoy (Polonnoje) formulated its literature.

Like the *Maggid* he received a traditional Torah education. The descendant of such renowned scholars as Rabbi Samson ben Pesah Ostropoli (d. 1648), Rabbi Yom Tov Lipmann Heller (1579–1654) author of the commentary on the Mishnah *Tosephot Yom Tov* ("The Additions of Yom Tov") and Joseph Katz, author of *Yesod Joseph*, the youthful Jacob Joseph was famed for his mastery of both the Talmud and Cabbalah. Jacob Joseph became Rabbi in Sargorod, where he remained until 1748. Like the *Maggid*, he at first resisted the growing influence of the Besht. But finally he, too, entered the magic circle.

It is told that when the Besht once visited Sargorod, the entire community flocked to him. Rabbi Jacob Joseph was already in the Synagogue, awaiting the worshippers for morning service, but he waited in vain. When he sent the beadle to investigate, the messenger hurried to the market place and promptly forgot his mission, remaining to listen with the others. So Jacob Joseph prayed in exasperated solitude, finding it harder than usual to concentrate. Later he summoned the Besht and demanded: "Are you the one who disturbed the communal prayer?" "Your Excellency, I am the one," answered the Besht mildly. "But I entreat you not to be angry with me. Let me tell you a story . . ." Rabbi Jacob Joseph listened to the words of the Master and many things became clear to him. Thereafter, he became a fervent disciple of the Besht.

The sudden conversion to Hasidism of the revered rabbi of Sargorod was regarded with marked disfavour by the community. Rabbi Jacob Joseph was the first Hasidic leader to suffer indignities, persecution and even expulsion. He moved to rabbinic posts in Rashkov (1748–52) and Nemirov (1752–70) finally settling in Polnoy (1770–82).

The Besht was aware of his new adherent's great potential. "The Blessed One will thank me for finding Him a Yosele (Jacob Joseph) like this." On another occasion, he remarked: "All Jacob Joseph's works are pleasing to the Creator, Praised be His Name, and all his doings are in the Name of God."

Jacob Joseph followed the practices of the Lurian Cabbalists. He fasted each day until nightfall, and this continued for five years. In the sixth year, during one of Jacob Joseph's week-long fasts, the Besht heard a heavenly voice urging: "Hasten to your Jacob Joseph, otherwise he will die." The Besht rode with such speed that his good horse, worth twenty ducats, fell exhausted and died on the way. On arrival the Besht caused his ascetic disciple to break his self-destroying fast:

"My horse died on the road for your sake. Let it, therefore, be an atonement for you."[3]

Unfortunately, few letters of the Besht have been preserved. But one of these rare letters express the Master's deep affection for his "Yosele". It opens with the salutation: "From the community of Medzibozh . . . to my beloved, beloved of my soul, the Rabbi, the great luminary, right-hand pillar, strong hammer, renowned in piety, perfect scholar, he who is full of wonder and works wonders, who is bound up in the chambers of my heart, more close to me than a brother—our teacher Joseph Ha-Kohen."[4]

Yet Jacob Joseph was not chosen as the Besht's successor. At first he rather resented the *Maggid*, but he quickly came to acknowledge the wisdom of "our teacher, the Hasid Dov Baer."

After the death of the Besht, Rabbi Jacob Joseph devoted himself to writing and produced four monumental works: *Toledot Yaakov Yosef* ("The Generations of Jacob Joseph"), a commentary on the weekly portions of the Torah, which was first published in 1780 in Medzibozh and Korzec and has since appeared in many other editions; *Ben Porat Yoseph* ("Joseph is a fruitful vine"), published in 1781 in Korzec, which contains a commentary on Genesis, *Halakhic* material, responsa and the letter of the Baal Shem Tov to Gershon Kutover; *Zafnat Paneah* ("Revealer of Secrets"), printed in 1782 as a commentary on Exodus; and *Ketonet Passim* ("A coat of many colours"), which was printed in 1866, in Lvov.

The keen intellect and phenomenal erudition of Rabbi Jacob Joseph enriched the movement. Myths gave way to perceptive homilies and illuminating *Midrashim*. As the Baal Shem Tov had brought Cabbalah to the hearts of the people, so his disciple opened the minds of the scholars to the profundities and potentialities of Hasidism. Scrupulously he acknowledged his debt to the Besht. The formula, "I heard from my master," or "I heard from my master of blessed memory," occurs no fewer than five hundred and thirty-six times in the works of Rabbi Jacob Joseph.[5]

Patience and forbearance were not characteristics of Rabbi Jacob Joseph. He believed that attack was the best form of defence, and to defend Hasidism it was necessary "to demolish the citadel of the rabbinate." Severely he censured the rabbis, calling them the "little foxes who despoil the vineyard,"[6] for their sophistry, materialism and inaccessibility. "In former times when men were engaged in piety and learning for their own sake and not for the sake of honours and rewards, the scholar would seek the company of the uneducated and would conduct himself with modesty and humility so as to draw the plain folk nearer to their Father in Heaven; but it is not so in this generation, when there is no bond of feeling and unity between the learned and their less cultivated brethren."[7]

The teachers are castigated for their lack of dedication.[8] Slaughterers are reproved for relying solely on technical knowledge of the laws of *Shechitah*. Scholars are accused of pride and egotism. "Each one puffs up, saying: 'I shall rule. I am a greater scholar'."

Who, then, could counteract the effect of the hypocrites, the sycophants, the false prophets, "the satyrs", the "demons in the vineyard of the Lord?" Why the *Zaddik*, of course, the self-appointed mediator between man and fellow man, as well as between God and man. For Jacob Joseph, as for the *Maggid*, the *Zaddik* was a medium through which the Creator works. His feet must be firmly rooted in reality but, like Jacob's ladder, his thoughts must soar to the heights. Deep humility was needed, for he must walk and work in harmony with the plainest folk in order to set aflame the "holy sparks" and raise their spiritual status. The *Zaddik* was like Abraham, who pleaded for the doomed cities of Sodom and Gemorrah. He is not like Noah, who was totally indifferent to the fate of his generation and built an Ark to safeguard himself and his family without so much as a prayer for the rest of the world.

Rabbi Jacob Joseph died in Polnoy in 1782. He added new dimensions to Hasidic lore and his works are a valuable guide to Jewish socio-religious life in the eighteenth century. From Rabbi Jacob Joseph's prolific writings, the student can determine the Hasidic attitude to almost any problem. The opponents of Hasidism burned his works. Hasidim revered his writings. "Hitherto" declared Rabbi Phinehas of Korzec, "there have never been books such as these in the world." "Even in the days of the Messiah," said another Hasidic scholar, "there will not exist a mind like this."

Rabbi Phinehas of Korzec

Many stars revolved in the orbit of the Besht. One outstanding personality was Rabbi Phinehas Shapira of Korzec (Koretz). In 1708 Shklow was sacked by the Swedes under General Lowenhaupt, and the Shapira household took refuge in Miropole, in Volhynia. Phinehas son of Abba, a learned Lithuanian rabbi, was born in Shklow in 1726.

The young Phinehas studied mathematics and grammar as well as rabbinics. With particular passion, however, he applied himself to mystical studies, and the *Zohar* became the light of his life. "The Zohar", admitted Rabbi Phinehas, "has kept me in the Jewish faith.[9] The exile is very painful for me to bear. I can only find relief from it during the hours when I study the *Zohar*." To study the *Zohar* was the best remedy against pride. Study of the *Zohar* was more important to him than study of the Talmud, because the former had originated in the Holy Land, whilst the Babylonian Talmud was formulated in the Diaspora.

Diligently Phinehas pondered the works of Moses Cordovero and Isaac Luria. A book that rarely left his desk was *Maggid Mesharim* ("The Preacher of Righteousness") by Rabbi Joseph Caro, containing the secrets divulged to him on one hundred and thirty-five occasions by his heavenly mentor (the *Maggid*). Rabbi Phinehas suffered great privations. To earn a minimal livelihood, he taught children near Polnoy. Eventually he settled in Korzec, a centre of Talmudic learning, and there he came under the influence of Rabbi Isaac ben Joel Ha-Kohen, author of the Cabbalistic essays, *Brit Kehunat Olam* ("The covenant of the everlasting priesthood").

Rabbi Phinehas met the Besht three times and these meetings changed his life. It dawned on him that self-deprivation was not the only path to God. However, Rabbi Phinehas remained an innovator, and many of his customs were decidedly non-conformist. Unlike the Besht, he would don his phylacteries on the intermediate days of the Festivals without the customary benedictions.

Rabbi Phinehas favoured Rabbi Jacob Joseph as the successor to the Besht. He greeted the writings of Rabbi Jacob Joseph as "Torah from the Garden of Eden," classing them with the *Zohar* and the *Etz Hayim* ("Tree of Life") by Hayim Vital. He regarded Dov Baer, the *Maggid* of Mezhirichi, as a recluse, living in a manner that was the negation of the Besht's philosophy. He differed with the *Maggid* on basic approaches. Whilst the *Maggid* stressed the importance of wisdom, Rabbi Phinehas put the accent on practical ethics.

During this period (1708–70), the Haidamack gangs revived the grim memories of the Chmielnicki massacres. The onslaughts of these wild Ukrainian bands in the provinces of Kiev and Podolia culminated in the Uman massacre in 1768, and many Jews fled from the lawless Ukraine. Rabbi Phinehas urged them to remain in their homes. "Were it not for me," he later asserted, "not one Jew would have remained there."

Rabbi Phinehas himself was far from being a recluse. He followed political developments very closely and grieved over the disintegration of the Polish state. All his life he prayed for the preservation of Poland. "I am not strong enough," he once remarked, "to prevent the danger. Only Rabbi Nahman of Horodenka was strong enough to do this . . . So long as Rabbi Nahman was there this nation (i.e., the Russians) could not cross the Dnieper . . . When Nahman, however, crossed the Dniester (on his way to the Holy Land), I remained alone."[10]

"To pray," maintained Rabbi Phinehas, "means to cling to God. . . . When a man considers his prayers to be something apart from God, he is like a supplicant whose petition the king grants. But he who knows that prayer in itself is God, such a man is like the king's son, who takes whatever he needs from his father."

When the Baal Shem Tov lay dying, his disciple David of Ostrog sadly asked: "Rabbi, how can you leave us behind alone?" Comfortingly, if cryptically, the Master replied: "The 'bear' (i.e. Dov Baer) is in the woods and Phinehas is a sage." Phinehas had his adversaries among them Rabbi Solomon of Lutzk, who published the *Maggid*'s writings. To Solomon, the *Maggid* could do no wrong and Phinehas could do no right. Yet, when the Rabbi of Koretz died in 1791 in Sheptovka, his adherents vastly outnumbered his detractors.

Chapter 5

The Great Defender

"A noble and holy soul has descended into the world, and it shall be an eloquent advocate for the House of Israel". Rabbi Israel Baal Shem Tov is said to have greeted the birth of Rabbi Levi Isaac of Berdichev (1740–1809) with this prophetic proclamation. And the prophecy was fulfilled.[1]

Levi Isaac was born in Husakov, Galicia, into a family renowned for scholarship. His mother, Soshe Sarah, was a descendent of Rabbi Samuel Edels (1555–1631). His father, Meir, was rabbi in Zamosz. From his early years little Levi Isaac showed phenomenal aptitude for study. Soon he was known as a prodigy, the "Illui" of Jaroslaw.

When he married the daughter of Samuel Israel Peretz of Lubartow (near Lublin), he moved to his father-in-law's town. There he met men like Rabbi Joseph ben Meir Teomim (1727–93), author of the *Peri Megadim*, a commentary on the codes *Orah Hayim* and *Yoreh Deah*. It was Rabbi Shmelke Hurwitz (1726–78), later to become rabbi of Nikolsburg, who introduced Levi Isaac to Hasidism. Rabbi Shmelke and his brother Phinehas (1731–1805), later to become Rabbi in Frankfurt on Main, devoted followers of the *Maggid* were remarkable men. To guard against over-sleeping, Shmelke always slept in a most uncomfortable position, sitting upright with his head resting on his arms. In his hand he would hold a candle and, when it burnt low, the flame would awaken him and he would instantly resume his studies. His prayers were often impassioned improvisations. "Alas, Lord of the Universe!" he exclaimed one New Year's Day, "all the people cry out to you, but what of all their clamour! They think only of their own needs, and do not lament the exile of Your glory!"

On his death bed, in 1778, Rabbi Shmelke confided to his disciples. "Today is the day of my death. You should know that the soul of the

prophet Samuel is within me. For this there are three outward signs:
my name is Samuel, as his was; I am a Levite, as he was; and my life
has lasted fifty-two years, as his did."

Rabbi Shmelke fired Levi Isaac with the desire to visit the *Maggid*
in Mezhirichi, but his father-in-law, Israel Peretz, put many obstacles
in his way. Then Peretz suffered such severe financial setbacks that
he was imprisoned by the squire for falling in arrears with his payments.
Levi Isaac set out to raise redemption money, and one of his journeys
brought him to the *Maggid*. At once a new world opened for the ardent
young scholar, a world in which he felt at home, and thereafter he
came frequently to Dov Baer to drink deeply from the fountain of
Hasidism.

At twenty-one, Levi Isaac succeeded Rabbi Shmelke as Rabbi in
Rychwal and shortly afterwards, in 1771, he became rabbi of Pinsk.
But the fierce and mounting opposition to Hasidism forced him to
leave. For a time he stayed with Rabbi Israel of Kozienice, and in 1780
he became rabbi in Zelichow, Poland, where he stayed for five years.
He took part in a debate which took place in Praga, Warsaw, in 1774
and forcefully defended Hasidism, while Rabbi Abraham Katzenellenbogen of Brest-Litovsk set forth the case for the opposition.

In 1784 Levi Isaac finally found peace in Berdichev, "the Jerusalem
of Volhynia", where he lived for the rest of his life, loved and honoured
for some twenty-five years. Here he wrote *Kedushat Levi* ("Sanctity of
Levi"), which was printed in Slavuta in 1798. And when he died in
1809 it seemed that "the light of the world had been extinguished," to
quote Rabbi Nahman of Braclaw. Just as Vilna could not replace
Elijah Gaon, so Berdichev could not replace Levi Isaac.

Levi Isaac was a *Melitz Yosher* ("Defender") par excellence, a mediator who tempered justice with compassion. Suffering did not embitter
this eternal optimist, who harboured a passionate belief in the inherent
goodness of men. For good reason he was called the *Darbarimdiger*
("the merciful one"). With abundant and overwhelming love, the
rabbi gazed upon his people. He could not behold "iniquity in Jacob
nor perverseness in Israel" (Numbers xxiii. 21). He regarded every
member of the House of Israel as a letter in a *Sepher Torah* ("Scroll of
the Law") sacred and above reproach.

Many tales are told of the Rabbi of Berdichev's boundless compassion. Even the most blatant transgressor was given the benefit of the
doubt. When he happened to meet a young man eating in public
on the Fast of *Ab* (the Ninth of *Ab*, the day on which both the First and

the Second Temples were destroyed) the Rabbi mildly questioned him: "Have you forgotten that to-day is the Ninth of *Ab*? Or are you perhaps not aware that it is forbidden to eat on the Ninth of *Ab*?" "I have not forgotten what day it is and I am well aware of the prohibition," answered the young man. "Possibly, my son, you are not in good health and have been advised by your doctor to eat?" the rabbi of Berdichev asked. "No, I am in excellent health," was the reply. "See, O Lord," exclaimed the sage with joy, "how admirable Your children are! Even when they transgress Your Commandments, they do not stoop to falsehood."

When he saw a coachman clad in a *Tallit* and *Tephillin* (praying shawl and phylacteries) reciting psalms as he oiled the wheels of his wagon, the rabbi of Berdichev's comment was in character: "How noble is this people You have chosen. Even when they oil the wheels of their wagons, they are mindful of You and commune with You." When the rabbi heard a thief bragging to confederates of the haul, the rabbi murmured: "It is still a long time to *Selihot* (Special penitential prayers recited from the Sunday before *Rosh Hashanah* until *Yom Kippur*) yet the man has already begun to confess his sins."

The Rabbi's ideal was "to love a good Jew as much as God loves a wicked one." To one inveterate evil-doer, he confided: "I envy you, for if you would only repent and return wholeheartedly to the Almighty, a ray of light would stream forth from every one of your transgressions and you would be altogether luminous."

Only on behalf of the House of Israel was his anger kindled. Fiercely he defended the people against the itinerant *Maggidim* who harangued and harrowed them. Yet even this wrath was muted by compassion. Once, in semi-humourous fashion, he "explained" the situation: "Lord of the universe! This poor *Maggid* reviles and rebukes Your people because that is how he earns his livelihood. Give him, I beg of You, his daily bread, so that it will no longer be necessary for him to defame Your holy people." With distress he heard another rabbi publicly admonish a congregant for worshipping in a hasty and seemingly indecorous manner. "It is wrong to criticise a Jew on such grounds," maintained the Rabbi. "God will surely understand him, just as a loving mother understands the mumblings, often unintelligible, of her little child."

On the solemn Days of Judgement, *Rosh Hashanah* ("New Year") and *Yom Kippur* ("the Day of Atonement"), when the House of Israel was on trial before the Heavenly Court, Rabbi Levi Isaac prepared his case and presented it with the skill of an experienced lawyer.

Like many great advocates, he would frequently use an anecdote to illustrate his argument. And sometimes he would call witnesses. On the Day of Atonement, he once urged the town's humble tailor to speak up in front of the whole congregation; and publicly the man made his confession: "I, Yankel, am a poor tailor who, to tell the truth, have not been too honest in my work. I have occasionally kept remnants of cloth that have been left over and I have occasionally missed the afternoon service. But You, O Lord, have taken away infants from their mothers, and mothers from their infants. Let us on this Day of Days, be quit. If you forgive me, then I will forgive you." At this the Rabbi benevolently sighed: "O Yankel, Yankel, why did you let God off so lightly?"

Sometimes, when the rabbi had no case to present, he counterattacked and even dared to question the very validity of the Heavenly Tribunal. "Do not our Sages tell us that a childless person may not be appointed a member of the *Sanhedrin*, since he may be devoid of pity? How then are the Angels qualified to constitute a tribunal and to sit in judgement on men?"

A rare *rapport* seemed to exist between Rabbi Levi Isaac and his God, with whom he communed in terms of remarkable intimacy and warmth. The famous monologue, which has been set to music goes like this:

> Good morning to you, Lord of the Universe.
> I Levi Isaac, son of Sarah of Berdichev,
> Have come to You to plead on behalf of Your people, Israel.
> What have you against Your people, Israel
> And why do you oppress Your people, Israel?
> No matter what happens, it is 'Command the children of Israel!'
> No matter what happens, it is 'Speak to the children of Israel!'
> Dear Father, I ask You, how many other peoples are there in the world?
> Babylonians, Persians and Edomites among others.
> The Germans—what do they say? 'Our king is the king!'
> The English—what do they say? 'Our Sovereign is the Sovereign!'
> And I, Levi Isaac, son of Sarah of Berdichev, say:
> 'Hallowed and magnified be the name of God!'
> And I, Levi Isaac, son of Sarah of Berdichev, say:
> Lo o'zuz mim-koi-mee! I will not stir from here! There must be
> an end to the sufferings of Your people, Israel. Hallowed and
> magnified be the name of God.

Diligently Israel's advocate sought evidence which could be used on his client's behalf. Once, on the eve of the Day of Atonement, he searched the streets for a Jewish drunkard: since Jews are specifically enjoined by the rabbis to eat and drink on the day before *Yom Kippur*, it might be expected that some would fulfil this particular precept with over-enthusiasm and over-indulgence. Yet not a single drunkard could be found in the whole of Berdichev. The Rabbi marvelled at the sobriety of his people and brought this astounding testimony to the attention of the Supreme Judge.

On the Day of Atonement, Levi Isaac would present his heartfelt plea to the Almighty: "I have no strength to pray, but surely You have the strength to say, 'I have forgiven' (*Salahati*)." On one occasion, when he was unable to blow the *shofar* ("ram's horn"), he exclaimed: "If You do not care for my *shofar* blowing, let Ivan (an eponym for a Gentile) blow!"

Many are the moving prayers that Levi Isaac composed. Among them is *Gott vun Avrohum* ("God of Abraham"), a touching farewell to the Sabbath, which Jewish women took instantly to their hearts. In the soft Sabbath twilight, pausing on the threshold of a new week, hundreds of thousands of devout wives and mothers have recited these weighty words:

"God of Abraham, of Isaac and of Jacob. Protect Your beloved people Israel from all evil for the sake of Your name. Now that this beloved Sabbath is departing, may the new week come to us with complete faith, with faith in the Sages, with love for our fellow men, with attachment to the Creator. Blessed be He, so that we may truly believe in Your thirteen principles, in speedy redemption in our days, in the resurrection of the dead and in the prophecy of our teacher Moses, peace be upon him. Lord of the World, who gives strength to the weary, give strength also to Your dear Jewish children, who praise only You and who serve only You; so that the new week will come to us with health, with good fortune, with success, with blessing, with peace, with the gifts of children, life and sustenance, for us and for all Israel and let us say, Amen."

Equally famous is the *Dudele* ("the You Song"), based on the one hundred and thirty-eighth Psalm.

> *Where I wander—You!*
> *Where I ponder, You!*
> *Only You everywhere, You, always You.*

You, You, You.
When I am gladdened—You!
And when I am saddened—You!
Only You, everywhere You!
You, You, You!
Sky is You!
Earth is You!
You above! You below!
In every trend, at every end
Only You, everywhere You!
You! You! You!

In *Kedushat Levi*, his commentary to the Torah, the rabbi stresses the importance of inwardness and authenticity. "When we perform the *Mitzvot* with great enthusiasm and desire, we cleave to the inner content of the *Mitzvot*, which is a flaming fire, and according to the intensity of our ardour, we remove ourselves from materialism and approach closer and closer to the true understanding of the Creator." Man is to find a way for the worship of God (*Abodat Ha-Bore*) in all acts of life, maintained Levi Isaac. "When a man desires some material thing, such as money or honour, he should reason thus: 'If I have such a strong desire for some things which are so ephemeral, how much stronger should be my desire for God, who is eternal and the source of everlasting joy.'"[2]

When the time came for him to join his fathers, Levi Isaac was prepared. Apparently, he even received a brief extension, for at the end of the Day of Atonement, he told his community: "My life has now run its course and I should be leaving the world at this very hour. Yet since I grieved at not being able to fulfil the Commandments of dwelling in a booth and reciting the benedictions over the *Esrog* ("Citron"), I prayed that my time might be extended until after the Festival of Tabernacles, and our Merciful Master granted my prayer."

It was said of Rabbi Levi Isaac—and it is a fitting epitaph—that he loved God and he loved Judaism, but that his love of the Jews surpassed his love for God and Judaism. "Every day I set aside a time to thank our Heavenly Father," said Rabbi Jacob Isaac of Lublin, "for sending to the world a soul as unique as Levi Isaac of Berdichev."

Chapter 6

The Wrath of Elijah

Elijah ben Solomon, the Gaon of Vilna (*Der Vilner Gaon*), has left a remarkable imprint on Jewish history. Although he spent most of his life within the "four ells of *Halakhah*", he wielded extraordinary power as the greatest rabbinic authority of East European Jewry. Venerated by his contemporaries, he became a legend in his lifetime. By reason of his intellect and personality, he loomed like a colossus over the great men of his generation.

Legends and miracles were not a Hasidic monopoly. Just as the *Shibhe Ha-Besht* ("Praises of the Besht") weaves a garland of legends around the founder of Hasidism, so *Aliyot Eliyahu* ("The Ascent of Elijah") gathers together the stories that grew up around the Gaon. Elijah was born on the first day of Passover, April 23, 1720, in Vilna or nearby Seltz. A descendant of such renowned rabbis as Moses Kramer (d. 1688) and Moses Rivkes, Elijah was a prodigy in an age when *Illuim* ("prodigies") were almost commonplace. At six and a half he is reputed to have delivered a Talmudic discourse of astounding profundity. One of his teachers was probably Moses Margolit, rabbi of Kaidan and commentator on the Palestinian Talmud (*Yerushalmi*). At a very early age Elijah married Hannah, daughter of Rabbi Judah Leib of Kaidan, and she bore him two sons, Aryeh Leib and Abraham.

When Elijah was about twenty years old, he journeyed "incognito" through Poland and Germany for eight years as part of a self-inflicted penance known as "going into exile" (*Golut uprichten*). From Königsberg he wrote to his family a letter of such ethical content, that it was later published under the title *Alim li-Terufa* ("Leaves for Healing"). The fatherly admonitions include the suggestion that his daughter should recite her prayers at home. In the Synagogue she might be distracted by the finery of her friends and envy them.

Elijah's capacity for study was almost superhuman. "In this world only that which is acquired by hard labour and through struggle is of value," was one of Elijah's maxims. Unswervingly, without the tiniest deviation, he followed the path of the Torah. This was the sum total of his life, and to its study he dedicated mind, heart and soul. Yet his general knowledge was encyclopaedic and his range of interest wide. In addition to Hebrew grammar, he also studied biology, astronomy, trigonometry, algebra and medicine. Furthermore, he encouraged Barukh of Shklov (1740–1810) to translate into Hebrew the six books of Euclid's *Geometry*. "If one is ignorant of the secular sciences, one is a hundredfold more ignorant of the wisdom of the Torah," maintained the Gaon, "for the two are inseparable."[1]

The Gaon aimed at literal interpretation (*Peshat*) rather than dialectics (*Pilpul*). "With a single shaft of the light of truth he would illumine the darkness, and with a single word could overthrow heaps of *pilpulim* hanging by a hair."[2] In his eulogy of the Gaon, Rabbi Abraham Danzig (1748–1820), author of *Haye Adom* ("Human Life"), credited him with the authorship of seventy books,[3] among them commentaries on the Bible, The *Mishnah*, the Palestinian Talmud, *Sepher Yetzirah*, the *Zohar* and *Shulhan Arukh*. He also wrote critical notes on *Tannaitic Midrashim*, as well as treatises on astronomy, trigonometry, algebra and Hebrew grammar. Not all his works have seen the light of day and many have been lost. A number of his manuscripts, including parts of the *Mishnah* commentary, have not been traced.

Almost a century before the *Jüdische Wissenschaft* ("scientific inquiries into Jewish history, literature and religion"), the Gaon of Vilna was analysing rabbinic texts with scientific skill, reducing problems that had baffled scholars for centuries. His intuition compensated for his lack of original manuscript material.

The Gaon declined a position of rabbi and lived on a small legacy from his great-great-grandfather, Moses Rivkes. Unlike the physician and scholar, Maimonides, whose days were occupied with the Court of the Vizier Al-kadi al-Fadil, with private patients and with communal affairs, as well as with philosophic study and research, the Gaon lived in virtual isolation. When accused of Sabbetianism by Rabbi Jacob Emden, Jonathan Eibeschütz, rabbi of the triple community of Altona, Hamburg and Wandsbeck, applied to Elijah for support. But with firmness and humility, the Gaon remained aloof. "I wish I had wings like a dove. I would then fly to restore peace and quench the strange fire of dissension. But who am I that people should listen to me?" the Gaon self-deprecatingly replied. "If they ignore the instruction of their rabbis and heads of holy congregations, how will they listen to the voice of an unknown person who lacks the virtue of age?"[4]

"Do not regard the views of the *Shulhan Arukh* as binding, if it is your opinion that they are not in agreement with those of the Talmud," was the Gaon's rather revolutionary advice to his disciples.[5] Yet he was, in his intolerance, a child of his generation. When one *Maskil*, Abba of Hlusk, remarked that the authors of the *Midrash* occasionally infringed the rules of grammar, Elijah would not let him go unpunished. "I was sentenced to forty strokes," writes Abba to Moses Mendelssohn. "I was led to the threshold of the Synagogue and my neck was enclosed within the iron rings attached to the wall . . . Everybody who had come for the afternoon service stopped and called to me: 'Traitor to Israel'. But even more, they nearly spat into my face."[6]

It is one of the ironies of history that the Gaon who was called "the Hasid" and who was the author of works on mysticism, became the ruthless antagonist of Hasidism. Small Hasidic groups had been established in Brest-Litovsk, Grodno, Troki and Lutzk, and the fiery activities of Rabbi Aaron of Karlin (b. 1736) near Pinsk sent sparks flying far and wide. Some of these sparks reached Vilna. There, too, the "Klaus of the Karliner", headed by Rabbi Issar and Rabbi Hayim, was beginning to attract attention. It also attracted the attention and roused the ire of Elijah who became the arch-opponent, the *Mitnagid* of Hasidism. For more than two decades he waged a bitter battle against the upstart group.

Although firmly and faithfully rooted in Jewish tradition, Hasidism was in a sense a revival movement. Not differences of principles but differences of practice created discord and inevitably met strong opposition from the establishment. For instance, the Hasidim adopted *Nusah Ari*, the liturgy of the Cabbalist Isaac Luria, in preference to *Minhag Ashkenaz*, the German ritual. Thus they had to establish their own houses of worship. The Gaon feared that such separatist tendencies would disrupt and demoralise the House of Israel.

Elijah Gaon insisted upon punctilious observance of the minutiae of all rabbinical laws and regulations. To him it was intolerable that some Hasidim should disregard the prescribed hours of worship. He did not believe that *Devekut* and *Kavanot* could make up for belated services and remained unconvinced when the Hasidim reasoned thus: "Can a child be told when to approach his father?" Neither did he accept the thesis that spontaneity ranks higher than punctilious recitation.

The Gaon was deeply concerned with the conduct of Synagogue services. He himself deleted many *piyutim* ("liturgical compositions") in order to shorten the lengthy services, and he encouraged communal singing: but he abhorred the undisciplined way in which many Hasidim worshipped, swaying and dancing, singing, sighing, sobbing or laughing as the mood seized them.

To the eyes of the unsympathetic outsider, the Hasidic way of prayer was strange and unusual. "They are engaged," reported the philosopher Solomon Maimon (1754–1800), "in all sorts of mechanical operations, such as movements and cries to bring themselves back into the state of ecstasy once more and to stay in that state without interruption during the whole time of their worship. It was amusing to observe how they often interrupted their prayers with all sorts of extraordinary tones and comical gestures, which were meant as threats and reproaches against their adversary, the Evil Spirit, who tried to disturb their devotion."[7] To Maimon, the way of the Hasidim was amusing. But the Gaon was not amused. To him this behaviour was not only unseemly but utterly abhorrent. It is said that the Hasidim in and around Vilna did, in deliberate defiance of their persecutors, conduct themselves somewhat indecorously: "They poured scorn on the students of the Torah and upon the learned, inflicting all manner of ridicule and shame on them, turning somersaults in the streets and market places of Kalisk and Liozno and generally permitting themselves all sorts of pranks and practical jokes in public."[8]

Dr. Solomon Schechter describes the Gaon as *Der Ewige Student* ("the perpetual student"). For him the "Torah is to the soul of man what rain is to the soil."[9] To a man so dedicated to scholarship, no amount of Torah study could be adequate, let alone excessive, and in his eyes the criticism of intensive study expressed by some of the Hasidic leaders threatened the very survival of Judaism. Neither the vast erudition of the *Maggid* nor the intellectual brilliance of Jacob Joseph of Polnoy could allay Elijah's fear that "the Torah would be forgotten in Israel." Vehemently he opposed the advice of the Hasidic rabbis that "a man must not pass all his time in study," and he was probably in complete disagreement with the dictum of the Besht that the "Evil inclination, (the *Yetzer Ha-Ra*), persuades a man to study the Talmud with all its commentaries in order to prevent him following other studies which might lead him to the fear of God."[10]

In counter-attack the Hasidic leaders accused their Rabbinic opponents, of "exhibitionism, hypocrisy, sophistry and learning not for the sake of Heaven." Jacob Joseph let fly many sharply-pointed arrows, and many were on target. These counter-attacks were bitterly resented. "There are rabbis," he wrote, "who do not accept the Torah interpretations of another scholar but only their own, and when they hear the Torah of others, they pass it off as something of no interest."[11] Similarly, Rabbi Judah Leib, Preacher of Polnoy (d. 1770) and author of *Kol Aryeh* ("The Voice of a Lion"), censured the Talmudists for their pride and intellectual arrogance. "They are wise, understanding and God-fearing in their own estimation."

The cult of the *Zaddik*, too, was also alien to the Gaon, for it produced a new type of teacher, whose powers stemmed from the heart rather than the head. His training ground was the court of his rabbi rather than the Yeshiva, since knowledge was not the chief qualification of leadership. Discourses about *Zaddikim* took the place of discussions on the Talmud. Instead of poring over the Tractates of the Talmud, instead of exploring the highways and byways of Jewish Law, Hasidim discussed with awe the miracles wrought by their wonder rabbis, and a rich new folklore sprang up. The eighteenth century saw the emergence of many remarkable rabbis. Many of the *Zaddikim* lived on a lofty spiritual plane to which they could raise their followers. Among them were such outstanding personalities as Rabbi Meir Margulies, Yehiel Meir of Zloczew, Ze'ev Wolf of Zbaraz and Mordecai of Nezhizh. Yet the Gaon of Vilna was neither able nor willing to concede that such men deserved recognition, for him it was as if they did not exist.

Mystic though he was, the Gaon failed to discern in Hasidism a new and momentous phase in the evolution of Jewish mysticism. In taking isolated thoughts out of context, the Gaon misunderstood and distorted them. "All accusations by the Gaon against the *Maggid*," wrote a Hasidic teacher, "based on quotations referring to God as residing in material things, are without foundation. These statements are not to be taken literally, for they are intended only to indicate the extent and intensity of God's providence."[12] The Gaon associated Hasidism with Sabbetianism and Frankism rather than with Lurian Cabbalah. For Elijah's knowledge of the Hasidic doctrines and dogmas came to him from devious sources and were frequently unreliable and invariably biased. To the Gaon, the acquisition of learning was an intellectual exercise: it had broadened his knowledge but not his outlook. He was intolerant of anyone whose views differed from his own.

So the forces against Hasidism were marshalled under the banner of the Gaon and a *casus belli* was soon found.

In 1771 an epidemic broke out in Vilna and many children died. A scapegoat had to be found, and the community chose the Hasidim for this role. The Hasidic leaders were accused of "defaming the Gaon of Vilna," and the Hasidic Rabbi Hayim was compelled to do public penance. In vain he pleaded with the Gaon for forgiveness. The Gaon would not relent. Rabbi Hayim was forced to leave Vilna, the Hasidic synagogue was closed, Rabbi Issar was imprisoned and Hasidic works were burned. Harsh though these penalties were, the Gaon was still not content.

In the spring of 1772, the *Kahal* of Vilna, with the consent of the Gaon, issued a *Herem* ("a decree of excommunication") against the "godless sect". The *Herem* was the most powerful weapon which the Jewish authorities possessed, and it was used primarily to maintain communal discipline. In a bygone age, when the synagogue was the centre of the community, the mere threat of the *Herem* would often subdue unruly elements. The weird ceremony, complete with the lighting of wax candles and the sounding of the ram's horn, was designed to strike terror into the heart, and the recitation of the appropriate formula produced the chill horror of a death sentence.

The *Herem* was widely used and even more widely misused. Scholars even employed it against each other, and the rabbi who did not invoke the ban at every pretext was regarded as a rare phenomenon. The most celebrated cases of excommunication in the seventeenth century were those of the noted rationalist Uriel Acosta (1585–1640) and of the philosopher Benedict Spinoza (1632–1677) who was formally excommunicated on July 27, 1656 by the *Sephardi* community of Amsterdam. In eighteenth-century England, the *Herem* helped enforce the *Ascamot* ("the civil laws of the Congregation").

The *Herem* of Vilna was not merely against an individual, but against a whole movement. Even this mass excommunication of the Hasidim did not satisfy the Gaon. "Had I the power," he declared, "I would have punished these infidels as the worshippers of *Baal* were punished of old."[13] A month after the proclamation of the *Herem* a letter was circulated through all the communities in Lithuania and White Russia:

"Our brethren in Israel, you are certainly already informed of the tiding whereof our fathers never dreamed, that a sect of the 'suspects' (*Hashudim* instead of Hasidim) has been formed . . . who meet together in separate groups and deviate in their prayers from the text valid for the whole people . . . They are the same who, in the middle of the *Shmoneh-Esreh* prayer, interject obnoxious alien words (Yiddish) in a loud voice, conduct themselves like madmen, and explain their behaviour by saying that in their thoughts they soar in the most far-off worlds . . . The study of the Torah is neglected by them entirely and they do not hesitate constantly to emphasise that one should devote oneself as little as possible to learning and not grieve too much over a sin committed . . . Every day is for them a holiday . . . When they pray according to falsified texts, they raise such a din that the walls quake . . . and they turn over like wheels, with the head below and the legs above . . . Therefore, do we now declare to our brethren in Israel, to those near as well as far . . . All heads of the people shall robe themselves in the raiment of zeal, of zeal for the Lord of Hosts, to extirpate, to destroy, to outlaw and to excommunicate them. We, here, have already, with the help of His name, brought their evil intention to nought; and as here, so should they everywhere be torn up by the roots . . . Do not believe them even if they raise their voices to implore you . . . for in their hearts are all seven horrors . . . So long as they do not make full atonement of their own accord, they should be scattered and driven away so that no two heretics remain together, for the disbanding of their associations is a boon for the world."[14]

The scribes of Vilna were kept busy. A second circular followed almost before the ink on the first was dry—adding more fuel to the raging fire. It purported to supply additional proof of heresy. "A manuscript has been found in the possession of a certain Issar which pointed out the misdeeds of which he had already made a full confession and that 'soul-snatchers', such as these, were destroyers in a double sense, as they not only beguiled people to forsake the Torah, but sought to seize the money of their youthful followers, whose dowry (i.e., of their wives) was squandered in wandering from town to town and in orgies."[15]

The Vilna authorities wrote urgently to Brody urging instant action and they responded without delay. On *Sivan* 20th the Brody leadership excommunicated the Hasidim. All the curses of the Pentateuch in Hebrew and in Yiddish were heaped on those who deviated from the "established custom".[16] Similar steps were taken by other communities. The Hasidim were forbidden to set up separate places of worship and were even debarred from celebrating *Seudah Shelishit* (the third Sabbath meal) together.[17]

That same year, 1772, saw the publication of *Zemir Aritzim v' Harbot Zurim* ("Uprooting of Tyrants and Flinty Swords") by Aryeh Leib ben Mordecai, a collection of all the bans issued against the Hasidim. In 1775 two of Hasidism's finest scholars, Shneur Zalman of Liady and Menahem Mendel of Vitebsk, came to Vilna and sought a personal interview with the Gaon. "We set out towards the saintly Gaon's house," recorded Shneur Zalman, "to discuss the whole matter with him in order that all misunderstanding might be removed. I myself took part in this mission as well as our saintly master the deceased Rabbi (Menahem) Mendel. But twice the Gaon locked the door against us. The leaders of the community approached him saying: 'Our Master, their chief spokesman has come to discuss the matter with you and when he is convinced of the error of his ways assuredly peace will again prevail in Israel'; but the Gaon gave evasive replies. When his followers started to plead with him, the Gaon left the city and stayed away until we returned home."[18] However, there is little accuracy in Solomon Maimon's assertion that "scarcely any trace of the Hasidim can be found."[19] The *Herem* could be devastating when wielded against individuals, but was ineffectual when applied to large groups of people who could ignore with impunity threats that could not be enforced. The publication of the *Toledot* gave additional ammunition to its opponents. Hasidic presses sprang up in Medzibozh, Slawuta and Korzec specifically for the printing and reprinting of Hasidic and Cabbalistic works.

In 1781, nine years after the proclamation of the first *Herem*, Vilna proclaimed a second *Herem* against the Hasidim. Once more the Gaon was in the forefront. "Although it was not my custom to trespass beyond my province," writes the Gaon, "yet I also give my signature mindful of the saying: 'When the Torah is being annulled, it is time to act'."[20] From Vilna two envoys, Rabbi David and Rabbi Joshua Segal, were sent throughout Lithuania to warn the people against the Hasidim. Most communities followed the leadership of Vilna. On *Elul* third 1781, the Rabbinical Assembly at Zelva (near Grodno) endorsed the Herem.[21]

In Shklov and Mogilev in White Russia, a circular was issued that the Hasidim were condemned with severity: "Because of our many sins, worthless and wanton men who call themselves Hasidim have deserted the Jewish community and have set up a so-called place of worship for themselves. And thus, as every one knows, they worship in a most insane fashion, following a different ritual which does not conform to the religion of our holy Torah, and they tread a path which our fathers did not tread. In addition to this, the works of their teachers have, unfortunately, recently been published, and it is obvious to us that all of their writings are opposed to our holy Torah and contain misleading interpretations. The exaggerations and stories of miracles that are described in their books are particularly transparent and obvious lies, and far be it from us to place any trust in any such exaggerated statements. And behold, as a result of this great misfortune, a fire has been kindled in the midst of Jewry, and there is a breaking away from the obligations imposed by the Torah.

"Therefore, we the undersigned, are in agreement that every community is most urgently bound to adopt rigorous measures—carrying with them every possible penalty—in order to put into effect all the protective and defensive measures described below. And these details are to be officially recorded in the minute-books of every community and city that they may serve as a charge and as a memorial for future generations, so that our Jewish brethren may avoid the evil customs and laws of the Hasidim:

"The following are the protective measures which were adopted in our session:

1. A day of fast and public prayer is to be instituted on January 15, 1787.
2. All possible measures are to be adopted to put an end to the prayer-meetings of the heretics in all communities, so that they will be deprived of the possibility of common assembly.
3. Careful watch is to be maintained that no one should study their literature, and search is to be made with this purpose in mind.
4. We fully confirm the validity of the ordinances which were issued in Brody and Vilna dealing with the prohibition of pilgrimages to the heads of the sect.
5. That which their ritual slaughterers kill may not be eaten, the meat of such slaughtering is to be considered carrion, and the instruments used are to be considered polluted and forbidden. Meat brought into one city from another place is to be considered

carrion, unless it is accompanied by a certificate from a reliable person who is not a member of the Hasidic group.

6. In every city supervisors should be appointed to see that all the above-mentioned provisions are carried out.

7. No one is to shelter any member of this sect.

8. No member of the above-mentioned sect may bring a suit in a Jewish court. No community may permit any one of them to hold a position as cantor or rabbi, and it goes without saying that no one of them may teach our children.

9. It is to be announced in all communities that anyone who knows anything, good or bad, about the Hasidim must bring this information to the Court."[22]

In 1794 both the *Toledot Yaacob Yoseph* and the *Testament of the Besht* were burned in public in front of the Great Synagogue in Vilna. Hatred and bitterness raged in hitherto peaceful communities. Even acts of physical violence were not uncommon.

In May 1796, it was related in Vilna that a Hasid was journeying through the country, purporting to be the son of the Gaon, publicly proclaiming that his father deeply regretted his harshness towards the Hasidim and was now making atonement for his grievous errors. Fierce and fearsome was the wrath of the Gaon. In letters, dated June 22 and October 14, 1796, the Gaon thundered: "These dolts who have sown so much evil should be chastised before the assembled people with whips and scorpions and brought to reason. No man should have pity upon them and take their part, but rather they should be cast out from all the tribes of Israel as evil-doers."[23] Clearly the Gaon saw himself in the role of his namesake, the prophet Elijah. The Hasidim were to the Gaon of Vilna what the worshippers of *Baal* were to Elijah the Tishbite.

On the third day of *Succot* (October 9, 1797) the Gaon died and "the joy of the festival was turned into mourning and all the streets of Vilna resounded with lamentation."[24] Some of the Hasidim, however, would not allow the death of the Gaon to diminish "the Season of Rejoicing", particularly since "the Light of the Exile" had been their most merciless persecutor. Incensed at this heretical conduct of the Hasidim, the *Kahal* set up a special committee to deal with it. But two decades of relentless warfare, waged by the greatest exponent of Talmudic Judaism in modern times, had failed to destroy or even weaken the movement. Stronger measures were necessary.

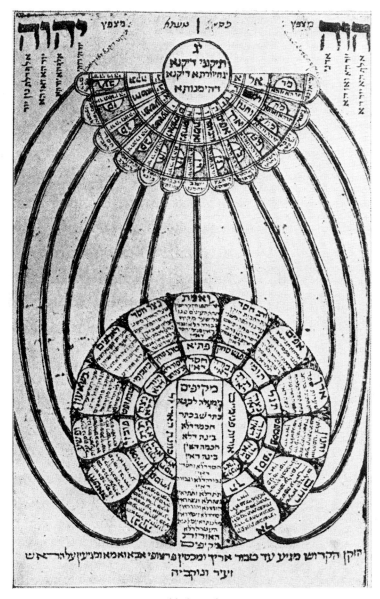

A Cabbalistic design

The grave of the Besht's Mother

With the connivance of the *Kahal*'s special committee, a certain Hirsch ben David drew the attention of the Prosecutor-General in St. Petersburg to the "political misdeeds perpetrated by the chief of the Karliner (Hasidic) sect, Zalman Borukhovitch (son of Borukh)".[25] The Russians acted on this information with practised speed. In October 1798, Shneur Zalman of Liady and twenty-two of his followers were arrested. The other Hasidim were soon released, but Shneur Zalman was taken to St. Petersburg. In a Hebrew memorandum, which had to be sent to Vilna to be translated into French, Shneur Zalman protested his innocence. He must have pleaded with convincing eloquence. On *Kislev* the nineteenth the *Yahrzeit* of the *Maggid*, he was released and recited the verse from Psalm iv. 19: "He hath redeemed my soul in peace."

The ordeal did not alter the temperament or outlook of the compassionate sage, who still urged his followers to be patient and forbearing with their opponents. His pleas were in vain. The persecuted Hasidim of Vilna, provoked by the tactics of the *Kahal*, reacted accordingly. In counter-accusation, they accused the *Kahal* of diverting to other purposes monies collected for taxation, and on this charge, which they soon disproved on February 4, 1799, the elders of the *Kahal* were arrested. Eight Hasidim were subsequently elected to the Council and for a time a Hasid, Meir Raphael, headed the community.[26]

The Hasidic victory was cut short by Avigdor ben Joseph Hayim (Haimovitch) a vindictive and unscrupulous man, formerly rabbi in Pinsk, who had alienated the Hasidim and been deposed by them in 1793. When his demands for restitution and compensation were unsuccessful, the ex-rabbi turned informer. In a lengthy report to the Russian Emperor Paul I in St. Petersburg, he described the Hasidim as a "pernicious and dangerous sect", supporting his accusations with a wealth of distorted data, and malicious misquotations. "I endeavoured through preaching to persuade them to return from their errors to the right way," wrote Avigdor to the Czar, "but when I saw that this effort had no effect on them at all, and when there came into my hands their clandestinely printed books in which law and justice were most insolently distorted, I was perplexed in mind, for I did not know how to frustrate their designs."[27]

A second warrant for the arrest of Shneur Zalman was issued on November 9, 1800, and once more the rabbi of Liady was taken to the prison of St. Peter and Paul at St. Petersburg. Here he was confronted with nineteen charges, all of which he successfully refuted. Three weeks later, on November 27, Shneur Zalman was released from prison. Yet it was not until March 29, 1801, that he was free to leave the Russian capital and return home.

The internecine war was finally settled, ironically enough, by State intervention. "The Statute Concerning the Organisation of the Jews" of December 9, 1804, granted every Jewish community the right to build separate synagogues and to choose its own rabbis. The rabbis were authorised to supervise all religious ceremonies and to settle all disputes relating to religion, but without recourse to "anathemas" and "excommunications." The struggle was over. Hasidim and *Mitnagdim* had to learn to live and let live, to worship and let each other worship as each saw fit.

Chapter 7

The Legacy of Lubavitch

Rabbi Shneur Zalman ben Barukh, "the old *Rebbe*", as he was affectionately called, was born, in 1747, in Liozno, White Russia. In sharp contrast to the weath of detail which surrounds every aspect of his adult life, little is known about his parentage and early upbringing. "This young lad," said one of his teachers, Issahar Baer Kobilink of Lubavitch, "is fit to be my friend and companion, not my disciple. He needs no guidance in the study of Talmud. His intellect is such that he can make his own way through the 'sea of the Talmud', and its commentaries."

At the age of thirteen, Shneur Zalman became an associate of the *Hebra Kaddisha* ("The Holy Society", which supervised burial arrangements). He had a methodical mind and methodical was his acquisition of knowledge. "When I was thirteen years old," he writes, "I studied by myself most of the time, devoting eighteen hours a day to my studies. For three consecutive years, I allotted two-thirds of my time during the week to the study of the Talmud and the Codes and the remaining third I utilised for the study of Scripture, *Aggada*, *Midrash* and *Cabbalah*. On the Sabbath, I divided the day equally between the Talmud, Codes, Scripture and *Aggada*, and finally *Midrash*, *Zohar* and Cabbalah."[1]

Soon men of wealth were competing for this desirable son-in-law, and at the age of fifteen he married Sterna, daughter of a businessman, Yehuda Leib Segal of Vitebsk. Nothing could quench or abate his thirst for knowledge. By the age of eighteen, the youthful scholar had mastered the Talmud with all its commentaries, and still he studied with an unmitigated ardour that seemed excessive to his materialistic father-in-law. In mean and petty ways, Yehuda Leib Segal gave vent to his resentment and even begrudged Shneur Zalman the candles he needed for his night-time studies. Yet, undaunted, Shneur Zalman pursued by moonlight his far ranging explorations of rabbinical and mystical Judaism. At midnight and in the other-worldly stillness of the dawn, the city of Vitebsk could hear the musical voice of the wakeful *Matmid* ("diligent student") as he chanted to himself.

Like the Gaon of Vilna, Shneur Zalman applied himself to astronomy and trigonometry also, and he paid special attention to Hebrew grammar, which he regarded as essential to the understanding of the Torah. Alone, without colleagues or teachers, the nineteen-year-old became restless. Moreover, he became aware that there were "two luminaries shining in the world", the light of Mezhirichi, the rallying ground of the Hasidim, and the light of Vilna, the *Mitnagdic* stronghold. "In Vilna the Torah is studied, but in Mezhirichi they learn how to pray. My soul," he declared, "desired Torah, so I set out for Vilna. But, on the way, I changed my mind. A little knowledge of the Torah I had already acquired, but of the principle of true worship I had yet learned nothing. I needed a guide who would show me how to serve God. Such a counsellor would I find in Mezhirichi."[2]

At the age of twenty, he left Vitebsk, armed with little but intellectual curiosity and the six roubles that his brother had given him for provisions on that arduous journey. But at journey's end in Mezhirichi, he found the guidance he was looking for. "Blessed be the Lord," he exclaimed, "Who hath led me along the true path." The *Maggid*, like the Besht, possessed great powers of discernment and soon perceived the rare quality of his new disciple. Hasidim relate that, as the *Maggid* was passing through the students' dormitory one night, he paused at the bed of Shneur Zalman. "Miracle of miracles," he remarked softly, "that so much spiritual strength resides in so frail a dwelling! This young man, sleeping so serenely, will one day become the rabbi of all the provinces of Russia, with multitudes listening to his voice."

Just as the master honoured the disciple, so the disciple honoured the master and repeatedly acknowledged his indebtedness. "When we learn Torah from the *Maggid*, it is as though he teaches us the Written Law." Close were the bonds between them. "The Besht I see only in a dream and then only on the Sabbath and on Festivals," Shneur Zalman remarked, "but my teacher, the *Maggid*, I behold both when I dream and when I am awake."

For three years, Rabbi Shneur Zalman sat at the feet of the *Maggid*, following him from Mezhirichi to Annopol. Here, he found colleagues of calibre of Rabbi Elimelekh of Lezajask, Rabbi Levi Isaac of Berdichev, and Rabbi Nahum of Czernobiel. Such fellowship was stimulating and instructive for the youthful Shneur Zalman. "Torah," he gratefully acknowledged, "I learned from the *Maggid*, who was my counsellor in ethics. From Rabbi Phinehas Shapiro of Korzec, I learned to seek truth and to value humility. And from Michael (Yehiel) of Zloczew (1726–80), I absorbed melodies which he had heard from the Besht himself."

Shneur Zalman also benefited from his role as companion and tutor of Rabbi Abraham (1741–77), the *Maggid*'s son, who was customarily called "Avraham ha-Malakh" ("Abraham the Angel"). "Not in vain," commented Rabbi Levi Isaac of Berdichev, "did they call him 'the Angel', for he is as pure as his deeds." Though heir to the non-ascetic traditions of Hasidism, "the Angel" spent his days in fasting, self-affliction and solitude. But for six hours a day, the young ascetic and Shneur Zalman studied together, devoting three hours to Talmud and three hours to Cabbalah, and both of them benefited from these studies. "Let my son go his own way," instructed the *Maggid*. "Explain the Torah to him as you understand it and he will interpret it according to his own conception. Show him the Talmud according to the letter and he will explain its meaning to you according to the spirit."[3]

Although one of the youngest and newest of the disciples, Rabbi Shneur Zalman was encouraged by the *Maggid* to compile a new *Shulhan Arukh* ("A Code of Jewish Law"). "Our dear Shneur Zalman's immediate grasp of any problem is tantamount to minor prophecy," was the *Maggid*'s exalted evaluation of his disciple's potential. Shneur Zalman was qualified for this challenging task. His phenomenal familiarity with Rabbinic literature was allied with a gift for lucid exposition. His logical and highly-trained mind could not tolerate ambiguity or obscurity. Shneur Zalman was twenty-five when he completed the section *Orah Hayim* ("Way of Life").

The youthful codifier marshalled ancient authorities with masterly skill and thoroughness and the "Rav's *Shulhan Arukh*", as his *magnum opus* was called, won high praise from his contemporaries, who called him "Prince of the Torah" and "unique in his generation". "He is like an iron pillar," they said of him "on whom one can depend."

In general, Rabbi Shneur Zalman followed *Ashkenazi* scholars rather than the *Sephardic* school, just as he opted for the *Halakhic* authorities in preference to the mystics. Thus the "Rav's *Shulhan Arukh*" was weighty evidence that contrary to the accusations of the *Mitnagdim*, the Hasidim were not attempting to lighten the "yoke of the Mitzvot." For Shneur Zalman stressed that man is bound to fulfil minor precepts as meticulously as major ones.

After the death of the *Maggid*, in 1773, the disciples dispersed, and many established their own courts. Rabbi Shneur Zalman lived in Liozno, a loyal supporter of his former pupil, young "Abraham the Angel", and of the venerable Rabbi Menahem Mendel of Vitebsk, who had actually beheld the glory of the Besht; but it was not long before Rabbi Menahem Mendel made his way to the Holy Land and Rabbi Abraham died at the age of thirty-six. With this double bereavement, Rabbi Shneur Zalman reverted for a time to the solitary life he had led before entering the home of the *Maggid*. Caring little for honour or recognition, he withdrew from the world of people into the world of books. It is related that even at the age of forty, he still shrank from the homage of the Hasidim who flocked to him. His wife however, made this homage more acceptable. "They are coming," she explained with subtlety, "to hear the Torah of the Maggid."

It was at this time that the Gaon of Vilna launched his mighty offensive against Hasidism. Maligned and menaced, the movement desperately needed a powerful leader. From afar, Rabbi Menahem Mendel realised this, and he wrote from the Holy Land urging his followers to turn to Shneur Zalman: "Revere him. . . . Honour him. He has laboured hard to hear the words of the living God. Him we have anointed to be a teacher of righteousness in the country, so that the Congregation of the Lord should not be like sheep without a shepherd. For, as guide and teacher, there is none to compare with him." In time of crisis there is room neither for hesitation nor for excessive humility. Rabbi Shneur Zalman rose to the occasion. Before long, he was the acknowledged head of the Hasidic communities in White Russia and his followers were numbered in thousands. Yet he continued to live in modest, almost Spartan, style. For he attributed the sufferings of the diaspora to the people's yearning for material things.

From Rabbi Menahem Mendel came sympathy and encouragement. "We have heard," he writes, "the groaning of the children of Israel. By His Name I swear that our doctrines and beliefs are blameless. We forgive those who provoke us and harm our person."[4] Rabbi Shneur Zalman preached patience and advocated forgiveness. However, peaceful overtures were neither appreciated nor reciprocated. Rabbi Shneur Zalman became the "Suffering Servant" of Hasidism. Twice arrested, his detention in St. Petersburg gave rise to many legends. His bearing impressed the mistrustful dignitaries, and his ready wit stood him in good stead.

It is related that one of the State prosecutors asked the prisoner to explain the meaning of the Biblical verse: "And the Lord God called unto the man and said unto him: 'Where art thou?'" (Gen. ii. 9). "Surely," reasoned the prosecutor, "the Lord knew where Adam was, so why did He ask his whereabouts?" Shneur Zalman replied: "The question, 'Where art thou?' did not apply only to Adam in the Garden of Eden. The question is of timeless relevance. Whenever a man sins and deviates from the right path, God calls him to repentance with the searching words 'Where art thou?'".

Ceaselessly Rabbi Shneur Zalman worked for peace and reconciliation with his opponents. To the leaders of Mogilev, he lamented "We have been sold alive. We cannot even be ransomed for money. We implore you do not cast us aside." Vindictiveness was alien to him. He preferred to forgive rather than to avenge, and he tried to influence his Hasidic disciples in the hope that they would adopt this spirit of magnanimity, for their conduct was a matter of great concern to him. Repeatedly, he pleaded that the movement should not suffer for the misdeeds of individual members. Every single Hasid was, of course, to see that his conduct was above reproach, since the actions of a minority can easily be misinterpreted. High standards of conduct were the best defensive measures that Rabbi Shneur Zalman could devise to avoid antagonising the rest of the community. Such conduct would prove to the *Mitnagdim* that their accusations were unfounded. To convince rather than to coerce the *Mitnagdim* of the baselessness of their accusations, Shneur Zalman himself visited a number of Rabbinic scholars and made friendly contact with many *Mitnagdic* scholars. Many of the opponents were won over by the erudition, the fervour, and the fiery eloquence of the scholarly rabbi who, by sustained personal effort, succeeded in mitigating in some measure the schism in the House of Israel.

He also tried to appease Rabbi Barukh of Tulchin: "What cause is there for any misunderstanding between us? Have I not suffered martydom and twice been dragged in chains to St. Petersburg, all so that the name of your grandfather might be vindicated? Might I not have said: 'There is his grandson Rabbi Barukh in Medzibozh. Send for him, that he may come and answer for his grandfather.'"[5]

Yet, Shneur Zalman was not destined to enjoy the tranquillity for which he yearned. The phenomenal exploits of Napoleon revolutionised the position of European Jewry. As the Napoleonic armies marched through Italy, the "walls of the Ghettoes began to dance". The Yellow Badge gave place to the tricolour cockade, and the gates of the Ghettoes were torn off their hinges. In 1799, while Napoleon was in the East, he is said to have invited the Jews of Asia and Africa to rally to his standard in order to regain possession of Palestine. Eight years later, on February 8, 1807, he summoned a *Sanhedrin*, commanding it to "reveal again to the people the true spirit of its laws and render proper interpretations of all mistaken conceptions." The *Sanhedrin* obliged by releasing soldiers in the French army from their religious obligations. Although few Jews accepted the pronouncements of the *Sanhedrin* as authoritative and binding, the Emperor was for the moment satisfied with his experiment. "To me at least, the *Sanhedrin* is useful," was his comment.

Although Napoleon was the hero of Polish Jewry, who regarded him as their liberator, the Hasidic rabbis of Poland were divided on this issue. Among staunch Napoleonic supporters was Rabbi Menahem Mendel of Rymanov (d. 1815). While Rabbi Mendel baked *Matzot* ("unleavened bread") for the festival of Passover, he would explain every time he put the dough into the oven: "Another Muscovite regiment goes into the fire." On the other hand, Rabbi Jacob Isaac of Lublin and Rabbi Israel of Kozienice prayed for the victory of the Czar, and Rabbi Naftali of Ropczyce (1760–1827) similarly opposed French dominion, for they regarded Napoleon as the symbol of heresy and agnosticism.

Mindful of his just treatment in St. Petersburg, Rabbi Shneur Zalman aligned himself with the anti-French faction. To Moses Maisels he writes: "It was revealed to me during the *Musaph* ("The Additional Prayer") on *Rosh Hashanah* that if B.P. (Bonaparte) is victorious, there will be great material prosperity in Israel, but the Jews will become estranged from God. But should A.A. (*Adonenu Alexander*, "Our Lord Alexander") be victorious, even though they would suffer great poverty, yet the hearts of the Children of Israel would draw closer to their father in Heaven."[6] According to a Lubavitch legend, Napoleon used to say: "Whenever I ride, that blond Jew rides before me." (Shneur Zalman was fair-haired).

In 1812, to elude the advancing French armies, Rabbi Zalman hastily left home with his entire family, twenty-eight souls in all, leaving most of his possessions behind. Wearily they journeyed from Liady to Krasny and then to Smolensk. "I would die rather than live under him (Napoleon)," wrote Shneur Zalman. He died that year on December 28, 1812, in Pena, a small town near Kurst and was buried in Haditz near Poltava. His last words were: "Soon I will no longer be with you. My children do not act proudly. Do not rely upon me to plead for you before the Heavenly Court. Do not depart, God forbid, from the way of the Torah and the Commandments."

The "Old Rebbe" left a vast literary treasure house: the Rav's *Shulhan Arukh*; *Torah Or* ("Torah's light"), homilies on Genesis, Exodus, *Hanukah* and *Purim*; *Likute Torah* ("Gleanings of Torah"), homilies on Leviticus, Numbers and Deuteronomy; *Beure Ha-Zohar*, a commentary on the *Zohar*; and a Cabbalistic commentary on the Prayer Book. His most important contribution to Jewish philosophy, was, however, the *Tanya* ("It has been taught") after the initial letters of the book *Likutei Amarim* ("Collected essays") or *Sepher shel Benowim* ("Book of Intermediaries"), which met with instant acclaim. Even his contemporaries greeted it with reverence. "With the *Tanya*, declared Rabbi Zusya of Annopol, "the Israelites will go forth to meet the Messiah."

The *Tanya* is divided into five sections. Section one consists of fifty-three chapters; section two, *Shaar Ha-Yihud ve-ha-emunah* ("Portal of Unity and Repentance"), and section three, *Iggeret Ha-Teshuvah* ("Epistle of Repentance"), each contain twelve chapters; section four *Iggeret Ha-Kodesh* ("The Holy Letter"), has thirty-two chapters, and section five, *Kuntres Aharon* ("Latest Discourse"). Fifty-five editions have so far appeared and it has been translated into Yiddish and English.[7] The fifty-three chapters of part one correspond to the weekly Torah reading, and the *Habad* Hasidim, to this day, religiously study a chapter of the *Tanya* every week.

Rabbi Shneur Zalman has been described as the Maimonides of Hasidism, for he represents the synthesis of Lithuanian intellectualism with Hasidic fervour. Emotion and *hitlahavut* ("ardour"), rich legacies of the Baal Shem Tov, are fused with philosophy and intellectualism. Yet, whilst Maimonides sought to harmonise Mosaic teachings with Aristotelian principles, the main concern of Shneur Zalman was to guide those "who are in pursuit of righteousness and seek the Lord . . . whose intelligence and mind are confused as they wander about in darkness in the service of God and are unable to perceive the beneficial light that is buried in books."[8] The proof for the existence of God, creation *ex nihilo*, Revelation and similar analogous matters which concerned Maimonides were not examined by Shneur Zalman. What to the philosopher is a question, is to the mystic a certainty, and Shneur Zalman was wholly mystic.

Shneur Zalman devoted twenty years to the preparation of the *Tanya*, and part one clearly demonstrates his mystical orientation, when he refers to the *Zohar* no fewer than forty-nine times, to Luria ten times and to Hayim Vital twenty-nine times.[9] He analyses the various facets and components of the soul, differentiating in true Cabbalistic tradition between the Divine Soul (*Nephesh Elohit*) and the Animal soul (*Nephesh ha-bahamit*). He examines the role of man in the cosmic order, the purpose of human existence, the concept of the Messianic era, the resurrection, the qualities of fear and love in relationship to God and the Lurian doctrine of *Tzimtzum*.

According to Rabbi Shneur Zalman, the intellect consists of three kindred faculties, *Hokhmah* ("Wisdom"), *Binah* ("understanding") and *Daat* ("knowledge"), the first, second and third of the ten *Sephirot*, and they form the root letters of the (Hebrew) word *Habad*. The prophets and the rabbis taught that "God desires the heart' and Rabbi Shneur Zalman stressed that God also desires the mind. Reason was elevated above emotion, for, just as it is impossible to beget children without a mother, so *Hokhmah* and *Binah* are the father and the mother that together give birth to love of God. "It is well known to all who have basked in the fragrant doctrines of the Besht and his disciples," wrote Shneur Zalman in this homely metaphor, "that understanding is the mother of children. These 'children' are love and fear, born of knowledge and profound contemplation of the greatness of God."[10]

A man is neither a static nor a passive entity. He is a dynamic being who must strive to develop his potential talent and perfect himself. For here there is no aristocracy of birth, and all men are capable of scaling the heights. Every Jew has the making of a *Zaddik*. In every soul there are sparks of potential goodness but often these are in a state of "suspended animation". These sparks can be reclaimed, for the "gates of repentance never close". "Within the soul dwells the light of God, which is not subject to the variations and determinations of time."

Within the framework of *Habad*, as Shneur Zalman's doctrines were called, the *Zaddik* is neither an intermediary nor a pillar of the world. He is a supervisor rather than a superior, a teacher of morality rather than a worker of miracles. It is permissible to lean on a friend for support, but it is better to stand by oneself. Trained to spiritual self-sufficiency and not to total dependence on the *Zaddik*, *Habad* Hasidim visit their rabbi regularly for guidance and instruction, pay him respect rather than homage. For the bond between them is one of mutual affection and esteem.

Habad attached great importance to Torah study and regarded it as equal to the observance of all the Commandments. Through the study of the Torah man can reach the highest stage of development and self-perfection, for the Torah illumines and elevates the mind. It is food for the soul, and the soul cannot live without it. Rabbi Shneur Zalman once remarked to Rabbi Joshua Zeitlin: "The Hasidim, too, set aside time for study. The difference between them and the *Mitnagdim* is this: the latter set time for study and they are limited by a time factor, whereas the former make the Torah their path of life."

From every chapter that a man studies and from every *Mitzvah* that he performs an angel is created. When the Torah is studied with ardour and when a *Mitzvah* is performed with joy animated angels are created. When there is no ardour, the angels are joyless and dispirited. The "animal soul" emanates from the *Kelipot* ("Shells"), known as *Nogah* ("light"), which is an amalgam of good and evil, and man cannot entirely escape from its source. The concern of Shneur Zalman was not with the *Zaddik* ("righteous person"), nor with the *Rasha* ("wicked person"), but with the *Beinoni* ("average man").

Whilst the eighteenth-century philosophers grappled with doubts and perplexities, Rabbi Shneur Zalman formulated his philosophy of Judaism with clarity and cogent conciseness. Moreover, his style is both lucid and lively, avoiding technical terms, and his material is presented with freshness and originality.

No other Hasidic rabbi left such a distinctive imprint on the movement as this "Suffering Servant". He established a dynasty, Lubavitch; he formulated a philosophy, *Habad*; he added fuel to the fire kindled by the Besht, and the flames burned with a new brilliance.

Chapter 8

Hasidism's Great Story Teller

"The Holy One Blessed be He sends the cure before the malady," so says the *Midrash*, and this saying comes to mind when one considers the life and works of Rabbi Nahman of Braclaw. For Nahman was born a year before the *Maggid* of Mezhirichi died, the year during which the Gaon of Vilna issued his *Herem* against the Hasidim. Poet and seer, one of the most remarkable of all the Hasidic rabbis, Rabbi Nahman was the greatest story-teller in the annals of Hasidism. Indeed, the tales of Rabbi Nahman rank with the classic tales of Jacob Ludwig Carl (1785–1863), Wilhelm Carl Grimm (1786–1859) and Hans Christian Andersen (1805–75).

Nahman was born on a Sabbath in 1772, in Medzibozh. His father, Simha, was the son of Rabbi Nahman of Horodenka, a devoted follower of the Besht and a reader in the Besht's synagogue. His mother Feige was the daughter of Udel, the only daughter of the Besht. Together with Meir of Przemysl, Nahman of Horodenka emigrated to the Holy Land in 1761. Nahman's grandmother Udel was also the mother of two sons, Barukh of Medzibozh and Moses Hayim of Sudlikov. The brothers were totally different in temperament. Rabbi Moses Hayim was a fine scholar of retiring disposition, while the turbulent Rabbi Barukh was quarrelsome, boastful and exceedingly vain.

Nahman was brought up in conditions of great poverty, but the glory of the Besht had not departed from Medzibozh. It was crowded with memories of his great grandfather and he spent many hours at the ancestral tomb lost in dreams. For little Nahman, the Besht lived on. An assiduous student, the lad learned fast. With increasing eagerness he applied himself to Talmud, Bible, *Zohar* and the writings of the Cabbalists. Both *Halakhah* and *Aggadah* were equally dear to him. Almost from the cradle he absorbed the legends and the wonder tales of

76

the Talmud and medieval literature, as well as the stories of the Besht. *Halakhah* sharpened his intellect, while *Aggadah* fired his imagination. When Nahman was but thirteen years old, his uncle, Rabbi Moses Hayim Ephraim, predicted that he would be "the greatest of all the *Zaddikim.*" That year, he married Soshia, daughter of Ephraim Ber of Zaslav, and settled with his youthful bride in Husiatyn, Podolia.

Marriage did not change his way of life. Nothing could divert him from his studies. "Great was his mastery," records his disciple Nathan, "of the Bible, of *En Yaacov* (an annotated compilation of the *Aggadic* sections of both the Palestinian and Babylonian Talmud by Jacob Ibn Haviv, 1460–1516), of Lurian literature and of the *Zohar*". Nahman did not believe in short cuts to Heaven. He chose the long, hard way, the ascetic way. "No limits are set to the ascent of man and each can scale the very highest peaks," he believed. Heir of the Besht though he was, he adopted the austere practices of Luria.

The frail Cabbalist indulged in prolonged fasts. Often, he abstained from food for days on end. In one year he fasted eighteen times "from Sabbath to Sabbath" and these fasts were followed by immersions in icy cold *Mikvaot* ("Ritual Baths"). Often he wandered alone for days through the fields and in the forests meditating on the mysteries of mortality, contemplating undisturbed the wonders of nature. Contrasting sharply with his indifference to his own health was the deep concern he displayed for the physical, as well as the spiritual well-being of his Hasidim. Premonitions of his short life span were always with him. Not an hour was wasted, not a minute lost. He regarded every single day as if it were his last, nor did he rest on the spiritual laurels of his distinguished ancestor. "The world imagines," he said, "that I have attained a high status because I am a descendant of the Besht. It is not so. I have succeeded because I have afflicted my body. Whatever I have achieved is due to my own endeavours."

To broaden his experience, Nahman tried new ventures and new challenges. He knew nothing about boats, but without hesitation stepped into one and sailed for hours down the river. By trial and error, he learned what other people learn from teachers. Thus it was from experience that he could say: "Everyone can reach the top, provided that he strives and works for it."

It was said that King Solomon understood the language of the flowers, birds and animals. In a different way, nature spoke to Nahman and through nature spoke God. "When a man becomes worthy to hear the songs of the plants, how each plant chants the praises of God, how beautiful and sweet it is to hear their singing! And therefore, it is good to serve God in their midst, roaming over the fields among the growing things, pouring out one's heart before God in truthfulness."[1]

The death of Ephraim Ber, his father-in-law, spelt the end of financial security for the young scholar and his family. He settled in Medvedavka, near Uman, and there at the age of eighteen, Nahman became a *Rebbe*. But he was in every way a non-conformist *Rebbe*. "I shall make a path through the desert," he proclaimed. "I shall hew down one by one the trees which have stood for thousands of years, so that no obstacle stands in our path."[2]

With an overwhelming passion, Rabbi Nahman, Hasidism's staunchest Zionist, yearned for the Holy Land. "All holiness is concentrated in the Holy Land. Only there is it possible to ascend the ladder to holiness. The holiness of *Eretz Yisrael* strengthens a man's faith and patience and helps him to subdue anger and to banish melancholy."[3] Aphorisms were no substitute for action. At the age of twenty-six, on the eve of Passover 1798, he decided to undertake this momentous journey. "In this year," he announced, "I shall certainly be in the Holy Land . . . I shall set forth immediately, whatever the conditions and even without money. Perhaps those who take pity on me will aid me."

The decision distressed his family. In vain his daughter pleaded: "Who will look after us while you are away in the Land of Israel?" He was unswerving in his determination. So powerful was the call of the Holy Land that nothing could disuade him and he steeled himself against the plaintive plea of his children. "Go to your parent-in-law," he replied. "Your older sister will become a servant. People will have compassion on your younger sister. Your mother will become a cook. I shall sell some household goods to raise money for the journey. My heart is already there." The knowledge that the Besht did not succeed in visiting the land of his fathers strengthened the resolve of the Besht's forceful great-grandson. "I know that I will have to surmount innumerable obstacles. As long as my soul is within me and the breath of life is in my nostrils, I will not give up. I am willing to die in order to reach the Land of Israel."

In poor health, and almost penniless, ready to face the untold hazards that lay ahead, Rabbi Nahman set out on his journey. First he went to Kamenetz, where he celebrated *Shavuot* ("The Feast of Weeks"). He embarked at Odessa, and four days later, after a stormy voyage, he reached Istanbul. Great were his sufferings in Istanbul. A plague was ravaging the community and Rabbi Nahman barely escaped infection.

"Before one rises," he commented with resignation, "one must first fall." It was only with difficulty that he managed to obtain a passage on a boat. Eventually (some four months after leaving home) he arrived in Haifa, on the eve of *Rosh Hashanah*, 1799.

Now the young mystic was in his element. After walking for but four cubits on the hallowed soil he felt that he had already attained a high degree of spirituality. Rabbi Nahman visited Tiberias and Safed, the homes of his spiritual counsellors, the Cabbalists. Wherever he went, he was honoured and made many friends, among them Rabbi Abraham of Kalisk. He even assumed the role of peacemaker and brought about a reconciliation between Rabbi Abraham and Rabbi Jacob Shimshon of Shepetovka. Mindful of his family obligations, Nahman betrothed his daughter to the grandson of Rabbi Menahem Mendel of Vitebsk. Reluctantly he returned home, via Rhodes, where he spent the Passover. But he always spoke with love and with longing of the Holy Land. "My place," he declared, "is only in the Land of Israel. If I travel anywhere I shall travel only thither."

In an age of rationalism, the age of which produced Moses Mendelssohn (1729–86) and Solomon Maimon, Rabbi Nahman valued faith above philosophy, simplicity above sophistry. Nahman, whose instinct was sure and whose intuition was reliable, had little patience for subtle dialectics. "It is better to be a believer, although unlettered, than a scholar and a sceptic." He despised philosophy. "Happy is he who knows nothing of their books, but who walks uprightly and fears retribution." Even Maimonides, the greatest Jewish philosopher of all time, did not escape censure.[4] "He who looks into the *Moreh* (Maimonides' "*Moreh Nebukhim*" "Guide to the Perplexed")" pronounced Rabbi Nahman severely, "loses the Divine image of his being."[5] "There are some who pass today for great philosophers," he added, "but in the world to come it will be revealed that they were in reality nothing more than heretics and unbelievers."[6]

Confession occupied a significant place in Nahman's world. Rabbi Nahman's Hasidim were called *Vidnicks* ("Confessors") because they went to confess their sins to the *Zaddik*. The private prayer of the *Vidnicks* was: "In Thy mercy make me worthy to confess before the *Zaddik*, in order that he may make atonement for me by means of his wisdom and humility."

In physicians, as in philosophers, Rabbi Nahman had little faith. Healing came from God. "Even where there are distinguished doctors, one should neither rely on them nor put one's life in their hands. They are liable to err and can easily do damage which can never be rectified. How much more is this the danger with the majority of doctors that are to be found in our country, who cannot distinguish their right hand from their left and are veritable killers . . . It is well to avoid them."[7] Jestingly he remarked: "It was difficult for the Angel of Death to kill the whole world by himself so he appointed deputies—the doctors."[8]

Although he did not glorify poverty, he disapproved of the acquisition of wealth and advocated modesty. In many ways Rabbi Nahman himself was modest and unassuming, yet he was deeply conscious of his own special qualities and unique mission. "Since the Jews were dispersed from the Holy Land," he declared, "there have been four great periods of learning, and at the centre of each epoch stood a chosen one. There are four chosen teachers: Rabbi Simeon ben Yohai, Rabbi Isaac Luria, the Besht and myself."[9] "All *Zaddikim* after reaching a certain degree of spirituality remain static; I, however, with the help of God, become another person every day." "In the world to come", he told his disciples, "you may be worthy to understand the hidden meaning that underlies my most casual remark."[10]

He warned against the heretical *Maskilim* and the new ideas that were infiltrating from Germany. "Heresies are spreading," he said. "Happy is he who strengthens himself by faith."[11] "Master of the Universe, help us to resist the temptations," he prayed "that are to be found in the writings and languages of the Gentiles . . . Annul the evil decrees, especially the decrees that compel our young people to study the ungodly writings."[12]

Rigorous, indeed, were the standards that Rabbi Nahman set for the *Zaddik*, for the role of the *Zaddik* was of transcendent importance. Rabbi Nahman believed that only through the *Zaddik* could a man attain understanding of the Divine. The *Zaddik* could perform miracles in heaven and on earth. The words of the *Zaddik* were more precious than the "words of the Torah and prophets." Thus for the Hasid to visit his *Rebbe* sporadically was not enough, for close communion between the two was essential. So exalted was Nahman's concept of the *Zaddik* and so exacting were his standards that few of his contemporaries passed muster. "The evil spirit finds it hard to lead all of mankind astray, therefore he appoints such pseudo-*Zaddikim* in various places to help him."[13]

Nahman was no false prophet to cry "Peace! Peace!" when there was no peace. His criticism was scathing when he felt that criticism was called for, and he cared nothing for consequences or repercussions. No one could ignore this dynamic, non-conformist descendant of the Besht, this great rebel of Hasidism.

His contemporaries, for their part, either loved or loathed him. Among his adversaries was the "Grandfather" of Shpola, known affectionately as the "Shpoler Zeide". To him the Besht attributed the lofty soul of Rabbi Judah Löw ben Bezalel (Der Hohe Rabbi Löw) of Prague. "You were sent to redeem lost souls. There are many outcasts in the world," said the Besht. "You alone can reclaim them." The *Shpoler Zeide* lived to the age of eighty-seven (he died in 1812) and was well advanced in years by the time Rabbi Nahman came to live nearby. Having known the Besht, Rabbi Phinehas of Korzec and the *Maggid*, Rabbi Aryeh Leib was regarded as the "Lion of the *Zaddikim*." Yet, friendly and unpretentious, he travelled from village to village, bringing a message of hope to the people. He was a popular *Zaddik*, with many miracles to his credit.

In 1800, eighteen months after his return from the Holy Land, Rabbi Nahman settled in Zlatupola, which was near Shpola. Repeatedly, the older *Zaddik* clashed with the turbulent newcomer. Rabbi Aryeh Leib regarded Rabbi Nahman as irresponsible and presumptuous, seeking to destroy from within what the Gaon of Vilna had failed to destroy from without. "This is not the way a *Zaddik* should conduct himself," he remarked, "nor is this the manner in which a *Zaddik* should converse." The mantle of the Gaon of Vilna had fallen on the octogenarian of Shpola. The struggle between the *Mitnagdim* and the Hasidim was over, but now "civil war" broke out within the Hasidic movement itself. Its aim had been the "close fellowship" of Hasid with Hasid, but now it was torn by jealousies and hatreds. Rival factions exchanged recriminations, and the accusations once levelled at the founder of *Habad* were now hurled at Rabbi Nahman. He was even accused of following Shabbetai Zevi and Jacob Frank. "Curse Nahman," urged the sage of Shpola, losing much of the serene benevolence that had characterised his life, "and I will assure you a portion in the world to come."[14]

Rabbi Levi Isaac of Berdichev tried to make peace, but without success. For, having antagonised his contemporaries, Rabbi Nahman made no attempt to pacify them. He accepted such persecution and vilification as almost inevitable. "How is it possible," he asked, "that they should not quarrel with me? I am not really of this world, and therefore the world cannot understand me[15] . . . All that has been before is as the life within the fruit before it is ripe . . . There has never been one like myself in the world . . . I am like unto a fruitful tree whose branches and foliage are fresh and green . . . I have kindled a torch that will never be put out . . . The righteous redeemer will be one of my descendants . . . In the world to come all men will be Hasidim of Braclaw."[16]

Such sentiments were hardly conciliatory. Clearly, he was not destined to live a peaceful life, nor did he seek it. "I assure you," Rabbi Nahman told his followers, "I could live at peace with everybody, but I am not fated to do so. There are certain steps that one cannot take without causing dissension." Rabbi Nahman did not stand completely alone. Among his supporters were Barukh of Medzibozh, Abraham of Kalisk and Hayim of Krasni. "If only I knew that the world would listen to me," declared Rabbi Levi Isaac of Berdichev, "I would cry aloud, in a voice that could be heard from one end of the universe to the other, that whosoever wishes to be upright and to serve the Lord in truth should attach himself to Rabbi Nahman."

In 1802, Nahman settled in Braclaw, Podolia, on the River Bug. There he met Rabbi Nathan ben Naphtali Hirz (d. 1830) of Nemirov, who became his Boswell. "Had I come to Braclaw merely to find you, that in itself would be reward enough," he once remarked. "Nathan, Nathan," he exclaimed, "you have the power to make my Torah live for ever." It was Rabbi Nathan who minutely recorded the aphorisms, the discourses and the tales of his master. "Great mysteries are contained in these fables," maintained the scholar-scribe, for whom every word was sacred.

Intimate was the relationship between Rabbi Nahman and his followers. They needed a charismatic leader and he needed their loyalty and devotion. "How can I ever forget you?" he writes. "Every one of you has a place in my heart. Every one of you has a share in my Torah." "Eat or do not eat, sleep or do not sleep, pray or do not pray, one thing you must do," he told his followers, "and that is to come to me." For mysterious reasons that he hinted at but did not divulge, Rabbi Nahman travelled from place to place. He visited Lvov, Ostrog and Zaslav. "If the people knew only the purpose of my journeys they would kiss my very footprints," he confided to his followers.[17]

In 1808, Nahman's health deteriorated even further, and he began to suffer from tuberculosis. The following year when his house in Braclaw was burned down, he settled in Uman, the scene of the notorious Haidamack's massacre led by the Cossack Zhelyeznyak in the spring of 1768. Here, Nahman became acquainted with such notable *Maskilim* as Hayim Heikel Hurwitz (c. 1750–1822) and his son Hirsch Ber Hurwitz (Hermann Bernard, 1785–1857) who later settled in England and was appointed in 1837 "Praeceptor Linguae Sacrae" at the University of Cambridge. "Hirsch Ber Hurwitz read and explained the German classics to Rabbi Nahman," writes a contemporary *Maskil*, "and Nahman listened with great eagerness. When he was pleased by an idea, he immediately incorporated it into his work and attributed it to a *Zaddik*."

Rabbi Nahman's days were now numbered, and for three years he lived in the shadow of death. But for him, death was merely a change of activity. "After my demise, any man" he told his Hasidim, "may come to my grave and recite ten chapters from the Book of Psalms and contribute to charity on my behalf. Then, even if his sins are many, I will do my utmost to intercede for him." With deep sorrow, the faithful Nathan watched his beloved mentor fading. "Rabbi, Rabbi, with whom are you leaving us?" he asked in anguish. The master comforted his Hasidim. "I am not, God forbid, leaving you. I will be with you always." He died on the third day of *Hol Ha-Moed Succot*, 1810, and was buried in Uman.

Seven children were born to Nahman, two boys and five daughters. His elder son, Shlomo Ephraim, died in infancy. "My heart is broken," wept the bereaved father. His younger son, Jacob, born in 1796, died at a very early age. Thus, there was no son to succeed Nahman. And he had no successor. His disciples became known as the *Toite Hasidim* ("Dead Hasidim") because they remained so faithful to the living memory of their departed Rebbe.

Yet the intra-movement feud did not die with the death of Rabbi Nahman, and for some time the leaderless Hasidim were vilified and persecuted. Rabbi Moses Zevi of Savran, the leader of the opposition, called them "sinners who caused others to sin," and warned his followers not to intermarry with them. "Moreover, a Hasid of Braclaw should not instruct your children . . . A *Shohet* ("Ritual Slaughterer") of Braclaw is disqualified from *shehitah* ("Ritual slaughter")." Rabbi Nathan of Nemirov pleaded with Rabbi Moses Zevi: "Do not shed innocent blood", but he pleaded in vain.

Braclaw Hasidim scattered, but they made it a practice to gather together once a year to recall in fellowship the days and the ways of their remarkable *Zaddik*. "Before the New Year, each Hasid lays aside his business and often makes a financial sacrifice to come to Uman, where he worships, weeps and remembers. The extent of the joy, weeping and dancing in the holy chapel cannot be described. It is a time of mutual enlightenment and inspiration." After the Russian Revolution of 1917, the gatherings at Uman came to an end. Until the outbreak of the Second World War "the Dead Hasidim" met regularly at Lublin.

Rabbi Nahman was a prolific author, but few of his books were published in his lifetime. Most appeared posthumously, lovingly edited and transcribed by Rabbi Nathan, who, in 1821, opened a printing press in Braclaw especially for this purpose. These works include *Likute Tephilot* ("A Collection of Prayers"), *Likutei Halakhot* ("A Collection of Legal Rulings") on the *Shulhan Arukh, Orah Hayim, Yoreh Deah, Hoshen Mishpat* and *Even Haezer*; *Sepher Ha-Midot* ("A Treatise on Morals") arranged alphabetically, and *Sippure Maasiyot* ("Stories).

It is only recently that Nahman has been accorded his rightful place in Yiddish literature, particularly with regard to his contribution to folklore, for he has been described as "the greatest story-teller of the Jewish people" and the "classical story-teller of all times, not only in Hasidism, but in the whole range of Jewish lore, with few, if any, equals in other literatures."[18]

It was in Braclaw that Nahman began to tell his stories. An original and gifted story-teller, he spoke in Yiddish, and in Yiddish the stories were faithfully recorded by Nathan of Nemirov. "Every word written in this holy book is sacred," wrote Rabbi Nathan. "These stories emanated from the mouth of the great *Zaddik* himself." Undoubtedly, Rabbi Nahman gathered material from many far-flung sources, recasting it in a form original and fresh, unmistakably the production of his own fertile mind. His knowledge was encyclopaedic. He shows familiarity with animal life, with marine life and with many branches of natural science.

Some tales were brief; others were virtually novelettes. Altogether some thirteen long stories and twenty-one short stories have been preserved. Among the most famous are: "The Lost Princess," "The Broken Betrothal," "The Cripple," "The King's Son and the Servant's Son," "The Wind that overturned the World," "The Bull and the Ram," "The Prince," "The Spider and the Fly," "The Rabbi's Son" and the "Seven Beggars."

Often Rabbi Nathan describes the occasion that inspired a particular story, the rise of Napoleon, for instance. "We were astonished by the exalted position to which that one (Napoleon) had been raised, so that from a lowly man (literally "servant") he had become an Emperor. We spoke with our Master about it. And he said: 'Who knows whose soul is his? In the Castle of Transformations souls are at times exchanged.' And he began to tell the tale of the king's son and the maid's son whose souls were exchanged."[19] Probably the story of the "Lost Princess" was inspired by the death of his daughter Sarah.

On another occasion, Rabbi Nahman saw a reader of a Synagogue wearing torn garments. "Are you not a master of prayer, through whom the blessings are brought down to earth?" he asked. He then told the story of the Master of Prayer." The stories reveal the story-teller's own views and attitudes. "The Sage and the Simpleton" reflects his attitude towards the *Maskilim,* for in this story he maintains that wealth leads to idolatry and that the truly pious do not strive for riches. For those who pursue wealth are always in debt, "slaves to their desires and ambitions and the slaves of others. Would it not be better if they turned away from their idols of gold and silver and learned to serve God?"

Sometimes perplexing, sometimes illuminating are many of these allegorical narrations. "Each tale," comments the writer, Meyer Levin, on the "Seven Beggars," "is an intricate maze; the reader follows several different paths, only to find himself suddenly standing still, bewildered and triumphant, at their common crossroads. The meaning is hidden, yet shining clear, for each person in each tale is a symbol, as abstract as a numeral, and in the end, the symbols seem miraculously to have taken their places in the pure formula of a given theorem."[20]

The tales have been printed in innumerable editions in both Hebrew and Yiddish. In the twentieth century they have been edited by S. A. Horodezky, David Kahana and Eliezer Steinman.[21] Martin Buber was the first to introduce Nahman to the Western world. He translated the tales into German. These were translated into English by Maurice Friedmann.[22] "I have not translated these stories," Buber confesses, "but retold them with full freedom yet out of his spirit as it is present to me." Some of Nahman's stories are to be found in Meyer Levin's "Golden Mountain."[23] However, no verbatim translation of the stories has yet appeared.

Chapter 9

"The Second Baal Shem Tov"

Chronic constitutional weaknesses rendered the Polish State an easy prey for predatory neighbours. The Three Partitions (1772–95) erased the name of Poland from the political map of Europe, and the subjugated territory was divided between the mighty encircling triumvirate of Russia, Prussia and Austria. Galicia was acquired by Austria in 1772, and the 1789 census revealed 178,072 Jews among the 3,039,391 inhabitants, with Lvov, Cracow, Brody and Tarnopol having large Jewish communities.

The civil emancipation of the Jews began in the last decades of the eighteenth century. In his Edict of Toleration (*Tolerantpatent*) of January, 1782, the Emperor of Austria, Joseph II, proposed "to grant to all his subjects, Jews as well as Protestants, freedom of worship." He abolished the yellow patch, the "Jews' Badge", and repealed discriminatory laws that dated back to the Middle Ages. Jews were permitted to send their children to State schools "to learn, at least, reading, writing and arithmetic". They became liable for military service and were no longer prevented from pursuing careers in industry.

This period saw the rise of the "Enlightenment" (*Haskalah*), movement aimed at integrating Jews into the main-stream of modern European culture. One of the Enlightenment's most famous exponents was Moses Mendelssohn, the "German Socrates", who wished to lead the Jews "out of the narrow labyrinth of ritual theological casuistry into the broad highway of human culture". With his translation of the Bible into German with a Hebrew commentary, *Biur*, the *Maskilim*, as men of the enlightenment were called, launched vitriolic attacks upon Talmudists and Hasidim alike. The Hasidic leaders were caricatured as ignorant magicians whose followers "walked in the darkness." Such invective was largely ineffective. In a rationalistic era, the era of

Voltaire, Rousseau and Locke, East European Jews in surprising numbers sought to enter the moonlight gardens of Hasidism.

"And a river went out of Eden to water the garden; and from thence it divided and became four streams." This verse from Genesis (ii. 10) has been interpreted by Rabbi Zusya of Annopol as follows: "'Eden' represents the Baal Shem Tov; 'the river' is the *Maggid* of Mezhirichi; 'the garden' is Rabbi Elimelekh of Lezajsk (Lishensk), and the four streams are Rabbi Israel of Kozienice, Rabbi Mendel of Rymanov, Rabbi Joshua Heshel of Opatov and Rabbi Jacob Isaac of Lublin."

Elimelekh of Lezajsk was born in 1717, in Lapacha, near Tiktin, one of the seven children of a wealthy landowner called Eliezer Lipmann. The family traced its descent back to the commentator Rashi (1040–1105), and even farther back, to the second-century *Tanna* Johanan Ha-Sandelar, "the shoemaker". Eliezer and his wife, Meresh, were kindly, charitable people, who tried to ease the poverty of their hard-pressed neighbours. Their house was always open and all were welcome. "My mother," said Zusya, "did not pray from a prayer book, because she could not read. But she knew by heart how to recite the benedictions. And she recited them with such fervour that, where she had recited the blessings in the morning, in that place the radiance of the Divine Presence rested the whole day."[1]

Elimelekh and his brother Zusya studied in Tiktin, where they came into contact with Rabbi Shmelke Hurwitz, who was then living with his grandfather, Meir ha-Levi Hurwitz. From Shmelke, one of Hasidism's great scholars, Elimelekh learned to study with single-minded diligence. Also beneficial to Elimelekh was his meeting with Shmelke's brother, Rabbi Phinehas, the author of *Sepher ha-Mikneh*, novella on Tractate *Kiddushin*.

The most dominant force in Elimelekh's life, however, was his own brother, Meshullam Zusya of Annopol (d. 1800), a remarkable man even in an age of remarkable men. He lived a life of unmitigated penury, yet he would say: "I have never experienced suffering." His humility was equalled by his kind-heartedness and his single-minded devotion to the service of God and man. "No matter when I lift my soul to Heaven," said Rabbi Nathan Adler (1741–1800), the German Cabbalist of Frankfurt-on-Main, "Zusya is always ahead of me." But Zusya was never content with his spiritual achievements, and strove ceaselessly to improve and perfect his way of life. His favourite saying was: "In the world to come, they will not ask me: 'Why were you not Moses?' But they will ask me, 'Why were you not Zusya?'"

"Exile atones for everything," said Rabbi Johanan in the Talmud.[2] So Elimelekh decided to go into "exile" with his brother Zusya, to atone for their misdeeds, and to bring others to repentance. Wandering incognito, for three years they suffered the rigours of the road, often weary and hungry, often endangering their lives. Generally, communal leaders were reluctant to permit unknown "wanderers" to occupy the pulpit, and it was only infrequently that Elimelekh preached in a local synagogue. They traversed Poland and reached as far as Ushpitzin—on the borders of Germany, spreading Hasidic teachings wherever they went. In the words of Rabbi Noah of Kobryn: "You will find Hasidim up to the point that the brothers Rabbi Zusya and Rabbi Elimelekh reached in their long wanderings. Beyond that you will not find Hasidim."

Hasidim delight in recounting the adventures of the two roaming *Rebbes*. It is told that they once arrived at an inn. Rabbi Elimelekh lay down to rest against the wall, with Rabbi Zusya beside him. In came a crowd of drunken peasants who took Zusya and pummelled him. After a while, they let him slide to the floor. Anxious to shield his brother, Elimelekh said to him: "Dear Zusya, now let us change places. Let me lie in your place and you sleep in my corner. It is time for you to rest. It is my turn to suffer their blows." So, quickly, they changed places. However, after another round of drinking, the peasants said to one another: "It is not fair to beat only one. Let the other one have his share." So they dragged out Zusya and again rained blows upon him. "If a man is destined to receive blows," philosophised Zusya, "he will receive them, no matter where he puts himself."[3]

Zusya and Elimelekh shared their thoughts as well as their sufferings, and their dialogues were instructive. "Dear brother," said Zusya once, "we believe that the souls of all men were contained in Adam. So we, too, must have been present when Adam ate of the Tree of Knowledge (Genesis iii. 6). How could we have permitted him to commit such a sin?" "I could easily have prevented it," replied Elimelekh, "but I refrained from doing so. Had Adam not eaten, the poisonous suggestion of the serpent would have haunted him for all eternity, for he would have believed that, had he eaten, he would have become like God himself."[4]

When the Besht died, Elimelekh was forty-three years old. Medzibozh lost its attraction for him. He devoted himself completely to his studies and to ascetic practices, fasting from Sabbath to Sabbath for fourteen years. At the urging of his brother Zusya, Elimelekh visited the *Maggid* Dov Baer at Dubno. Elimelekh hailed the *Maggid* as "my teacher", who then became his true mentor. At Dubno, he renewed his acquaintance with Rabbi Shmelke, and there he met Rabbi Levi Isaac of Berdichev and Michael of Zloczew.

After the death of the *Maggid* in 1773, Elimelekh reigned for the next thirteen years as the "uncrowned" head of Hasidism. He was loyally supported by most of the *Maggid*'s great disciples, among them Rabbi Jacob Isaac, the Seer whom Elimelekh called "Messiah the son of Joseph", Rabbi Israel of Kozienice, Menahem Mendel of Rymanov, the witty Rabbi Naftali of Ropczyce and Rabbi Kalonymos Kalman Epstein the author of *Maor Va-Shemesh* ("The Light and the Sun").

Elimelekh's home town of Lezajsk became the Jerusalem of Hasidism, and Elimelekh proved to be an ideal *Rebbe*. Like the Besht, Elimelekh could establish instant rapport with both scholars and the masses. No curtain divided him from the people. The *Maggid* had remained in his own home, waiting for the people to come to him. Like the Besht, Elimelekh took up the wanderer's staff and visited many villages and distant hamlets. In this way he came to understand the economic struggles, as well as the spiritual needs of the people. He was deeply concerned over the plight of orphans and it gave him particular pleasure to arrange marriages for them. There was never any money in the house of Elimelekh, for all gifts were promptly distributed among the poor.

Paramount, of course, was the need for faith—rock-like, unfaltering faith in God. But man must also have faith in the *Zaddik*. With the cessation of prophecy, the *Zaddik* was the true heir of the prophets. Who, then, is a *Zaddik*? Any man who observes the Sabbath with true devotion, according to Rabbi Elimelekh. The role of the *Zaddik* is to strengthen his followers in their struggle against the Evil Inclination.

A key weapon in this struggle is prayer, and all that the *Zaddik* achieves is through the power of prayer. Rabbi Elimelekh himself composed a special prayer to be recited before the statutory services: "May it be Thy will to remove all barriers between our souls and Thee, our Father in Heaven. Keep us from conceit, anger, ill temper . . . Plant Thy Holy Spirit within us and save us from all envy and jealousy. Endow us with vision to see in everyone his good qualities and to close our eyes to his defects. Then shall our prayers cause us to rise to even higher levels and bring us nearer to Thee." Many Hasidim recited these words. In the Court of Biala, this prayer was recited just before *Kol Nidre* on the eve of the Day of Atonement.

At a time when Hasidism was suspect and Hasidim were regarded as renegades, Rabbi Elimelekh drew up a code of conduct for his followers. "He who adopts this liturgy (*Nusah Ari*)," his son Eliezer reported in his name, "should not utter falsehood or curse his neighbour in his heart . . . He should not be guilty of pride or jealousy, nor should he covet wealth." Rabbi Elimelekh counselled moderation in all things, and as far as liquor was concerned he counselled abstinence. In particular, he warned his followers to abstain from alcohol on the last two days of *Succot* (*Shemini Atzeret* and *Simhat Torah*), so as not to allow strong drink to be mixed with the Holy Spirit.

Under the direction of Elimelekh, Torah study was intensified at Lezajsk. Hasidim were exhorted to apply themselves, each according to his ability, to Scripture, *Mishnah* and *Gemara*, with the commentaries of Rashi and *Tosaphot*. The "curriculum" included the books of *Musar* ("ethical literature") the *Shelah* (*Shnei Luhot Habrit*) by Isaiah Horowitz and *Hovat Ha-Levavot* ("Duties of the Heart") by the religious philosopher, Bahya ben Joseph Ibn Pakuda (c. 1050–1120).

A perfectionist, he was tormented by self-doubts and feared that he had not fulfilled his mission. "I am old. I am nearly sixty years of age, and I have not managed to carry out even one *Mitzvah* with proper devotion," grieved Rabbi Elimelekh. "A new *Gehinnom* (hell) will have to be created for me. The present hell that now exists cannot purge my sins and transgressions." It did not seem to the self-doubting *Zaddik* that he could possibly be worthy of inheriting the world to come. "If I were asked in the world to come 'Have you learned?' I would have to answer, 'No'. To the question, 'Have you prayed properly?' I would also have to answer negatively. All that could be said in my favour would be that I was telling the truth." Constantly, he pondered the matter. "If I am directed to enter Gehinnom, I will ask, 'Who ordered this?' And if they tell me, 'The Almighty', I will hasten into hell to fulfil the will of God."

Despite the opposition of both the Besht and the *Maggid* to asceticism, Elimelekh never entirely discarded the Lurian way of life, yet he persuaded Rabbi David of Lelov to discontinue such practices. However, he agreed with the *Maggid* that "learning two pages of the Talmud with the commentaries of *Rabbenu* Asher ben Jehiel (1250–1327) is preferable to fasting, and reciting the Book of Psalms thrice daily is more beneficial than fasting a whole week." Elimelekh stressed that repentance was not to be associated with melancholy, for "sadness prevents a man from serving his Creator."

When the Vilna authorities excommunicated the Hasidim, Elimelekh, like the *Maggid*, advised restraint. Even when he was physically assaulted by an over-zealous *Mitnaged*, his reaction was mild: "Master of the Universe! I forgive him with my whole heart. Let no man be punished on my behalf." But when Rabbi Levi Isaac of Berdichev was persecuted, Elimelekh rallied to his support. And similarly, Shmelke, in his eloquent defence of Hasidism, stressed that "the Hasidim are dedicated to the service of God. They pray and study Torah at every available moment . . . Have we not all one Father? Has not one God created us? Why do we deal treacherously every one against his neighbour?"[5] Shmelke's defence of Hasidism brought considerable criticism in his own community. Travelling to Nikolsburg, Elimelekh delivered passionate discourses and was able to reconcile the rabbi and his community.

Two letters, written at this time and included in Elimelekh's book, *Noam Elimelekh* ("The Pleasantness of Elimelekh"), throw some light on the "civil war" that was raging so fiercely in Galicia between *Mitnagdim* and Hasidim. In one letter, his son refutes the accusations of Rabbi Abraham Katzenellenbogen of Brest-Litovsk and justifies the adoption by the Hasidim of the *Nusah Ari* ("The Lurian Liturgy"). Another letter stresses the high calibre of the *Zaddikim*. "They serve God in truth without any pride . . . They engage ceaselessly in the study of the Torah for its own sake. They study in order to fulfil the Commandments . . . Their whole purpose is to purify themselves and their thoughts."

Elimelekh died in 1786. His grave became a place of pilgrimage, and for over one hundred and fifty years right up to World War II, Hasidim would place *Kvitlekh* ("petitions") at the tomb.

His most important work, *Noam Elimelekh*, ("The Pleasantness of Elimelekh"), a commentary on the weekly Torah reading, is one of the classics of Hasidic literature. It was published in Lvov two years after his death, by his son and successor, Eliezer. It was instantly acclaimed for its power and profundity, and has since appeared in over forty editions. Rabbi Mendel of Rymanov used to say that only on the eve of Sabbath, after emerging from the ritual bath, was he able to grasp the meaning of *Noam Elimelekh*.[6] Rabbi Hayim of Kossov went further, declaring that only "a person who is able to revive the dead is able to understand this book."[7]

Elimelekh also wrote *Likute Shoshana* ("Gatherings of the Lily"), comments on Biblical passages and rabbinic sayings which appeared in

1778, and *Iggrot Ha-Kodesh* ("Holy Letters") and *Hanhagot Yeshurot* ("Right Conduct"), both of which appeared in 1800. The latter tract carried an epilogue *Zetel Katan* ("small paragraph"), which advised the reader to repeat it at least twice a day and to explain every word in Yiddish."

In the course of thirteen years, Elimelekh armed his followers with weapons that enabled them to survive the onslaught of the *Mitnagdim* and the *Maskilim*. The weapons were prayer, study, kindness and compassion. Not undeservedly was he called "A Second Baal Shem Tov."[8]

Chapter 10

The Polish Pioneers

1. The Fatherly Maggid of Kozienice

During the last quarter of the eighteenth century, the period of the Partitions of Poland (1772–95), over seven hundred thousand Jews lived in Poland and in Lithuania,[1] and their life was fraught with hazard and hardship. Under the terms of the First Partition, Russia secured parts of White Russia. The Second Partition (1793) gave Russia half of Lithuania and the rest of White Russia. In the Third Partition (1795), Russia took Courland and the rest of Lithuania. The decree of December 23, 1791 set up the so-called Pale of Settlement, consisting of the Western and South-Western provinces, to which the Jews were confined in very straitened circumstances.

Much of their social misery, ironically enough, stemmed from the corruptness of the community leaders. "They consume the offerings of the people," records one rabbi,[2] "and drink wine for the fines imposed by them. Being in full control of the taxes, they assess and excommunicate their opponents. They remunerate themselves for their public activity by every means at their disposal, both openly and in secret. They take no step without accepting bribes, while the destitute carry the burden. . . . The learned cater to the rich, and, as for the rabbis, they have only contempt for one another. . . . The rich value the favour of the Polish lords above the good opinion of the best and the noblest among the Jews." Inevitably, the Polish Constitution of May 1791, although it improved the lot of the Polish peasantry, in no way bettered the lot of the overburdened Jews.

Despite its impoverishment, Poland was still *Akhsaniah shel Torah* ("Home of the Law"), and her *Yeshivot* produced some of Jewry's greatest Talmudists. Many of Europe's key Rabbinical posts were occupied by Polish scholars: Rabbi Jacob Joshua ben Zevi Hirsch (1660–1756), rabbi of Frankfurt-on-Main and author of *Pene Joshua*, novella on the Talmud, was born in Cracow; Rabbi Jonathan Eibeschütz was born in Cracow; Rabbi Ezekiel ben Judah Landau (1713–93), rabbi in Prague, was born in Opatow; Rabbi Joseph Ben Meir Teomin (1727–93), author of *Peri Megadim*, a commentary on the *Orah Hayim* and Rabbi of Frankfurt-on-Oder, was born in Lvov; Zevi Hirsch, son of Aryeh Leib (Hart Lyon), rabbi of the Great Synagogue in London (1758–64), was born in Rzeszow, in 1721.[3]

In Poland itself dwelt such scholars as Ephraim Zalman Margolioth (1762–1828) of Brody, and Rabbi Jacob Meshullam Ornstein (d. 1839) of Lvov. However, the scholarly élite had little contact with the masses, who were, to a large extent, far removed from the Torah, drowning in a dark flood of suffering and superstition. Desperately they grasped at a lifeline, and the lifeline was Hasidism. One of the earliest leaders was Rabbi Israel Hopstein, *Maggid* of Kozienice. Israel was born in 1746, in Opatow, near Sandormiersz, to Shabbetai, a poor book-binder. His mother, Perl, had been childless for many years, and Israel was born only after she had received a blessing from the Besht. The boy received his early Talmudic training from the rabbi of Opatow, Dov Berish Katz, a grandson of Rabbi Shabbetai ben Meir ha-Cohen. One of Israel's fellow students, Isaac Abraham Katz, later author of the Responsa *Keter Kehuna* ("Crown of the Priesthood") and rabbi of Pinczow, recalls the diligence with which Israel pursued his studies. After this he studied in Ostrowiec under Rabbi Ezekiel and in Horschow, Volhynia, under Mordecai Zevi Hurwitz, son of Isaac Halevy Hurwitz, rabbi of Hamburg and Altona.

After the death of his father, in 1761, Israel settled in Przysucha where he came under the influence of Rabbi Abraham of Przysucha (d. 1800) from whom he acquired not only knowledge of the Talmud and Cabbalah but also the art of *Maggidut* ("Homiletics"). He was a gifted student, and even the *Mitnaged* Hayim ben Isaac of Volozhin (1749–1821), founder of the Yeshiva of Volozhin (a townlet in Lithuania) testified to Israel's phenomenal mastery of Talmud and Codes.

Like his namesake, Rabbi Israel Baal Shem Tov, Israel became a teacher. He loved and understood children, and many of his pedagogical ideas were far in advance of his time. Rabbi Shmelke Hurwitz became Israel's guide to Hasidism and Israel quoted him frequently, often referring to him as "the Gaon, the Hasid, the Prince of God."

The time came for Israel to journey to Mezhirichi, then the Zion of the movement. "I studied eight hundred books of the Cabbalah," the newcomer to Mezhirichi remarked with humility, "but, when I arrived in the presence of the *Maggid*, I realised that I had not yet begun to study."[4]

"Our teacher the *Zaddik*, interprets the Torah through the Holy Spirit which rests upon him," wrote Rabbi Israel. The *Maggid*'s response was instant and ardent. "Blessed be the Holy Name!" he exclaimed. "The Almighty has provided a young man who can edit the manuscript of Rabbi Isaac Luria's Prayer Book." The *Maggid* realised that Israel would be more than an inspired editor and that through him Hasidism would spread through Poland. "Now that you have arrived here," he prophesied, "*Keter Yitnu* ("They will give a Crown") will be recited in Warsaw as well," (meaning that more people would adopt the Lurian Liturgy and become Hasidim).

After the death of the *Maggid*, Israel came under the influence of Rabbi Elimelekh of Lezajsk. "My knowledge of the Cabbalah may be superior to that of my teacher Elimelekh," Rabbi Israel admitted, "but I am not able to serve God in the way that he does, in a spirit of self-sacrifice, love and awe." Rabbi Israel often refers in his writings to the "holy book of our rabbi and teacher, *Noam Elimelekh*".[5] In touching symbolism, Elimelekh before his death, bequeathed his "heart" to Israel. To his colleague, Mendel of Rymanov, the dying sage bequeathed his brain; his intellect he gave to Rabbi Joshua Heshel, and to the Seer he gave his vision.

Eventually, Rabbi Israel became *Maggid* in Kozienice, a small town north-east of Radom, with a population of only one thousand three hundred Jews. To supplement his meagre stipend, he preached in the neighbouring towns of Magnuszew and Grice, and multitudes flocked to hear him. His tone was gentle and persuasive, his use of Torah texts apt and illuminating. His love of learning and the depths of his scholarship were apparent from every word he spoke. "He who studies Torah for its own sake," he once said, "becomes a chariot riding in the Name of God. Holiness rests upon him and all the angels listen to him."

Rabbi Israel wrote prolifically, and among his many works are *Avodat Yisrael* ("Service of Israel"), discourses on the Pentateuch and *Ethics of the Fathers*,[6] *Or Yisrael* ("Light of Israel"), *Nezer Yisrae* ("Crown of Israel"), a commentary on the *Zohar*, and *Tehilat Yisrael* ("Praises of Israel"), comments on the Psalms.[7] He was particularly fascinated by the personality of Rabbi Judah ben Bezalel Löw, of

Prague, the reputed creator of the *Golem*, and Israel wrote *Geulat Yisrael* ("Redemption of Israel") about him. The writings and *responsa* of Rabbi Israel demonstrate his mastery of *Halakhah*, which earned him the respect of his contemporaries. Rabbi Israel was most careful to acknowledge his sources, giving credit wherever it was due.

His literary productivity and manifold communal commitments are the more astonishing when one considers that all his life, Rabbi Israel was frail in physique and beset by many ailments. Often, he was too weak to rise from his bed, and many blankets were needed to warm him. Every day, he was carried to the Synagogue in a litter. But his indomitable spirit overcame his physical disabilities.

Rabbi Israel never forgot the poverty of his early days. He was virtually a father to many orphans, and brought up a number of them in his own home. All the money he received from his Hasidim was promptly distributed among the poor. When, in 1778, a fire ravaged the Jewish quarter of Kozienice, he financed the rebuilding of a whole street, which became known as "the *Maggid*'s Street", and allocated the houses to the poor. The *Maggid* himself lived in austere surroundings, for he had no desire for physical comforts. However, he did not prescribe such austerity for others. "Tell me," he once asked a wealthy Hasid, "what do you eat every day?" "Very little," replied the rich man. "My needs are simple. Bread with salt and water are enough for me." "Your way is not a good way," reproved the *Maggid*. "You should eat fattened chickens and drink wine. For if you eat well, you will give bread to the poor. But if your menu consists of dry bread, you will begrudge the poor even stones." Kozienice became a place of pilgrimage and the frail *Maggid* won many adherents to the movement.

Unassuming and modest in his ways, devoid of worldly ambition, Rabbi Israel was revered by his colleagues. "I have heard a *Bat Kol* ("A Heavenly Voice")," declared the Rabbi of Rymanov, "proclaim that 'he who lives in the generation of the *Maggid* and has not looked upon his face will not be worthy to welcome the Messiah when he comes'". The *Maggid*'s fame spread beyond the Jewish community, and he was visited by such Polish nobles as Adam Chartoryski, Josef Poniatowski and Prince Radziwil. Adam Chartoryski was childless, and Rabbi Israel offered special prayers on his behalf. "O Master of the Universe," he reasoned, "You have so many Gentiles, let there be another one." Chartoryski was, indeed, blessed with a child, and never forgot his debt to the Rabbi. There are allusions to the *Maggid* in the writings of the Polish writers, Anna Potocka and Leon Dembowski.[8]

Rabbi Joseph Isaac Schneerson of Lubavitch

Rabbi Menahem Mendel Schneerson

Rabbi N. D. Rabinowicz, the Rebbe of
Biala

Rabbi Israel was deeply concerned with the welfare of Jewry as a whole. He was one of the twenty-four delegates who urged the Government to abolish the tax on *Shehitah* (a tax imposed by the Government on the Jewish ritual slaughter of animals). When the State arbitrarily decreed military service for Jews between the ages of twenty-four and twenty-eight, he was among the community leaders who negotiated for exemption, and arranged instead for the payment of seven hundred thousand gulden. In many such situations, Rabbi Israel's connections with the Polish nobility proved advantageous.

Closely, the *Maggid* watched the ever-changing political map, as each change drastically affected, but seldom improved, the situation of the Jews. "I like the Poles," declared Napoleon at Verona, in September 1796. "The Partitioning of Poland was an iniquitous deed that cannot stand. When I have finished the war in Italy, I myself will lead the French troops and will force the Russians to reunite Poland."[9]

These were not idle words. Under the treaty of Tilsit (1807), Napoleon's reconstituted Poland was styled the Grand Duchy of Warsaw. The Duchy covered thirty thousand square miles and had a population of two million and fifty thousand.

The new regime started on an admirably democratic footing, by abolishing serfdom and legislating for civil equality. Predictably, however, the nobility opposed the Bill of Civil Rights, and on October 17, 1809, Duke Frederick Augustus decreed that: "Those inhabitants of our Varsovian Duchy professing the Mosaic religion are barred for ten years from enjoying the political rights that they were about to receive, in the hope that, during this interval, they may eradicate the distinguishing characteristics which mark them off so strongly from the rest of the population." Assimilation was the price of emancipation, and for Rabbi Israel, this was too high a price. In common with most of his Hasidic contemporaries, he opposed Napoleon.

Rabbi Menahem Mendel of Rymanov was a notable exception. Hasidim believe that, just as the High Priest Simon the Just (4th–3rd centuries B.C.E.) was considered to be the guardian angel of Alexander the Great, so the Rabbi of Rymanov provided spiritual support for Napoleon. "I see the red Jew (the rabbi of Rymanov) walking by my side through the heat of the battle," Napoleon allegedly declared, "assuring me of victory." When Napoleon stood at the gates of Moscow, Menahem Mendel prayed for him. On the other hand, Naftali of Ropozyce mobilised Hasidim against the Corsican. According to Hasidic legend, the fate of Napoleon was decided not on the battlefields, but in the Courts of the Hasidic rabbis. Hasidim relate that Napoleon came in disguise to plead with Rabbi Israel, but it was no use, for the Rabbi interpreted the verse of Exodus (xviii. 18), *Navol Tibbol* ("Thou wilt surely wear away"), as *Nofol Tipol* (i.e., "Napoleon will fall.")[10]

Rabbi Israel attracted a number of important magnates to his court who negotiated for and represented the Jewish community. Josef Mandelsburg of Kazimierz obtained a salt monopoly, and over five thousand Jewish families were employed in his various enterprises. The *Maggid*'s friendship with Poniatowski enabled him to act as an intermediary in times of difficulty. Another influential Hasid was Samuel Zbitkover (1758–1801), the "Rothschild of Polish Jewry", who lived in a district of Warsaw called *Targo Wash*, where he owned houses, wine cellars and inns. This district was later called *Szmulowizna* in his honour, for Samuel financed the forces of King Frederick of Prussia and Poniatowski. During Tadeusz Kosciuszko's rebellion, in 1794, Samuel provided financial backing for a volunteer battalion of Jewish cavalry organised by Berek Joselewicz (c. 1765–1809). During the upheavals that followed, Samuel saved the lives of hundreds of Jews. His son Berek Dov Bergson was equally committed to Hasidism, and his wife, Tamarel, was a devout follower of the *Maggid*. A number of the *Maggid*'s disciples, among them Simha Bunam of Przysucha and Rabbi Isaac of Warka, were in the employment of the benevolent Bergsons.

A passionate bibliophile, Rabbi Israel rejoiced in a fine collection of early prints. He was instrumental in having hitherto unobtainable volumes reprinted, and it was through him that a number of Cabbalistic manuscripts first appeared in print.[11]

Like Levi Isaac of Berdichev, Rabbi Israel communicated with God as a friend. He even spoke to him in Polish, crying out in ecstasy *Moi Kochanka* ("My darling"). Like Rabbi Levi Isaac of Berdichev, Rabbi Israel, too, was persecuted and forced to take refuge at Zelichovo, home town of Levi Isaac. But the faith of the rabbi never faltered. "Perchance, Almighty God," he pondered, "You withhold Your mercy from the children of Israel because of the dearth of true *Zaddikim* to plead for them. Behold in Rymanov You have Rabbi Mendel, who is equal to all the *Zaddikim*; You have the Seer, who is equal to the *Urim Vetummim* ("Sacred means of Divination used by the early Hebrews whereby the Divine purpose is revealed", I. Samuel xxviii. 6) and finally you have me. I most sincerely repent and plead for forgiveness for all your children."[12]

Rabbi Israel died on the eve of the Festival of Tabernacles, 1815. His son, Rabbi Moses Elikum Beriah, succeeded him. So the verse, "And it came to pass when the Ark set forward that Moses said" (Num. x. 35), was interpreted by the Hasidim as follows: "When the Ark set forward (i.e., when Israel of Kozienice died), 'Moses said', he was succeeded by his son Moses."

A father to his Hasidim and to all Jewry, a statesman as well as a scholar, the *Maggid* of Kozienice was one of the powerful pillars of Polish Hasidism.

2. The Sad-eyed Seer of Lublin

Early in the nineteenth century, Lublin and Przysucha replaced Medzibozh and Mezhirichi as the key centres of Hasidism. The influence of the Besht, the *Maggid* of Mezhirichi, and Rabbi Shneur Zalman had been restricted to the Jews of Podolia and the Ukraine; the influence of Rabbi Elimelekh of Lezajsk was confined to Galicia; now, from Lublin and Przysucha, Hasidism spread to Polish Jewry.

The father of Polish Hasidism was Rabbi Jacob Isaac Hurwitz, known as *Ha-Hozeh* ("The Seer") of Lublin. He was born in 1745, son of Rabbi Eliezer Ha-Levi Hurwitz, Rabbi in Jusefow. A brilliant and restless student, Jacob Isaac was fifteen years old when the Besht died. Shortly after this, he made his way to Mezhirichi. "Such a soul has not made its appearance since the time of the prophets," the discerning *Maggid* declared.[13]

After the death of the *Maggid* in 1773, Jacob Isaac became a disciple of Rabbi Shmelke of Nikolsburg. Not given to idle conversation, Jacob Isaac immersed himself in his studies to the exclusion of all else. Even his teacher thought such single-mindedness excessive. Rabbi Shmelke urged his colleague Zusya of Annopol to "make our Itzikel (Jacob Isaac) a little lighter of heart." Like the *Maggid*, Rabbi Shmelke held the young man in high esteem: "When Jacob Isaac recites the benedictions," remarked Rabbi Shmelke reverently "the entire Heavenly court responds, Amen." Rabbi Zusya could not change the youthful Seer's meditative disposition, but he did prevail upon him to make his way to Lezajsk. "Only in the Court of my brother," declared Rabbi Zusya, "will you find perfection."[14]

At Lezajsk, Jacob Isaac found such like-minded associates as Menahem Mendel of Rymanov and Abraham Joshua Heshel of Opatow. Rabbi Elimelekh took a paternal interest in the newcomer, stating emphatically, "He is my equal." To this devout disciple Elimelekh bequeathed his "eyes", and Jacob Isaac did indeed seem to acquire his master's spiritual vision. Rabbi Elimelekh had lived a life of extreme self-denial, and his disciple followed this rather un-Hasidic model. To avoid seeing unseemly things, he literally shielded his eyes for seven years, and his eyesight was seriously impaired. However, he acquired the title "Seer" because of his inner vision.

Within the lifetime of Elimelekh, Jacob Isaac had established his own court at Lancut near Lezajsk. In 1800, no doubt in deference to Rabbi Eliezer, Elimelekh's successor, he moved to Lublin, and this had been the meeting place of the "Council of Four Lands" (*Vaad Arba Aratzot*).

Lublin, where the Seer established his *Bet Ha-Midrash*, soon vied in popularity with the old historic *Maharshal's Shul* (the Synagogue of Rabbi Solomon ben Jehiel, known as *Maharshal*, 1510–73). It became a training ground for Hasidic leaders. Gifted young men flocked there, as well as the founders of the most illustrious Hasidic dynasties in Poland and Galicia, such as that of Przysucha. Kock (Kotzk), Ger, Ropczyce, Dynov were all greatly influenced by the life and doctrines of the Seer. Even the iconoclastic Menahem Mendel of Kotzk, generally no respector of persons, referred to the Seer as *Urim Vetumim*. Rabbi Uri of Strelisk, known as the "Seraph" (d. 1826) declared: "Lublin is Eretz Yisrael; the court of the *Bet-Ha-Midrash* is Jerusalem; the *Bet Ha-Midrash* itself is the Temple; the study of the Seer is the Holy of Holies, and the *Shekhinah* speaks from his mouth." "The Seer saw the Holy Spirit as Samuel the prophet," said Rabbi Elimelekh of Dynov. "And the difference between him and the prophet was that he did not say: 'Thus saith the Lord'."

It was said that the moment a Hasid arrived, Rabbi Jacob Isaac would take out his soul and cleanse it carefully, remove all the rust and restore it to a state of pristine purity, so that its owner became as sin-free as a new-born babe. People left his presence comforted and hopeful. However, this was not a reciprocal process, and the *Zaddik* himself was generally of a sombre disposition. He inspired confidence in others, but had little confidence in himself. He had a smile on his face but no joy in his heart. For he was always afraid, afraid of sin, afraid of his own power. "There can be no man less worthy than I am," he sighed "The lowliest workman is more deserving."[15] "Woe to the generation", he lamented, "that looks to me for leadership."

Diligently and devotedly, the Seer served his community, and from this he derived special satisfaction. "I do not know what merit I have definitely acquired. Maybe I rejoice that I have performed at least one good deed in this life," the self-effacing Seer reflected. "I arranged the marriage of forty orphans. Whenever I arranged a marriage for a member of my own family, I also provided for a fatherless child." The Seer habitually brought home poor wayfarers and waited on them himself, for "is not carrying the spoons and the coal-pan from the Holy of Holies part of the services of the High Priest on the Day of Atonement".

The Seer took nothing for granted and even explained that there was a good reason for the acceptance of *Pidyonot* (money). "When a *Zaddik* petitions God on behalf of a Hasid, it is possible that this may be regarded as presumptuous. People may ask him: "Why does not the Hasid pray for himself? Now when the *Zaddik* accepts money he has a ready response: "I am praying on his behalf because he has given me a *Pidyan*."[16]

The Seer was the author of three books, *Divre Emet* ("Words of Truth"), printed in Zolkiew in 1808, and *Zot Zikoron* ("This is the Remembrance"), and *Zikoron Zot* ("This is remembrance") which were not printed before 1869. *Divre Emet* in addition has a number of novellae on the Talmudic tractates of *Sabbath* and *Hullin*.

On the night of *Simhat Torah* 1814 after the *Hakkaphot* ("Circuits") the Seer left the *Bet Ha-Midrash* and retired to his room on the first floor of his house. The room had only one small window. At midnight a Hasid, Rabbi Eliezer of Hmelnick, passed by the courtyard of the *Rebbe* and saw a body lying on the ground. "I am Jacob Isaac the son of Motel," the Seer whispered to him. He was taken into the house. "The evil powers pursued me," he told Dr. Bernard of Piotrokov. He was seriously injured, and died on *Tisha B'Ab* 1815. His mysterious fall has never been explained.

Chapter 11

The Way of Przysucha

1. The Holy Jew

The greatest of all the Seer's disciples, a giant among giants, was Jacob Isaac, "*the Yehudi Ha-kodosh*" ("the Holy Jew") or the "*Yid Ha-kodosh*", as he was called with affection and with awe. Many explanations have been offered for this appellation. Some explain that it was to differentiate between him and his master, the Seer, who was also named Jacob Isaac: an explanation which conforms with the rabbinic ruling that "it was forbidden for a disciple to call himself by the same name as his teacher."[1] Others maintain that the soul of Jacob Isaac was the soul of Mordecai, the hero of the Book of Esther, who is referred to in the Book of Esther (x. 3) as "Mordecai the Jew" (*Ha-Yehudi*). Why was Mordecai called *Ha-Yehudi* ("the Jew")? asks the Talmud,[2] with its customary rhetoric. "Because he repudiated idolatry. Anyone who repudiates idolatry is called a Jew." Pride, anger, avarice, slander and flattery are synonymous with idolatry. Throughout his life, the "Holy Jew" shunned such negative qualities, and for this reason he merited the title "Yehudi".

According to yet a third theory, Jacob Isaac would scrupulously identify all authorities he cited in his discourse and would even attribute his own ideas to others, with the modest disclaimer: "I heard it from a Jew". Perhaps the truth is that the "Holy Jew" was simply an apt description of this remarkable rabbi, for every day of his life Jacob Isaac strove to be a Jew in the fullest sense of the term.

Jacob Isaac was born in 1765 at Przedborz, son of Asher Rabinowicz (d. 1798) one time the rabbi in Grodzisk. Like Rabbi Israel Baal Shem Tov, the boy studied and prayed in secret alone for hours in the deserted *Bet Ha-Midrash* without the knowledge of his parents or his teachers. Whenever the *Bet Ha-Midrash* was closed, he would surreptitiously make his way there and spend hours in study. At the age of fourteen, he studied under Rabbi Aryeh Leib Harif Heilprin, afterwards a rabbi in Sochaczew and Warsaw. He also studied in the Yeshiva at Lissa, Prussia under Rabbi Tebele Horachow (d. 1792).

It was not only from his rabbis that Jacob Isaac learned wisdom. He liked to tell of the valuable lesson taught him by his neighbour, a blacksmith. Late one night, when the weary scholar was preparing to set aside his books, he heard the smith still hammering away. "If my neighbour can labour so industriously for material things," he reflected, "then surely I can work even harder in the service of the Lord." And at dawn the knowledge that the smith was already at the anvil drove slumber from the scholar's eyes. In these long hours of study he mastered Talmudics and Rabbinics to such an extraordinary degree, that he asserted that in the classical work, *Urim Vetumim*, by Jonathan Eibeschütz he only found "three remarkable passages."

While Jacob Isaac lived in Opatow (Apt) with his parents-in-law, he acted for a while as principal of the Talmudical College. Opatow was the home of Rabbi Moses Leib of Sassov (1745–1807) author of a noted *novella* on the Talmud.[3] With good reason he was called "the father of widows and orphans". He would spare no effort to help the needy and to raise funds for the redemption of captives. At Opatow, Jacob Isaac established cordial relations with Rabbi Moses Leib and also came into contact with the extraordinary *Rebbe*, Joshua Heshel (d. 1835), a disciple of both Rabbi Elimelekh of Lezajsk and Rabbi Yehiel Michael, the *Maggid* of Zloczew.

Rabbi Abraham Joshua Heshel implored his children not to inscribe extravagant epitaphs upon his tombstone. "Write only," he pleaded, "that I loved the House of Israel." A selection of his teachings are to be found in his books *Ohev Yisrael* ("Lover of Israel") and *Torat Emet* ("The True Law") both published posthumously. Although not a *Kohen* (of priestly descent), the rabbi of Apt believed that he had been a High Priest in an earlier life. In the order of service of the High Priest, recited during the additional service (the *Avodah*) on the Day of Atonement, the rabbi would change the prescribed text: "Thus did he (i.e., the High Priest) say", to "And thus did I say." *Kavanah* was the keynote of his life and he strove to serve God with single-minded and selfless dedication.

Jacob Isaac became a teacher and wandered from place to place in search of pupils. In the course of his wanderings he encountered the kindly Rabbi David of Lelov (1746–1814) a disciple of the Seer, known for his patience and for his forbearance, for his love of children and his concern for animals. During country fairs he would bring water to thirsty horses neglected by their owners. Rabbi David brought a number of talented men under the wings of Hasidism and the *Yehudi* was his greatest acquisition.

Rabbi David brought Jacob Isaac to the Seer and he found him the answer to his fervent prayer: "Let God, the Master of the spirits of all flesh, set a man over the congregation who will go out before them and who will come in before them" (Numbers xxvii. 16). The Yehudi was the answer to his prayer. The Seer was quick to recognise the quality of his new disciple and he lavished praises upon his new pupil. "His soul had already appeared three times: in our Patriarch Jacob, in Mordecai and in Rabbi Jacob ben Meir Tam (1100–71)." Other contemporaries acclaimed him with equal warmth. "The Rabbi of Lublin," said Uri of Strelisk, "can be compared to the phylacteries of Rashi. Jacob Isaac can be likened to those of *Rabbenu Tam*."[4]

To Hasidism, Jacob Isaac applied the dialectic approach of the Talmudists. Allied to his quick wit was a gentle disposition, for with humility he would expound his precepts to colleagues and disciples. He regarded pride as the source of all evil, and there was not a trace of it in the unassuming *Zaddik*. "Why," he asked, "is the word 'Justice' repeated twice in the injunction, 'Justice, justice shalt thou follow'" (Deut. xvi. 20). "Because," he explained, "only just means should be used to secure the victory of justice. Moreover, a man should never cease to pursue justice."

Yet the mild master had his detractors, among them the Seer himself, whose attitude towards him was, to say the least, ambivalent. Although he occasionally delegated authority to senior disciples, the Seer resented the growing influence of Jacob Isaac. Since the Seer ministered to the masses, he had little time for the "graduate" disciples. Consequently, men like Menahem Mendel of Kotzk, Simha Bunam of Przysucha and Dov Baer of Radoszyce transferred their allegiance to Jacob Isaac, who established his own court in Przysucha. This aroused the antagonism of the Seer, and the hostile flames were fanned by such mischief makers as Simeon Ashkenazi and Jehudah Leib of Zelechow. Jacob Isaac's every action was misrepresented and his visits to Lublin misconstrued. "He comes only to woo Hasidim away from me," was the Seer's unperceptive reaction, as he virtually banished Jacob Isaac from Lublin. Although yearning with all his heart for reconciliation, Jacob

Isaac practised patience and restraint. But to no avail. He even travelled to Rymanov to seek Menahem Mendel's intervention as peacemaker. But nothing helped. "Let that be," the Yehudi then said to Hayim Meir of Moglienice. "No good will come of our talk. They will soon say that I am acting like a *Rebbe*."[5]

On one occasion, the Seer presented Jacob Isaac with one of his shirts as a mark of esteem, and the gift was precious in the eyes of the disciple. But on his way to the Bath House, a ragged beggar fell at the feet of the Yehudi and wept bitterly. The compassionate sage was deeply moved. He had no money to give, so he took the shirt which the Seer had given him and handed it to the beggar. News of this incident quickly reached the Seer, who was grieved and angered at the apparent slight. Hurt by the estrangement, Jacob Isaac turned to the Seer. "Look into my heart" he pleaded. "Can you see there any anger or evil intent?" The Seer looked at him long and earnestly and turned away abashed. "There is neither anger nor evil intent in your heart."

It was revealed to Jacob Isaac, according to the hidden auguries in the mystical book of *Raziel* (a composite Cabbalistic book supposedly delivered by the Angel Raziel to Adam), that he was destined to die after *Rosh Hashanah*, and when the time came the Seer was distraught. "Stay with me" he implored, "and we will keep you alive." But Jacob Isaac declined. "The Seer could have kept me alive," mused the Yehudi, "but my soul would have paid a high price."

Jacob Isaac's domestic life, too, was not free from dissension. His wife, Sheindel, was difficult and quarrelsome, continually grieving her long-suffering husband. It is related, for instance, that once, on the first night of Passover, she refused to allow Jacob Isaac's aged mother to sit at her accustomed place next to her son, claiming this prerogative for herself. A tempestuous scene ensued. The dismay of the Yehudi and the chagrin of the Hasidim disrupted the serenity of the evening.

Jacob Isaac died in 1814.[6] His discourses appeared in various publications.[7]

The Przysucha doctrines, like *Habad* philosophy, brought about a new orientation in Hasidism. What Rabbi Shneur Zalman had done for White Russia and the Ukraine, Jacob Isaac did for Polish Jewry. The Hasidism of Elimelekh of Lezajsk, of Israel of Kozienice and of the Seer of Lublin was concerned with the masses. The *Rebbes* were preoccupied with the material, as well as the spiritual, well-being of their followers. Like faithful shepherds, the *Rebbes* could not be deaf to the cries of the flock. The *Rebbes* were practical idealists who were concerned to help as many as possible as much as possible.

The Rebbe is not "merely" a miracle worker. For it is considered no great effort to work miracles. It needs greater effort—and is a greater accomplishment—to be a good Jew. Therefore it is important to learn to be a good Jew. Through study of *Gemara* (Talmud) and *Tosaphot*, the mind is purified and ennobled.[8]

"Ye shall not lie to one another" (Leviticus xix. 11) enjoins the Torah, but it is equally essential for a man not to lie to himself. With all his strength, the Yehudi fought against superficiality, insisting on sincerity and total involvement in prayer, in study, and in every human relationship. For Rabbi Shneur Zalman it was possible to acquire the love of God and the fear of God only through the contemplation of the almost ineffable grandeur of Creation. Jacob Isaac, however, was not concerned with speculative research, but with man's study of his own soul. Neither through parental merit nor through the mediation of teachers could man reach the highest pinnacle, but only through pains-taking personal striving. Every deed should be performed in the spirit of truth, for truth is the seal of God. Falsehood and deceit must be completely eradicated. The Besht believed that there was a spark of divinity in every Jew. Jacob Isaac went even further and maintained that every Jew could be a Moses and should be satisfied with nothing less than aiming at the highest.

In Przysucha, services were not always recited at the prescribed times, for it was better to pray late than to pray without *Kavanah*. Regular hours are acceptable under normal conditions, but during an emergency, unconventional methods must be used. For the Hasid, life is always a battlefield, for there can be no armistice between those moral enemies, good and evil. The teachings of the Yehudi would seem to be in the mainstream of Hasidic thought, yet just as Rabbi Shneur Zalman was opposed by Rabbis Barukh of Medzibozh, Mordecai of Lehowitz and Abraham of Kalisk, so, too, Jacob Isaac had many adversaries who rejected his teachings as "revolutionary".

"The prayer of Jacob Isaac," commented Rabbi Jacob Aryeh of Radzymin, "was like the prayer of the Besht. The prayer of the Besht was like the prayer of Isaac Luria. The prayer of Isaac Luria was like the prayer of Rabbi Simeon ben Yohai, and the prayer of Rabbi Simeon ben Yohai was like the prayer of Adam before he sinned." Not only did Jacob Isaac establish a famous dynasty, but he also blazed a new trail through the multiplying maze of Hasidic lore.

2. Rabbi Simha Bunam, the Cosmopolitan Rebbe

In the early history of Hasidism, sons did not automatically succeed their father. The Yehudi had three sons, Yerahmiel, Nehemiah and Joshua Alter. Yet his Hasidim appointed Simha Bunam, the Master's favourite disciple, as their leader.

Simha Bunam Bunehart was born in Wodzislaw in 1765. His father, Zevi, was *Maggid* of the town and a scholar of note.[9] On his mother's side, Simha Bunam was a descendant of Joel ben Samuel Serkes (1561–1640). From his father, Simha Bunam acquired a basic grounding in Rabbinics and homiletics. Later, to widen and deepen his knowledge he studied in Mattersdorf under Rabbi Joab ben Jeremiah (d. 1807) and at Nikolsburg under Mordecai Benet (1753–1829), Chief Rabbi of Moravia. Benet was famous for his wide secular knowledge. Every day he would lecture on Maimonides' work *Yad Ha-Hazakah* ("Strong hand") or *Mishneh Torah* ("The Second Law") the Hebrew compendium of the *Halakhah*. Benet paid particular attention to Hebrew grammar and the medieval Jewish philosophers.

Returning from Hungary, Simha Bunam married Rebecca of Bendin, and soon the young scholar became attracted to Hasidism. Rabbi Moses Leib of Sassov, the Seer, Rabbi David of Lelov, and Rabbi Israel of Kozienice became his spiritual fathers. At the suggestion of the *Maggid* of Kozienice, Simha Bunam began to work for the industrialist, Berek Dov Bergson, and his wife, Tamarel, and travelled widely as their representative. The cosmopolitan rabbi frequently visited the Danzig and Leipzig trade fairs. He wore European clothes, spoke Polish and German, visited the theatre occasionally, and enjoyed playing cards.

After a few years as a timber merchant, Simha Bunam qualified as a practising chemist (magister pharmaciae) in Lvov. He opened an apothecary's shop in Przysucha, where he soon acquired a large clientele. He even supplied medicines to the Napoleonic forces in Russia.

His business preoccupations did not lessen his interest in Hasidism. Regularly he visited the rabbis of Kozienice, Opatow, Lelov and Lublin. "Stay with me," pleaded the Seer, "and I will endow you with the Holy Spirit."[10] In Przysucha and in Lublin, Simha Bunam fell under the spell of Jacob Isaac, and the master loved him dearly. "The young man," remarked Jacob Isaac, "is the core of my heart." Every night Simha Bunam would close his store and hasten to the Yehudi, where new stores of wisdom were opened to him. He accompanied the Yehudi to Rymanov, and when the Yehudi died, Simha Bunam was the heir apparent. Some could not forget his background. "How can he call himself Rabbi," sneered Rabbi Meir of Opatow. "Did he qualify for that in Danzig, in German theatres or in the pharmacy?" "Rabbi Meir does not know what sin is and he does not know how to sin" retorted Rabbi Simha Bunam. "I can understand temptation and can help men to withstand it. I can inspire my Hasidim with the fear of God."[11]

Just as Dov Baer developed the doctrines of the Besht, so Simha Bunam interpreted the ideas of Jacob Isaac. He, too, surrounded himself with a band of selected young men to whom he dedicated his life. They responded with equal dedication, forsaking all material interests (sometimes even wife and children) for his sake. "He never speaks an idle word," testified one disciple. Regular periods were set aside for the study of Talmud medieval philosophy and cognate subjects, while Cabbalah did not figure prominently in the curriculum. The school of Simha Bunam concentrated on Maimonides' *Guide to the Perplexed*, Judah ha-Levi's *Ha-Kuzari* ("The Khazars"), Jedidiah Berdesi's *Mivhar Peninim* ("Choice of Pearls") and the works of Judah b. Löw b. Bezalel, the *Maharal* of Prague, whom Simha Bunam regarded as his "Heavenly Teacher."[12]

Simha Bunam thought highly of the commentary on the Pentateuch by Abraham Ibn Ezra (1089–1164) whose linguistic textual analysis was the forerunner of Biblical criticism. "Through Ibn Ezra," asserted Simha Bunam, "one can acquire fear of God." It is not improbable that the return of Simha Bunam to primary sources of Judaic faith, and inspiration in the Bible, Talmud and the medieval philosophers, was to counteract the *Haskalah* movement. Hence Cabbalah occupied a very minor part of his curriculum.

Rabbi Simha Bunam did not lead an isolated life in Przysucha. He distrusted the "enlightened absolutism of Alexander I". Boldly, he told high Russian officials that "it was not the business of the State to interfere in the internal affairs of Jewry. These matters can safely be left in the hands of rabbis and spiritual leaders. As far as the Jews were concerned, the duty of the State was to improve their economic position and to alleviate the poverty that prevailed among them". Vehemently, he opposed the Committee of the Old Covenant (*Komitet Staroza-konnych*) and its assimilationist programme, particularly secular education for children and the censorship of Hebrew books, translation of the Talmud and the establishment of a Rabbinical training college. Supporters of this Committee, which was founded in Warsaw in 1825, included the mathematician, Abraham Stern, representing the *Maskilim* and Jacob Zunberg Bergson, son of Tamarel.[13]

In his later years, Rabbi Simha Bunam became blind, an affliction which he accepted with courage and faith. "I prayed to God," he said, "that He should deprive me of my sight in order that I might see the inner light . . . What is good for me to see I see with the inner light. What is not good to see I do not wish to see at all."

Rabbi Simha Bunam held that truth must permeate every thought, every word and every deed. Any action which is not based on truth does not exist. A man must be faithful to God and to his people. But first of all he must be faithful to himself. Preparation is the basis of prayer and study. A man must first cleanse his heart and mind. It is futile to pray when preoccupied with sensual desires and worldly thoughts. And it is useless to perform *Mitzvot* for ulterior motives. This is tantamount to idolatry. In order to strike the proper balance between overweening pride and false humility, "man should believe simultaneously, 'I am dust and ashes', and 'for me alone the world was created'".

Hasidim of Przysucha did not stress "congregational prayers" nor did they conform rigidly to regulated hours of worship. On the words of the morning prayer: "Let a man at all times revere God in private as in public, acknowledging the truth in his heart," Simha Bunam commented: "Only if a man acknowledges the truth and speaks the truth is he able to 'rise early' and pray at the appointed times laid down by the Sages."[14]

Miracles have no place in Simha Bunam's philosophy. "Had I known that through miracles I could bring men back to God, I would have planted the trees of Danzig in the streets of Przysucha." He tried to curb the cult of the *Zaddik*. "A fur hat and an illustrious father," he pointed out, "do not make a *Zaddik*. No doubt, Esau, too, wore silk garments and recited Torah at *Shalosh Seudot* (the third Sabbath meal)."[15]

Apart from the Besht, no other *Zaddik* has created as many parables as Simha Bunam. Here, to cite just one of them, is the parable of the deceitful *Zaddik*. A simple peasant was once fond of reeling drunkenly through the streets, and the authorities decided to have a little sport with him. They washed him, dressed him in the garb of a bishop, and brought him still unawares to the episcopal palace. When the dazed villager awoke from his stupor, he found himself dressed as a bishop and with deference addressed as such. Entering his chamber, the servants would bow down and, with great deference, greet him: "Peace, O, Lord Bishop." The peasant began to wonder who he really was. So he decided to see whether he could understand the theological writings on the bookshelves. The peasant looked through several pages but nothing made sense to him. However, when people paid him homage he came to the conclusion that he really was a bishop. As for understanding the meaning of the religious books, he concluded that all the other bishops could not understand them either. The analogy is clear. Similarly, not all who dress like *Zaddikim* are in actual fact *Zaddikim*. They dress like *Zaddikim*, so they appear to be *Zaddikim*, but they are far removed from the path of godly fear and love, and thus the people are misled.[16]

According to Simha Bunam, humility is born of knowledge and understanding. When a man ponders the greatness and glory of the Creation he becomes aware of his own insignificance. Yet it is not enough to be outwardly self-effacing. A man may appear unassuming even while his heart is filled with arrogance. Ideally, however, not the merest speck of pride should taint the heart. Before prayer it was particularly important to remove all traces of egoism and self-importance, for these impede true worship of God.

Inexplicably, the teachings of Simha Bunam aroused the antagonism not only of the *Mitnagdim* but also of a number of Hasidim. Rabbi Naftali of Ropczyce went as far as to call him "dangerous". "I am not saying anything against the Rabbi," Naftali rather unconvincingly explained. "He is a true *Zaddik*, yet his way is dangerous to those who follow him." In an equally enigmatic vein Rabbi, Uri of Strelisk remarked: "Rabbi Simha Bunam is a great *Zaddik* who wishes to show the world a new way to God, but he did it before the work was completed. As a result of this, those who followed him have taken a wrong course."

Many *Zaddikim* attended the wedding in Ostilla between the son of Rabbi Don b. Isaac of Radziwill and the daughter of Joseph ben Mordecai of Neshitz. Such opponents of Rabbi Simha Bunam as Simeon Ashkenazi, Moses of Kozienice and Meir of Opatow, seized the opportunity to seek the support of Rabbi Joshua Heshel of Opatow in undermining the status of Simha Bunam. But the Rabbi of Przysucha sent five of his disciples, among them Isaac Meir of Ger, Alexander Zusya of Plock, Issahar Dov Horowitz, Rabbi Feival of Grice, the son-in-law of Bergson, Eliezer Dov of Grabovitz, to present his side of the story to the Apter. As a result, the opponents of Simha Bunam met with a stern rebuke. "If you were living in a forest," the Rabbi of Opatow admonished them, "you would have quarrelled with the trees."[17]

Simha Bunam died in 1827. As he lay dying, he heard his wife Rebecca weeping. "Why do you weep?" he comforted her. "All my life I have been learning how to die."

Chapter 12

The Holy Rebel

Menahem Mendel of Kotzk is one of Hasidism's greatest enigmas.[1] He mystified his contemporaries, terrified his followers, baffled his biographers and intrigued Hasidic historians. Biographies, essays, novels and plays have been written about him, yet very little is known. So, whilst it is not easy to analyse his teachings, it is even harder to unravel the complexities of his character. The light of research has not dispersed the clouds in which he deliberately enveloped himself. But from innumerable anecdotes, aphorisms and discourses, gathered and transmitted by able disciples, there emerges the outline of a tragic and powerful figure.

Menahem Mendel (Heilprin) Morgenstern was born in 1787, in Gorey, near Lublin. His father, Leibish, was a poor glazier who earned a few inadequate roubles by travelling from remote village to village in search of employment. From infancy Mendel was a headstrong child determined to have his own way to the point of being almost unmanageable. Educating this unruly child was no easy matter. Mendel lived in a world of his own—a world of books and dreams, never wasting a moment in play or childish pursuits. So the child became increasingly introvert, an organised student and a highly independent thinker. The matrix of his personality formed and hardened. He was cold and reserved, unwilling to confide in anyone. "I am alone," he wrote rather sadly, "even when I am surrounded by friends and colleagues."

Mendel studied Rabbinics in the Yeshiva of Rabbi Joseph Hochgelernter at Zamosc. "Black Mendel," as his fellow students nicknamed the youthful introvert, devoted himself with complete absorption to his studies. He had little concern for family or friends. Only his teachers mattered to him, and he regarded with special reverence his very first instructor, the one who had taught him the alphabet. For this is the foundation of all other studies. The teachers of Scripture, *Mishnah*, Talmud and Codes deal with controversial matters, but there is no controversy over the *Aleph Bet* (the first two letters of the Hebrew alphabet).

His instructors were impressed and awed by his academic prowess. "Mendel does not make even a gesture without premeditation. His words are deep. His ways are hidden." Later his disciples spoke of him with even greater reverence. "What I have laboured over for many days," marvelled Rabbi Isaac Meir, "the Rabbi grasps in seconds. My knowledge does not even reach his doors." "He is the source of all wisdom and understanding," averred Rabbi Abraham of Sochaczew.

In 1807 Mendel married Glickel Nei of Tomaszow. Afterwards he made his way to Lublin. "An old man in Gorey," related Mendel, "was telling Hasidic tales in the *Bet Ha-Midrash*. He told what he knew and I listened. I became a Hasid." When his father reprimanded him for associating with a Hasidic rabbi, Mendel replied: "We read in the Torah (Exodus xv. 2) 'This is my God and I will glorify Him,' My spiritual father takes precedence over my physical father." But it was not easy to be a spiritual father to this determined youth. "What sort of rabbi do you want?" the Seer of Lublin asked him. "I seek a rabbi who is a good Jew, a plain Jew and who fears God," was the forthright reply. "Your way is the way of melancholy. Forsake it, for it has not found favour in my eyes."

Mendel changed not his ways, but his *Rebbe*. In Jacob Isaac of Przysucha, he found a leader with a kindred spirit, a *Rebbe* who scorned the elaborate ritual of the Hasidic court. For the first and only time in his life he felt that he was no longer alone. For Przysucha was a training ground for the perfection of the soul.

With Jacob Isaac's death Mendel was left a spiritual orphan. Hasidim relate that Jacob Isaac appeared to his bereaved disciple in a dream. "Now that I have been called to the 'Academy on High', you know not who will be your teacher, but be not dismayed. In the celestial spheres I shall continue to be your guide." Mendel, who was afraid of no man, living or dead, replied: "I do not want a dead teacher."

Like most of his colleagues, Mendel transferred allegiance to Rabbi Simha Bunam, the successor of Jacob Isaac. But peace of mind eluded him. In self-imposed penance he wandered through the countryside, suffering many hardships. In turn he visited Kozienice, Lelov, and Szydlowiec. Rabbi Simha Bunam was drawn to the brooding and intense young man. One Passover at the *Seder* table, Rabbi Simha Bunam handed him a handsome silver goblet, saying: "This fine goblet belongs to the man who has the finest brain."

After the death of Simha Bunam, Mendel settled in Tomaszow, where he became a legend in his lifetime. "A fire is burning in Tomaszow," Hasidim used to sing. "A new light is burning there." Toward this new light streamed Hasidim of all kinds, both the erudite and the unlearned, husbands virtually abandoned family and business. In vain the deserted women pleaded and wept. "Tears were created for women," the Hasidim of Kotzk unrelentingly rejoined, for they could not tear themselves away from the "burning bush" that blazed in Tomaszow. In the plain, austere synagogue they led a materially comfortless existence. Their clothes were threadbare. They were often hungry. But their hunger for knowledge was abundantly satisfied. Regularly their *Rebbe* delivered discourses on the Talmud and Maimonides, and all the Hasidim were involved in the mind-illuminating discussions that followed. There were no on-lookers at Tomaszow. All were participants.

Two years later the Rabbi moved to Kotzk, where he was welcomed by his disciple, Mathathiah Koroner, the rabbi of the town, and to Kotzk his devoted Hasidim followed. "To Kotzk one does not travel," they used to sing. "To Kotzk one ascends. For Kotzk takes the place of the Temple, and to the Temple one ascends."

Mendel was not a *Rebbe* in the accepted sense of the word. Not for him the stereotyped life that many of his fellow *Rebbes* led. He despised the humble Hasidim who begged for his blessing. He had just as much contempt for the wealthy followers who showered him, or were willing to shower him, with money or gifts. A man was not necessarily poor if he had no money. Nor was a man rich if he had money. Mendel had a different sense of values. There were, according to him, only two categories—"poor in knowledge" and "rich in knowledge".

Mendel's discourses were terse, each weighted word requiring a commentary. Provided that his train of thought was clear to him, the rabbi of Kotzk cared little whether others understood him. Yet despite his aloofness and detachment, perhaps even because of it, he could not keep throngs away. "Oxen, horses," he shouted at his Hasidim, "what do you want from me?" But the less they were welcomed, the more they came. His very protestations provoked and attracted them. Men made considerable sacrifices to finance a pilgrimage to Kotzk. And there, in the shadow of the master, they tarried for weeks, for months, forgetful of family and responsibilities. The avowed aim of their Master was to redeem the entire House of Israel and to make it "a kingdom of priests and a holy nation." And to do this he needed a *corps d'élites*, a small group of hand-picked aides.

Rabbi Mendel, like Maimonides, preferred one discerning disciple to a thousand ignorant men. "Would that I had ten white *Kaftans* and no more," he prayed. Through this small ruling class, an aristocracy of scholarship and piety, all Israelites would be led through the gates of knowledge and along the path of truth.

Usually impatient, often cruelly candid, Rabbi Mendel saw himself as a general deserted by his army in the heat of battle. He seemed to be fighting single-handed for truth and basic values. Naturally, his outspokenness did not endear him to his colleagues, nor did he court their friendship. "Do you think that I shall enjoy the world to come?" a rich follower once asked him. "You do not enjoy this world for which you have toiled so incessantly," came the forthright reply, "so how can you expect to enjoy the world to come—for which you have made no preparations at all?"

Following the traditions of Przysucha, the Rabbi of Kotzk attached no importance to miracles, believing that to transform a man into a real Hasid was the greatest miracle of all, more important and more difficult than creating a *Golem (homunculus)*. The God-given injunction (Gen. iii. 19), "By the sweat of thy brow shalt thou eat bread," applies even more to spiritual bread. Nothing could be achieved without effort, but if the effort were strenuous enough anything could be achieved. "If a man laments that he has striven but has not found," remarks the Talmud, "do not believe him," Mendel interpreted the Talmudic adage as follows: "Do not believe that he has really striven with sufficient diligence. For, had he really exerted himself, then he would undoubtedly have achieved his purpose. For, why did the second Tablets of the Law survive, whereas the first Tablets were shattered?" The only reason, according to the rabbi's interpretation, is that Moses himself fashioned the second Tablets with great effort and many prayers. Moreover, as far as the first Tablets were concerned, he was simply the recipient of the Tablets, which were given "ready made" and no human effort was needed. But Moses himself, with tremendous labour and earnest prayers, actually fashioned the Second Tablets.

"All or nothing" was the *credo* of Kotzk, and its protagonists scorned half measures and compromises. They believed that the half-way house is a resting place only for the indolent soul. Man must aim high, for he was created so that he might lift up the heavens. Only horses walk in the middle of the road. It was better to be thoroughly wicked than to be half a *Zaddik*. A perfect Gentile is better than an imperfect Jew. Sincerity is of the utmost importance, for God's name is truth. A rabbi is neither a king nor a high priest, but an ordinary human being who strives, as every man should strive, to achieve perfection. A man should increase his knowledge, even though by so doing he will inevitably lose his peace of mind. Mendel hated complacency. "He who learns Torah and is not troubled by it, he who sins and forgives himself, and he who prays today because he prayed yesterday—a very scoundrel is better than such a man."

"Where does God live?" Mendel was asked. "Wherever He is admitted," was his reply. Mendel was a dreamer. Reaching forth to the summit attained by the Besht, he hurled himself to the depth of melancholy. His dreams had strange dimensions. Magnificent and megalomaniacal were his visions. "I am the seventh. I am the Sabbath. Six generations preceded me: the first was Rabbi Dov Baer, the second was Rabbi Shmelke, the third was Rabbi Elimelekh of Lezajsk, the fourth was the Seer of Lublin, the fifth was the Holy Yehudi, the sixth was Rabbi Simha Bunam and I, Mendel, am the seventh." "My soul," he said, "is one of those that were created before the destruction of the Temple. I do not belong among the people of to-day. And the reason for my coming into this world is to distinguish between that which is holy and that which is profane." Severely Rabbi Mendel censured his Hasidic colleagues. None lived up to his standards. "All the week they do what is right in their own eyes. Comes the Sabbath, they attire themselves in *kaftans* and fur hats and, wearing piety like a mantle, they exclaim: 'Come, my beloved.'" Like the Yehudi and Simha Bunam, Rabbi Mendel did not always pray at the appointed hours. "In Kotzk," he said, "we have a soul and not a clock." Proper preparation is as vital as prayer itself. A woodcutter may spend most of the day sharpening his tools and laying the groundwork. Often it is not until the very end of the day that he actually proceeds to chop the wood that is to earn him his wages. If a man feels that by praying in private he can concentrate better than in public, then he should do so. Lengthy services were not held in Kotzk. On the New Year and the Day of Atonement, for instance, the *Piyutim* ("Liturgical Poems") were omitted and the focal passages, *Unesanneh Tokef*, prayer of the *Musaph Amidah*, were recited quietly and quickly.

Like the Besht, Mendel was fired by lofty idealism. Unlike the Besht, he isolated himself from his contemporaries. He regarded himself as a reformer, a revivalist, a man with a mission. And the knowledge of his own superiority kept him apart. He did not find in his fellow men "the image of God". He saw only their faults, their weaknesses. "The whole world is not worth a sigh," was his misanthropic verdict. But neither reality nor dreams could still his spiritual wanderlust or satisfy his restless soul. His life was one long struggle with himself, an unceasing attempt to attain his impossible ideals.

The *Rebbe* of Kotzk supported the Polish revolt of 1830, although his patriotism waned when the Minister of War, Morawski, declared: "We cannot allow Jewish blood to mingle with the noble blood of the Poles. What will Europe say when she learns that, in fighting for our liberty, we have not been able to manage without Jewish help." In spite of this, Joseph Berkowicz (1789–1846), son of Berek Joselewicz, urged the Jews of Poland to enlist, and similarly, Mendel urged wealthy Jews to aid the rebels. After the suppression of the revolt, he lived for a time in Galicia, changing his name to Morgenstern to deflect vicious Russian retaliation.

One Friday night in 1840, on the eve of Sabbath *Toledot*, an extraordinary incident took place in the rabbi's house. It is one of the great mysteries in the history of Hasidism. The followers of Kotzk never discuss the subject, referring to it merely as "that Friday night", but *Mitnagdim* and *Maskilim* have no such scruples. They allege that in a crowded *Bet Ha-Midrash* at midnight, Rabbi Mendel cast aside the *Kiddush* cup that was held out to him by his faithful beadle, Zevi Hirsch of Tomaszow. As if shattering the invisible chains that bound him, he cried out: "I demand justice. Have we not suffered enough? Why are you afraid, you flatterers and liars? Get away from here and leave me alone." Others assert that he shouted: "Get out of here, you fools. I am neither a rabbi nor the son of a rabbi."

The outburst exhausted him and he fainted. He was carried from the *Bet Ha-Midrash* to the adjacent room, where he was revived with difficulty. On *Shmini Atzeret* 1850, Rabbi Mordecai Joseph Leiner of Izbica, author of *Mai Hashiloah* ("The Waters of Siloam"), threw off the yoke of Kotzk. "The *Shekhinah* has departed from Kotzk," mourned the Hasidim. Together with a number of disenchanted Hasidim, Mordecai Joseph, a day after *Yom Tov*, departed for Izbica, where he established his own court. "In Kotzk they worship the broken tablets," was Mordecai Joseph's cryptic comment.

The majority remained loyal to their *Rebbe*. Among the faithful were:

Rabbi Isaac Meir of Ger, Mendel's brother-in-law; Rabbi Abraham of Sochaszew; Yehiel Meir, the Psalm Jew of Gostynin; Isaac of Warka and Rabbi Henoch of Alexander. For nineteen years, until his death in 1859, at the age of seventy-two, the rabbi of Kotzk remained secluded in his study. There he prayed, studied, ate and slept. Through an opening in his door he listened to the Reading of the Law and took part in congregational prayers. Even on the *Seder* nights, he sat alone in his room, alone with his God. At first the beadle would bring out *Shirayim* (morsels left over from the *Rebbe's* meal) but gradually this was discontinued. Only a very select number of disciples, such as his brother-in-law and his son-in-law, were able to enter the "Holy of Holies". Only once a year, on the day before Passover, did he leave his chamber, so that it might be prepared for the festival. Seldom did he appear in public. On the rare occasion when the double doors were opened and he entered the *Bet Ha-Midrash*, terror-stricken Hasidim fled or hid under the tables. Yet for nearly two decades, Hasidim from all over Poland, outstanding rabbis and scholars among them, continued to make their way to Kotzk. Even a number of defectors returned, preferring the curses of Kotzk to the blessings of Izbica.

Neither Mendel's terrifying silences nor his furious outbursts deterred them. They clustered in the *Bet Ha-Midrash*, studying, meditating and gazing at the closed doors of the rabbi's room, hoping against hope to behold the countenance of the stormy petrel of Hasidism. For they believed that their *Rebbe*, in his self-imposed isolation, was fighting a great and fearful battle against all the massed forces of evil. They believed that, in his small room in Kotzk, the rabbi soared through the seven heavens, struggling desperately to hasten the Coming of the Messiah.

Mendel destroyed all his manuscripts. Methodically, each year on the eve of Passover, as he cleared out the leaven, he destroyed everything he had written. His teachings, however, left a permanent imprint on the Courts of Sochaszew, Ger and Alexander and on Polish Hasidism in general. The slight corpus of Mendel's work contrasts sharply with its powerful originality and consequent influence. His disciples were ardent and extravagant in their praises of this most turbulent of the *Zaddikim*. "It is not possible to find another like him, he is as great as the Besht," avowed Rabbi Isaac Meir of Ger. "Just as there was thunder and lightning when the Torah was given on Mount Sinai, so there was thunder and lightning when the Torah was received in Tomaszow. There is no one to grasp the quality of his genius and the degree of his greatness."

"The *Zaddik* perished and no man taketh it to heart" (Isa. lxvii. 1), says Isaiah. "There is no one to impress the words of the *Zaddik* upon our hearts." Rabbi Abraham of Sochaczew went even further. "He is an Angel of the Lord of Hosts. From him I learned wisdom and understanding."

As Rabbi Mendel lay dying, he murmured: "With Him I speak mouth to mouth, even manifestly and not in dark speeches and in the similitudes of the Lord doth he behold." (Numbers xii. 8). The dream of Mendel of Kotzk was that every single Jew might speak face to face with his Maker, echoing the prayer of Moses, "Would that all the Lord's people were prophets and that the Lord would put His spirit upon them" (Numbers xi. 29).

The Rabbi of Kotzk was an enigma in his lifetime as he remains an enigma today. He baffled his contemporaries—and all that has been written in later years about him, both by those who knew him best and those who did not know him well at all, has not solved the mystery.

Chapter 13

The Royal Rebbe and the Militant Masters

The nineteenth century was Hasidism's golden era. This was the time when many East European villages had their own Hasidic courts. Many a remote little *dorf* ("hamlet") in Russia and Poland owes its immortality to the Hasidic Rabbi who lived there and adopted its name as his title. So it was with Belz, Rizhyn (Ruzhin) and Ger. From these hamlets shone brilliant luminaries who lit up the souls of men and added a new lustre, a new richness, a new depth to the Hasidic constellation. For more than a hundred years Rizhyn and Sadagora were focal centres—cities of refuge for Hasidim in Eastern Europe.

Israel Friedmann, founder of the Rizhyn-Sadagora dynasty, was born in 1793, in Przedborz (Kiev). His father, Rabbi Shalom Shakhnah (1771–1802), was the son of Rabbi Abraham "the Angel", and the grandson of Rabbi Nahum of Czernobiel (d. 1795). Shalom Shakhnah was six years old when his father, Abraham, died, and Israel was but five years old when he was orphaned. The child was brought up by his elder brother, Rabbi Abraham, who succeeded his father. At thirteen he married Sarah, daughter of Rabbi Moses, head of the Talmudical College of Berdichev and later Rabbi in Butchan. When his brother, Abraham, died childless in 1813, the sixteen-year-old Israel was his heir. The youthful *Rebbe* settled first in Skvira and then in Rizhyn, where he established his court.

According to legend, the Besht once said, "My soul will return to earth after forty years," and many Hasidim believed that this did, in fact, happen and that the soul of Israel Baal Shem Tov found a second home in Rizhyn.

For in many ways, Rabbi Israel resembled his great namesake. Like the Besht, he lost his father at an early age. Life was his teacher and nature his inspiration. Like the Besht, he was a man of joyous faith.

"He who does not serve the Lord with joy," he maintained, "does not serve the Lord at all." He opposed asceticism, believing that to afflict one's body was to endanger one's soul. Tolerant and kindly, he held the humblest individual in high esteem. "When a Jew takes his *Tallit* and *Tephillin* and goes to the Synagogue to pray, he is as important to-day as the Besht and my grandfather the Maggid were in their day."

"Just as the letters of the alphabet are mute without the vowel signs and just as the vowel signs are meaningless without the letters, so *Zaddikim* and Hasidim are bound up with one another." "All thy people Israel are righteous." Rabbi Israel did not write learned books nor did he make any notable contribution to Hasidic thought. It was neither scholastic discourses nor exegetical homilies that attracted people. As errant children come to a loving and all-forgiving father, so the people come to Rabbi Israel. He identified himself with the problems of each Hasid and in his hospitable house the doors were never shut. Hasidim from all walks of life mingled in true fellowship.

Even among the Rabbis of the day, there was remarkable unanimity in their affection for him and almost all his colleagues felt a reverential regard for the Rabbi of Rizhyn. At the famous Hasidic wedding at Ostilla in 1814, Rabbi Abraham Joshua Heschel, "the Moses of his generation", once bound Israel's girdle around his *kapote* with the words: "Heaven hath honoured me with *Gelilah* ("The *Mitzvah* of binding the *Sepher Torah*"). Israel has not forgotten what he learned in his mother's womb . . . We, his elders, should we not abase ourselves before this young man of Rizhyn because of his nobility and uprightness?" Even rationalist Rabbi Samson Raphael Hirsch (1808–88), leader of Jewish orthodoxy in Germany, remarked after meeting Rabbi Israel: "It is difficult to perceive how such a man could be born of woman, for the light of the *Shekhinah* shines in his face." "No one can compare with him," said the Seer of Lublin, "he has the soul of King Solomon."

When Rabbi Hayim Halberstamm (1793–1876) visited Rabbi Israel he gave this reason: "Why was the Temple built on Mount Moriah (where the binding of Isaac took place) and not on Mount Sinai (where the Torah was given to Israel)? Because the place where the Jew is willing to offer his life for the Sanctification of God's Name is more sacred than the place where the Torah was given. At all times Rabbi Israel is ready to offer himself for the Sanctification of God's Name."

Rizhyn spelt royalty. The Rabbis of Rizhyn were, virtually, the Exilarchs of Hasidism. They dressed with elegance and lived in the style that befitted descendants of the House of David. "If one appears before a king, one dons fine garments, how much more so should one prepare for the presence of the king of kings?" So outwardly Rabbi Israel adopted the life and style of a Polish landowner or a Russian nobleman. His residence was palatial. "Like the house of a prince", notes Professor B. Mayer in "The Jews of our Times", "and his clothes were costly." His coach was drawn by four horses and he employed a large retinue of servants. In "Brama Fakuta" ("The Gates of Repentance") a non-Jewish writer, Broniezky, notes that "the greatest architects, painters and decorators came especially from Paris and Italy to the little town of Rizhyn in order to build and decorate the Rabbi's house. The residence was most impressive from without and valuable materials were used to adorn the interior."

On July 13, 1866 the London "Jewish Chronicle" reported: "The luxury of the palace is truly Royal. Among other things there is a silver room full of the most splendid articles of all types and various shapes, the value of which is estimated at several hundred thousand roubles. The apartments contain most splendid Turkish and Persian carpets as well as most heavy damask hangings . . . his sons and sons-in-law wear the most magnificent kaftans. The smallest children and grandchildren have French, English, German and Russian nurses and governesses, and, moreover, have tutors like young princes."

"What can I do?" asked the Rabbi. "It is not my choice. I am forced from above to take the road of honour and glory and it is impossible for me to deviate from it." The poor were not intimidated by the kingly aura; they thronged to him and found him approachable and unassuming. The aristocracy was impressed and non-Jews often sought his guidance. Such were the claims on his time that Rabbi Israel slept only three hours a day. "One must not waste the time of the kingdom," He said. He would rise at dawn and spend many hours in prayer and study. He opposed asceticism, however, for when a man fasts, he harms himself not only physically but also spiritually. "When there is a little hole in the body," he said, "it eventually makes a hole in the soul."

The Russian Ukase of 1827 whereby boys were conscripted into the army at a tender age caused the Rabbi of Rizhyn considerable grief. He wept over the young boys, little more than children whom the ruthless recruiting officers often snatched off the streets. When the little conscripts, the Cantonists sadly confessed that they were forced to desecrate the Sabbath and to contravene the Dietary Laws, the Rabbi comforted them tenderly; "When the Messiah comes," he answered them "it is you who will take precedence over all the Zaddikim." Rabbi Israel's outlook might well be called ecumenical. Benevolent and flexible was his outlook. He believed that many—if not all—roads lead to Heaven. Some make their way heavenwards through study, others through prayer, some through teaching, others through learning, some through fasting, and others through eating.

In prayer, Rabbi Israel preferred the "still, small voice". To a Hasid praying loudly and violently, he once whispered: "My friend, try first the quiet way." He urged his followers to pray at the times prescribed by the Codes.

In the winter of 1838, two notorious Jewish informers, Isaac Uksman and Samuel Swartzman, were assassinated in Podolia. As a result, many Jews were arrested, including Rabbi Israel, whom the Governor of Kiev, General Bibikov, regarded as "wielding almost the power of a Czar". For twenty-two months, despite prodigious efforts by his Hasidim, the Rabbi languished in the prisons of Kiev and Kamenetz Podolsk, accepting his fate with resignation and realism. "Am I better than the head of our family, King David, who suffered persecution at the hands of kings and princes?" he asked. In 1840 on the day after *Purim*, he was released and allowed to return to Rizhyn. He was, however, under strict surveillance and, to forestall banishment to Siberia, Rabbi Israel escaped to Rumania, where he stayed first in Jassy and later in Scala. Meanwhile, his family in Russia though not in immediate danger, he advised to escape to France or England.

Unhappily, peace eluded the refugee Rabbi. The Russian Government demanded his extradition. To save their leader from imprisonment and possibly banishment to Siberia, the Hasidim maintained that Rabbi Israel was an Austrian citizen, born in Sadagora (Sadagura), to Hertz and Feige Donnenfeld. Eight people, both Jewish and non-Jewish, corroborated this claim, while the Russian Government produced documentary evidence to counter it. Austria's Salomon Mayer von Rothschild (1774–1865), interceded with Count Metternich, and the Austrian Government refused to accede to the Russian demands.

Rabbi Israel acquired an estate in Sadagora (Sadagura), near Czernowitz, and there the glory of Rizhyn was revived. Yet the expatriate yearned for his homeland and for the multitudes of Hasidim from whom he was cut off. "The Messiah," he said, "will first come to Russia." Rabbi Israel died, in 1851, at the age of forty-five. "Everyone leaves behind books," he mused. "I leave sons." Each of his six sons established a distinguished Hasidic dynasty. There were also four daughters.[1]

The Militant Masters of Belz

The founder of the dynasty of Belz, Shalom Rokeah, was born in Brody in 1799. He was a descendant of Eleazar ben Yehudah (1160–1238), author of *Rokeah* ("The Perfumer"), a treatise on ethics and Jewish law. Shalom's father, a follower of Rabbi Hayim Halberstam of Zanz, (Sacz), died at the age of thirty-two and Shalom was brought up by his uncle Issahar Baer, Rabbi of Sokal, whose daughter Malka he married.

Even before daybreak the dutiful Malka would wake her husband with the words: "Shalom, arise to the service of the Creator." "See," she would urge him, "all the labourers are already at their appointed tasks." Inspired by his wife, Shalom needed little urging, but appreciatively he applied to her the verse in Genesis (xiv. 18) "And Melchizedek, king of Salem," interpreting it "If Malka (his wife) is *Zeddeket* ("righteous"), then Shalom is king."

Through Solomon of Lutzk (d. 1813), a disciple of the *Maggid*, Shalom was drawn to Hasidism. Solomon became, in effect, the Boswell of the *Maggid* of Mezhirichi. He devoted his life to collecting and collating the sayings and discourses of the *Maggid*. Two important works, *Divrat Shlomoh* ("The words of Solomon") and *Maggid Debarav L'Yaakov*, (He declareth his words unto Jacob") are the results of his labours.

Shalom visited many of the leading Hasidic rabbis of his day, including Abraham Joshua Heshel of Opatow, Uri of Strelisk and the *Maggid* of Kozienice. Yet, while he appreciated the rare qualities of all the great *Zaddikim* he met, he remained an ardent devotee of Rabbi Jacob Isaac of Lublin. "He who knew the Seer glimpsed the heights to which a mortal could attain, and he who knew the Holy Maggid of Kozienice realised how much the love of God meant to the Jew." Whenever Shalom left Kozienice for Lublin, the *Maggid* would release him with reluctance. "Stay here," the *Maggid* pleaded, "and you will see the prophet Elijah." "Stay with me and you will behold the Patriarchs," the *Maggid* promised further. But Shalom withstood the temptations, and the reward was a warm welcome from the Seer. "He who deprives himself of the privilege of beholding Elijah and the Patriarchs, in order to return to his teacher," glowed the Seer, "he is indeed a true Hasid."

The Seer predicted that this young disciple would be "the head and leader of thousands," and honoured him in many ways, such as allocating to him *Shishi* (the sixth portion of the Reading of the Law), a *Mitzvah* much sought after by the Hasidim. Once when Shalom read the *Megillah* ("The Book of Esther"), the Seer afterwards commented: "I have heard this tale told many times but never as movingly as this." It was at the suggestion of the Seer that Shalom agreed to become Rabbi in Belz, a small town forty miles north of Lvov, and there he remained for forty years.

Belz had always been fortunate in its spiritual leaders. Among its renowned rabbis who had lived in Belz were Joel Serkes and Zehariah Mendel ben Aryeh Lob, a well-known commentator on the Codes. Under Shalom, Belz maintained its academic leadership. People came to him from Galicia, from Hungary and from Poland. He had many followers, and among his outstanding visitors were Rabbi Shalom Halevi Rosenfeld of Kaminka, Rabbi Hayim of Zanz, Rabbi Ezekiel of Shinova and Rabbi Joshua of Leczna. From the Rabbi of Belz they learned the importance of sincerity and simplicity.

The Rabbi of Belz did not dress in white garments, nor did he distribute *Kamayot* ("amulets"), but he was widely known as a worker of miracles. Men, sick in mind or body, hastened to him. Apparently, none was disappointed. For they came as supplicants and remained as Hasidim. "In Belz we discovered," Hasidim would say, "that a man can be a *Rebbe* without a *Zipice* ('the traditional white kaftan')." They observed Rabbi Shalom at prayer and discovered the meaning of devotion. For he worshipped with such intensity that phrases seemed to tumble over one another, and prayers were recited at lightning speed. Similarly his discourses were brief and to the point.

The Edict of Toleration did little to improve the severe economic problems of the Jewish community, and taxes continued to mount. A tax on *Kosher* meat was introduced in 1784, and increased in 1789, in 1810 and 1816, a year which saw the introduction of a candle tax. Enforced secularisation began in 1836, with the Government decree that no rabbi should be appointed who had not taken an academic course. Galicia became the centre of the *Haskalah* ("Enlightenment") movement, with Letteris, Krochmal and Rapoport as its key protagonists.

With seemingly disproportionate virulence, the *Maskilim*, as the enlightened were called, assaulted Hasidism as "a cancer that has to be eradicated from its very source". In his satires, *Megale Temirin* ("Revealer of Secrets") and *Bohan Zaddik* ("The Test of the Righteous"), ridicule was the weapon of satirist Joseph Perl (1774–1839). The *Zaddi-kim* were described as men who were ready to commit every crime. Hasidic discourses and homilies were distorted and misrepresented. But the assaults were not only verbal. A number of the *Maskilim* even became "informers", hurling accusations, true and false, at the Hasidim, accusing them of evading the candle tax, of illegally maintaining Synagogues and of printing Hasidic literature.

The high incidence of apostasy among the *Maskilim* convinced Rabbi Shalom that *Haskalah* represented a danger to Judaism. There is no half-way house in Judaism. "In the Codes of the *Shulhan Arukh*, in the *Orah Hayim* ("The Way of Life"), in the *Yoreh Deah* ("The Teacher of Knowledge") and in *Even Ha-Ezer* ("The Stone of Help"), works dealing with the relation between God and man, the term 'compromise' is not to be found. Only in the *Hoshen Mishpat* ("The Breastplate of Judgment"), which deals with monetary matters, does the word occur." Thus, the Rabbi of Belz refused to temporise with the Reformers, categorising as rank heresy the slightest deviation from the traditional path.

Rabbi Shalom was by nature a fighter. All his life he had fought spiritual battles. From boyhood he had excluded from his life all activi-ties that might distract him from his studies and his struggle for spiritual self-betterment. Now he devoted himself single-mindedly to the fight against the *Maskilim*. One way in which he did this was to stress the need for the thorough training in Torah for young children. "Days are coming," he warned, "when to rear a son in the Torah and in the fear of God will be as hard to accomplish as the Binding of Isaac."

Shalom was greatly revered by his colleagues as well as his disciples. Said Rabbi Israel of Rizhyn: "The Rabbi of Belz is the Master (*Baal Habayit*) of the world." Towards the end of his life, Rabbi Shalom lost his sight and his health failed, but his influence did not wane, nor did his campaign against *Haskalah* falter. He died in 1855, leaving five sons and two daughters.[2]

Joshua (1825–94), the fifth and youngest son, succeeded to the spiritual throne of Belz. He too was renowned both for his phenomenal Rabbinic knowledge and for his worldly wisdom. When a Hasid pleaded, "Help me to die as a Jew," Rabbi Joshua pointedly replied, "You are making the request that Balaam made. Balaam the wicked prayed, 'Let me die the death of the righteous and let mine end be like his' (Numbers xxiii. 10). This is understandable, for Balaam lived like a Gentile but wished to die like a Jew. You, however, should first try to live the life of a Jew. The rest will come naturally."

Rabbi Joshua believed that a Jewish leader is obliged to devise ways and means of attracting those who are far away and quite literally he did this. From distant lands men travelled to him, and all felt rewarded by the forthright counsel he offered. For him, no Jew was beyond redemption. Rabbi Joshua was the first Hasidic rabbi to engage actively in politics. The majority of Galician Jews were Hasidim and his aim was to enlist and co-ordinate this reservoir of Hasidic strength. Only in this way could he counteract the activities of the assimilationist *Shomer Yisrael* ("Guardian of Israel") Association and its organ *Der Israelit*, which was established in 1868 to disseminate the doctrines of the Enlightenment. The *Maskilim* now sought to establish a rabbinical seminary and to elect representatives to the city councils of Lvov and Vienna.

Rabbi Joshua met opposition on all sides, but in spite of it he formed the *Mahzike Ha-Dat* ("Upholders of the Faith") movement in 1878, opening branches in many cities, and through the intervention of Ignatz Deutsch of Vienna received Government recognition. Two journals *Mahzike Ha-Dat* and *Kol Mahzike Ha-Dat* ("The Voice of the Upholders of the Faith") were published in alternate weeks to alert readers to the anti-religious agitation of the *Maskilim*. In the face of the grave threat of assimilation the *Mitnagdim* set aside their own quarrels with the Hasidim and actively co-operated with Rabbi Joshua. Titular head of the *Mahzike Ha-Dat* was Rabbi Simon Schreiber (1821–83) of Cracow, son of Rabbi Moses Sopher. Chiefly on account of the efforts of Rabbi Joshua, Rabbi Simon was, in 1879, elected to the Austrian Parliament by sixteen Jewish districts of Kolomyja, Buczacz, and Sniatyn.

In his fight to preserve traditional Judaism, the energetic Rabbi of Belz enlisted the help of such leading rabbinical authorities as Rabbi Joseph Saul Nathanson (1808–75) of Lvov and Rabbi Isaac Aaron Ettinger, known as "Reb Itzsche" (1827–91), rabbi of Przemysl and Lvov, who sent to the Holy Land some 50,000 gulden annually. "We have six hundred and thirteen commandments. Every one is holy and dear to us. We cannot forgo even one of them," declared the Rabbi of Belz to the *Maskilim* of Lvov. Rabbi Joshua died in 1894, leaving five sons and two daughters.

Rabbi Issahar Dov (1854–1927), second son of Rabbi Joshua, continued the fight for Orthodox Judaism. For ten years he lived in

Czernobiel in the house of his father-in-law, Rabbi Zusya Twersky. Issahar Dov's manner was forceful, and in all things he favoured the direct approach. When it was decreed that rabbis should take State examinations, he reasoned as follows with the Governor of Lvov: "If your Excellency wishes to construct railways, would he not call in engineering experts to guide and to advise him? Surely in such matters he would not consult shoemakers? Similarly, in matters affecting the welfare and status of the rabbinate, only rabbis should be consulted."

At the outbreak of the First World War, Issahar Dov moved first to Ratzfeld (1914–18), then to Munkacs (1918–21) and then, owing to the violent antagonism of the *Rebbe*, Rabbi Hayim Eliezer, son of Rabbi Hirsch Shapira (d. 1914), to Halshitz near Jaraslov. In 1925, the *Rebbe* returned to Belz, where he lived for the rest of his life. Rabbi Issahar Dov employed a personal attendant, Jacob the *Maggid*, whose sole and singular duty was to rebuke his master at regular intervals. When they were dining together one day, Jacob the *Maggid* taunted him: "The Rabbi is seated. He eats and drinks, unmindful of townfolk who have no food. Immediately Rabbi Issahar left the table in order to collect money for the needy. He died in 1927. Hasidim all over the world mourned for the mild but militant Rabbi of Belz.

Rabbi Abraham Mordecai Alter and his family

Rabbi Aaron Rokesh of Belz in Tel Aviv

The Court of Rabbi Israel of Rizhyn at Sadagora

Rabbi Joel Teitelbaum of Satmar

Chapter 14

The Nineteenth Century—Age of Development and Dissent

In the nineteenth century outstanding personalities arose, men of vision and vitality who moulded and remade the lives of men. Many of the *Zaddikim*, as they were called, maintained huge households, receiving and entertaining hundreds of visitors. Many faceted was the role of the *Zaddik*. He was the attorney (*Melitz Yosher*) who pleaded for his clients before the august assembly of the heavenly court; and he was *Guhter Yid*, the friendly father figure, in whom his children could confide. Whether they needed spiritual strengthening or *gesunt und parnossa* ("health and sustenance"), the *Rebbe*'s blessing and his assurance that "the Almighty would help" fell like manna on the parched lips of the afflicted Jews sunk in the deep valley of despair. His power was far-reaching. His most casual utterances were invested with many layers of mystical meaning and his considered judgements were counsels beyond cavil. He wore infallibility like a silken *kapote* and his endorsement was thought to "guarantee" the success of any project.

The Hasidim lived in a world of their own. They were known by their apparel, their speech and their songs. In the eyes of a Gentile observer,[1] they formed an "immense mass of squalid and helpless poverty". This may well have been true, but a faith immovable and immortal as the mountains enabled them to inhabit simultaneously an inner invisible world which was a foretaste of the Golden Age to come.

Although in many ways diametrically opposed in their philosophy, Czernobiel and Lubavitch were the two dynasties primarily responsible for the expansion of Hasidism in Russia during the first half of the nineteenth century.

The dynasty of Czernobiel was founded by Rabbi Nahum (1730–98) author of the works *Yismah Lev* ("Rejoicing the Heart") and *Meor*

Einayim ("Light of the Eyes"). A disciple of the Besht, Rabbi Nahum himself practised self-denial to an almost unhasidic degree. He lived a life of asceticism and self-deprivation, his estate consisting of innumerable acts of charity and piety. However, with Nahum's son, Mordecai (1770–1837), son-in-law of Rabbi Aaron of Karlin, a disciple of the *Maggid* of Mezhirichi, the pendulum swung in the other direction. Rabbi Mordecai became one of the first Hasidic rabbis to live a life of luxury. Rabbi Mordecai's opulent way of life was financed by *Ma'amadot* (regular contributions from his Hasidim) and it was a way of life that his sons continued.

Each of Rabbi Mordecai's sons established "courts" in different localities: Rabbi Moses (b. 1789) in Korostshev; Rabbi Jacob Israel (b. 1794) in Cherkassy; Rabbi Nahum (b. 1804) in Makarov; Rabbi Abraham (b. 1806) in Turisk; Rabbi David (b. 1808) in Talnoje; Rabbi Isaac (b. 1812) in Skvira, and Rabbi Johanan (b. 1816) in Rachmistrovka. His oldest son, Rabbi Aaron (1787–1872) became the titular head of the dynasty and lived in Tarnopol. The sons of Czernobiel, especially Rabbi David of Talnoje, lived on a grand and almost regal scale and became the foundation stone of Hasidism in Russia.

While the rabbis of Czernobiel were somewhat particularist in their outlook, mainly concerned with the spiritual needs of their own followers, the dynasty of Lubavitch took the whole of the House of Israel under its protective wings.

"He taught the Torah in public to show men the way of the Lord, albeit in Cabbalistic wisdom. He composed many works on the Cabbalah which have spread to many communities in Israel. He was like the father of the *Sanhedrin* when teaching the Torah in public. All his people surrounded him on every side and they all united with one heart to hear the words of the living God flashing from his lips like sparks of fire." So Abraham Abele of Kherson described[2] Dov Baer (1773–1827), the successor of Shneur Zalman, known as "Der Mittler Rebbe", i.e. the Intermediary Rabbi, who later settled in Lubavitch.

Dov Baer's accession was contested by his father's star disciple, Rabbi Aaron ben Moses Halevi Horowitz of Staroselye (1766–1829). For eight years, Aaron had sat at the feet of Shneur Zalman, and his works, *Shaare Ha-Yihud Veha-Emunah* ("The Gates of Unity and Faith") and *Abodat Ha-Levi* ("The Levite's Worship"), are original and oustanding contributions to the understanding of *Habad*.[3] No doubt Rabbi Aaron felt that he was better qualified than Dov Baer to carry on the teachings of Shneur Zalman. However, the consensus of the Hasidim was to accept the leadership of Dov Baer. A staunch supporter of Dov Baer was his younger brother Hayim Abraham (d. 1848).[4]

During the "benevolent paternalism" of Alexander I, Dov Baer strongly advocated agricultural settlements. Under the Statute of 1804, those who settled in certain areas of farmland were exempted from taxes for five years.[5] By 1807, four Jewish colonies had been established in Southern Russia, and, during the reigns of Alexander I and Nicholas I, six hundred and forty-five families (3,618 people in all), were settled in newly-established Jewish colonies in Russia.[6] "My advice," wrote Dov Baer encouragingly, "is that men, women and children should learn how to perform various types of work such as weaving, spinning and all skills such as are required in the factories. The training of artisans should likewise be organised in an orderly manner and should be properly regulated especially for the children of the poor, and the middle class as well. They are to have teachers paid for by the communities and under communal supervision. Furthermore, many Jews should begin to engage in agriculture. They are to acquire good fertile lands, in large or small plots and to work on the soil, and God will surely send His blessings on the earth and they will at least be able to feed their children properly. But since the majority of our people are unfamiliar with farm work, they should at first engage experienced farmers (they may be non-Jews) to tend the soil carefully during the first few years. Jews should not be ashamed of engaging in farm work. For were not the fields and vineyards the source of all our subsistence in the Holy Land, the richer farmer using Jewish servants and good workers? Why then should we be different from our ancestors?"[7]

Like his father before him, Dov Baer was imprisoned by the Russian Government in 1826, on the trumped-up charge that he had "collected two or three hundred thousand roubles for the Sultan of Turkey". Through the good offices of Dr. Heibenthal and Jan Lubormirsky, he was released on *Kislev* the tenth, and to this day the anniversary of his release is celebrated by *Habad* Hasidim.

A prolific writer, Dov Baer wrote commentaries on the *Zohar*, on Genesis, on Exodus, *Pisuke Dinim* ("Legal Decisions"), and a "Tract on Ecstasy" (*Kuntres ha-Hithpaalut*). So far nineteen of his works have been published.

A gifted orator, his involved discourses were long and yet utterly absorbing and lucid. All could understand when he expounded the theories of *Habad*. "If you cut his finger," Hasidim said in awe, "you would find that not blood flowed in his veins but Hasidism." He died at Neyzhin (Chernigov) at the age of fifty-four, leaving two sons and six daughters.

It was known that Dov Baer preferred one of his sons-in-law to his sons, so Menahem Mendel, known as the *Zemah Zedek* ("Offspring of Righteousness") after the title of his works, became the third Rabbi of Lubavitch. Menahem Mendel was born in 1789 in Lubavitch. His mother was the second daughter of Shneur Zalman. Menahem Mendel's diligence was phenomenal. "I generally study for eighteen hours a day," he later recalled, "which includes five hours of writing, and in the past thirty years I have spent a total of thirty-two thousand hours studying the works of Shneur Zalman."

"With a few honourable exceptions," writes the sociologist, Jacob Lestschinsky, "the Jewish masses, together with their rabbis and Hasidic leaders, were buried in such obscurantism that the plans of the government, in essence progressive and, as regards the prevailing conditions of Jewish life, revolutionary, were remote from their understanding and psychology."[8] Menahem Mendel was one of these exceptions. Like his father-in-law, he actively encouraged agriculture and, in 1844, he bought from Prince Shezedrin 3,600 *Desyatins* (9,700 acres) of land at Shezedrin around Minsk, where he established a settlement for three hundred families.

One of the first problems which faced the third Rabbi of Lubavitch was the pitiful plight of the Cantonists, as the recruited child-soldiers were called. By the decree of August 26, 1827, Jews were made liable to military service and could be called up between the ages of twelve and twenty-five. Every year, the Jewish community had to supply ten recruits per thousand of the population. Among the non-Jews the proportion was seven per thousand. Recruits aged between twelve and eighteen were to be placed in establishments for military training. The Jewish community (*Kahal*) was instructed to appoint three to six persons who were responsible for selecting the recruits.[9]

These conscripts, mostly the children of poor families, were to serve for a period of twenty-six years, a term which started when the recruit reached the age of eighteen. Bitter, indeed, was the life of these young boys, often snatched away from their mothers' arms when they were but eight or nine years old and sent to distant and remote provinces. Unscrupulous agents roamed the streets and were known as the "hunters" or "snatchers". The bodies, the minds and the souls of these unfortunate children were at stake.

Menahem Mendel set up a special council to alleviate the sufferings of the youthful Cantonists. The *Hebra Tehiat Ha-Metim* "The Society for the Revival of the Dead") ransomed as many children as possible. Special Lubavitch delegates regularly visited army camps to bring comfort and moral support to the child soldiers and to lessen the likelihood of conversion.

At this time, the *Haskalah* movement raised its head in Russia and Isaac Ber Levinsohn (1788–1860), of Kamenetz Podolsk, known as the "Russian Mendelssohn", wrote such anti-Hasidic works as *Dibre Zaddik* ("The Words of the Zaddik") and *Teudah Be Yisrael* ("A Testimony in Israel"), published in Vilna, in 1828. On January 15, 1840, the *Maskilim* opened a school in Riga, under German-trained Rabbi Dr. Max Lilienthal (1815–82), who was aided by Mordecai Aaron Gunzburg (1795–1846), creator of modern Hebrew prose, and Aryeh Leib Mandelstam. In 1841, forty-five delegates of the "Lovers of Enlightenment" met in Vilna to plan expansion. The Minister of Public Instruction, Count Sergius Uvarov, welcomed these innovators, regarding the movement as the logical step towards assimilation.

To win the co-operation of the Jewish community "in support of the efforts of the Government", a Rabbinical conference was convened at St. Petersburg. Among the delegates were the head of the Yeshiva of Volozhin, Rabbi Isaac b. Hayim of Volozhin (1821–79), banker Israel Heilprin of Berdichev, Bezalel (Basilius) Stern, director of the Jewish school in Odessa, and Menahem Mendel of Lubavitch. A. L. Mandelstam was the official translator. Moses Montefiore, who had been invited, was not able to attend. The sessions lasted from May 6 to August 27, but the delegates agreed on very few issues. A law promulgated on November 13, 1844, stipulated that although they were not barred from the general school system, Jews could open their own schools, provided that they were self-supporting, and could also set up two theological seminaries. In a supplementary secret circular, the Government admitted that "the purpose of educating the Jews is to bring about a gradual merging with the Christian nationalities and to uproot those superstitions and harmful prejudices which are instilled by the teachings of the Talmud."[10]

Menahem Mendel fought the *Haskalah* movement both in private and in public. He sent emissaries throughout Russia to expose what he considered fallacies in the arguments of the *Maskilim*. Passionately, he opposed the idea of revising the liturgy and of editing the Scriptures. "The Torah," he wrote, "is from Heaven. We believe that every word of the Torah given by Moses came from God . . . We dare not edit it . . . One is obliged to teach one's son the written Torah in its entirety."[11]

Practical steps were taken, such as the expansion of Lubavitch Yeshivot in Bobrovna, Pasana, Lyozno and Kalisk. Rabbi Menahem Mendel travelled widely, and his friendship with Professor I. Bertenson, Court Physician to the Czar, often helped in delicate negotiations relating to the welfare of the community. Like many of his colleagues, Menahem Mendel suffered from the malevolence of informers like Herschel Hosech ("Darkness"), Benjamin the Apostate and Lipman Feldman, who tried unsuccessfully to trap him.

August 26, 1856, saw a number of improvements in the legal status of the Jews. The discriminatory system of Jewish conscription was abolished and the recruitment of Jews to the armed forces was placed on the same basis as for the other subjects of the Empire. Selected categories of Jews were permitted to reside with their families outside the Pale of Settlement. When Menahem Mendel died in 1866, he was succeeded by Rabbi Samuel, his youngest son. Rabbi Samuel, too, participated in discussions in St. Petersburg. This was a period of virulent antisemitic propaganda and fearful pogroms, and Rabbi Samuel's strenuous attempt to improve matters only resulted in his being placed under house arrest.

In the Lubavitch tradition, Rabbi Samuel's successor, Rabbi Shalom Dov Baer (1860–1920) continued to fight for equal rights for the Jewish community. He was particularly concerned about the welfare of the Mountain Jews (*Berg Yidn*) who lived in the mountains in Uzbekistan, a region far remote from the main centres of Jewish life. Rabbi Shalom Dov Baer deputed Samuel Ha-Levi Levitin, formerly Rabbi of Rakshik, to minister to their spiritual needs, and the *Sephardim* responded gratefully, much to the gratification of the *Ashkenazim*. Rabbi Shalom Dov Baer spent the years of the First World War in Rostov-on-the-Don, and there he died.

In Galicia, the dynasties of Rizhyn (Ruzhin) and Sadagora ruled supreme. Rabbi Israel of Rizhyn left six sons known as the "Six Orders of the Mishnah" or the "Six Wings of the Angel" (Isaiah vi. 2) and three daughters. Eight months after Israel's death, his eldest son, Shalom Joseph, died (1851), and his brother Abraham Jacob Friedmann (1820–83) succeeded him. To Abraham Jacob his loving father had applied the verse from Micah (vii. 20): "Thou wilt show faithfulness to Jacob."

Thousands of Hasidim, including rabbis and scholars, did show faithfulness to the new Rabbi and Sadagora became a thriving Hasidic centre. Like his father, Rabbi Abraham Jacob incurred the displeasure of the authorities and was imprisoned for fifteen months in Czernowitz. Sir Laurence Oliphant (1829–88), the English proto-Zionist who propagandised for Jewish resettlement in Transjordan, described his visit to the *Rebbe* in 1880. "When I was in Vienna, people I trusted told me about the Sadagorer *Rebbe*. I wanted very much to meet him. I thought, come what may, a man who by spirit alone rules thousands of people cannot be an ordinary, commonplace creature. Since I was then situated near Sadagora I advised the *Rebbe* that my wife and I would like to meet him. Immediately, he sent us his splendid carriage. The whole Jewish community of Sadagora awaited our arrival, lining both sides of the street to see the Gentile coming to their *Rebbe*. At the entrance of the *Rebbe's* house, his sons and sons-in-law, in Polish dress, greeted us. Inside, the rebbe's daughters were hostesses to my wife. I was led into a room, much like a princely court, furnished with precious gold and silver antiques. There I met the *Rebbe*, accompanied by two servants. Regal authority was in his face. He spoke intelligently about the situation of the Russian Jews. Though I did not quite understand his conduct, I was nevertheless convinced that he could lead and command his people with just the barest gesture."[12]

Meanwhile, Rabbi Abraham's brothers established their own Courts: Rabbi David Moses (1827–75) in Czortkov: Rabbi Mordecai Shragai (1834–94) in Husiatyn; Rabbi Nahum (1837–1933) in Stefanesti and Rabbi Dov in Leowie (Rumania).

Having survived the assaults of the *Mitnagdim*, Hasidism now had to cope with fratricidal internal struggles. A participant in one of these unedifying episodes was Rabbi Dov or Bereinu (1817–66) a son of Rabbi Israel of Rizhyn.[13] Carefully educated by private tutors in almost princely style, Dov had been married at the age of fourteen to the youngest daughter of Rabbi Motel of Czernobiel. The young couple, however, were incompatible. They were childless, and disharmony reigned in their home. After his father's death, Dov in 1852 settled in Husay, Rumania, and later he moved to Leowie. His was a sensitive and a brooding disposition, a prey to fits of melancholy. The only person with whom he had any real rapport was his brother Nahum, and Nahum's death in 1858 was a blow from which he never recovered.

Not for Dov was the conventional pattern of the Rabbi's life. He liked to gather around him a few intimates with whom he could commune and philosophise. He held himself aloof from the Hasidim.

They wearied him with their endless woes. He implored his attendants to keep the people away, but they would not be repulsed or rejected. Dov felt himself the victim of circumstance, persecuted by his wife and by his family. His constant companions were the local apothecary and a doctor. The day came when he refused to attend the services, and on one *Kol Nidre* night, in 1869, his attendants virtually carried him by force to the Synagogue. Alarmed at his conduct, his wife begged several trusted Hasidim to escort the *Rebbe* to his brother in Sadagora.

The rumour that Rabbi Dov was being held against his will in his brother's house, led the lawyer Dr. Judah Leib Reitman of Czernowitz to intervene with the civil authorities. As a result, Dov came to live with Dr. Reitman, a defector from the Hasidic milieu. This defection was widely exploited by the *Maskilim*. In a manifesto drafted by A. Orenstein and published in the Hebrew periodical *Ha-Magid*,[14] Dov declared that though he remained true to the faith of his fathers, he sought to escape from the "foolish crowd" that surrounded him and wished to "remove the thorns from the vineyard of the House of Israel and to free Judaism from senseless customs that have no source in the Law of Israel".

This statement from a son of the Rabbi of Rizhyn caused consternation among the Hasidim and jubilation among their opponents. Dov's brother-in-law, Rabbi Mendel, and his nephew, Shalom Joseph, eldest son of Rabbi Isaac of Bohush, were among those who attempted to reason with the renegade *Rebbe*. After eight weeks in Dr. Reitman's house, Dov did indeed have second thoughts, and, on *Shushan Purim*, he remorsefully returned to Sadagora. There, four months later, he issued a public statement (*Kol Kore*) expressing his desire to "return to the rock from which I was hewn . . .". I will hold fast to the deeds of my holy fathers . . . Their law is a lamp to my feet and their righteousness is a light to my path."

For six years until the day of his death in 1866, he lived in Sadagora, deserted by his wife, shunned by his brothers, and ignored by his former followers. He died as he had lived, without friends, one of Hasidism's most perplexing personalities.

But for the Sadagora dynasty, the cup of suffering was not yet full. Now followed seven years of bitter persecution. The mantle of the Vilna Gaon fell, surprisingly enough, on a Hasidic *Rebbe*, Hayim Halberstamm of Sans (Nowy Sacz) (1793–1876). At the age of eighteen, he was appointed Rabbi of Rudnick near Brody, a town where many Hasidim of Ropczyce lived, and Rabbi Hayim became a follower of

Rabbi Naftali Zevi Horowitz of Ropczyce. There he met Rabbi Shalom of Kaminka and Rabbi Meir of Opatow. In 1830, Rabbi Hayim became rabbi in Sacz, which the Hasidim call *Tzanz*, spelling it with a *Zaddik* (one of the letters of the Hebrew alphabet) to denote that it was the home of a *Zaddik*.

For forty-six years, Rabbi Hayim lived in Sacz. There he wrote such learned works as *Divre Hayim* (on the Talmudic tractates *Gittin* and *Mikvaot*), responsa *Divre Hayim* (on the four parts of the *Shulhan Arukh*), and *Divre Hayim* on the Torah. His responsa reflect the social and religious life of the Jews in Galicia in the mid-nineteenth century. "We concentrate," wrote Rabbi Hayim, "on Talmud and the Codes. We study Cabbalah when others are asleep." He was revered by *Mitnagdim* as well as Hasidim. Rabbi Saul Joseph Nathanson (1808–75) called him "Holy Gaon, Light of Exile."

When the "Light of Exile" stood in prayer, light seemed to radiate from him. He forgot the world around him, he even forgot his ailing foot, stamping it until it bled, as he poured out his heart before his Father in Heaven. He lived in an extremely frugal fashion, distributing to the poor all the monies that he received.

Then suddenly, "the Great Defender", as Rabbi Hayim was known, became the Great Accuser, though the cause of this transformation is exceedingly vague. Perhaps it was because the royal life style of the Sadagora dynasty was so alien to him. Perhaps it was personal pique at the disrespectful behaviour of Rabbi Mordecai Shragai of Husiatyn. At any rate the temporary defection of Rabbi Dov brought matters to a head. Rabbi Hayim issued an ultimatum requiring the Sadagora brothers to "change their way of life" or suffer the consequences. In the winter of 1869, Rabbi Hayim, supported by Rabbi Shlomoh Shapira (later Rabbi in Munkacs), declared war against the Hasidim of Sadagora. "They are rebels . . . Their scribes are apostates . . . one must not use their *Tephillin* and *Mezuzot* . . . It is forbidden to eat the meat of their slaughterers. The Almighty who preserved us from Shabbetai Zevi should preserve us from them. They are all apostates . . . They conduct themselves with arrogance . . . They walk in the ways of Gentiles . . . Their womenfolk transgress the law . . . They should be persecuted without mercy."

Rabbi Elimelekh of Grodzisk and Rabbi Mendele of Vishnitz rose to the defence, imploring Rabbi Hayim not "to pursue in anger this holy family". The Rabbis of Sadagora refused to launch counter-attacks and so their Hasidim took matters into their own hands. On

Nisan the fourth 1869, Nissan Back and forty-nine other Hasidim issued an *Issur* ("Prohibition") known as *Mishpat Katuv* ("Written Judgement") forbidding people to obey the dictates of the *Rebbe* of Sanz. The Issur was proclaimed at the Western Wall in Jerusalem and repeated in Safed and Tiberias.

Leading scholars, like Joseph Saul Nathanson, Rabbi Isaac Aaron Ettinger ("Reb Itzsche"), Rabbi of Przemysl, and Dov Berush Meisels (1798–1870), Rabbi in Warsaw, now rallied to the support of Rabbi Hayim. The day after *Shavuot* (Pentecost), 1869, the followers of Rabbi Hayim publicly excommunicated "Nissan Back and his followers". For seven years the "civil war" between Hasid and Hasid raged through Galicia, dividing families and splintering communities. These were indeed the seven lean years of Hasidism.

Chapter 15

Dynamic Dynasties of the Late
Nineteenth Century

Ninety per cent of all the Jews in Europe and America today, and eighty per cent of world Jewry originated in Eastern Europe. It was Poland, the main centre of Hasidism,[1] which produced the pietists, the Hebraists, the Yiddishists, the pioneers, the men of letters and the men of action.

During the nineteenth century, Jews in Czarist Poland clustered together in closely-knit communities. Differences of morals and of mores set them apart from their non-Jewish neighbours and they fought to preserve their identity. For the most part Polish Jewry refused to purchase civic equality at the price of assimilation, and an overwhelming majority clung with whole-hearted devotion to traditional Judaism.

The spread of Hasidism marked the emergence of a Jew for whom the Torah was all-embracing and all-sufficient. It was "hard to be a Jew", but it was compensatingly "good to be a Jew". In an age of systematic persecution and licensed discrimination, the Jew managed miraculously to retain a spiritual *joie de vivre*. Only in study of the Torah, in the fulfilment of Mitzvot, in communion with his Creator, could he find refuge and the strength with which to face the deadly decades. Poland proved to be fertile soil for Hasidism and in no other country did the movement spread so rapidly. It is possible to note only a few of the major dynasties here.

Inevitably much must be omitted, and events that merit meticulous analysis and personalities who deserve detailed biographies must receive but passing reference. Little short of a lifetime of collation could do justice to so panoramic and close-packed a canvas.

Rabbi Mordecai Joseph Leiner (1800–54) was the founder of the

Radzyn-Izbica dynasty which produced five outstanding teachers in the course of one century. The rabbis of Izbica believed in informed faith, rather than blind faith. For God should be served with intelligence as well as with devotion. It was necessary to love not only fellow Jews but also all men. First, man must aim at perfecting himself. In this way he could help prepare for the coming of the Messiah and hasten the dawn of the Apocalyptic era.

For thirteen years Rabbi Mordecai Joseph had sat at the feet of Menahem Mendel of Kotzk, but in 1840 he was among the disillusioned dissenters who left Kotzk. His work *Mai Ha-Shiloah* ("The Waters of Siloam"), written with great economy of words, maintains that the short-comings of the Biblical heroes were of minor importance and did not detract from their moral stature.

Rabbi Mordecai Joseph's son Rabbi Jacob (1828–78) wrote *Bet Jacob* ("The House of Jacob"), commentaries on Genesis, Exodus, Leviticus and on the Festivals and *Sepher Ha-Zemanim* ("The Book of Seasons") discourses on the months of *Nisan* and *Iyar* as well as a commentary on the Passover *Haggadah*. Mild, kindly Rabbi Jacob was heir to his father's rabbinate, but not to his father's fiery temperament. The *Rebbe* attracted many adherents. After living for thirteen years in Izbica he settled in Radzyn, where he established his "court".

His son, Rabbi Gershon Hanoh Heinokh (1839–90), brought Radzyn into the limelight. In the format of a Talmudic tractate he produced a monumental anthology called *Sidre Tohorot* ("The Section of Purity"), named after the sixth and the last sections of the Mishnah. Of the sixty-three tractates of the Mishnah, twenty-six and one half tractates are not accompanied by the explanatory Babylonian *Gemara*. To compensate for this, Gershon Heinokh collated the relevant comments and interpretations of the Sages. Every single page bears the acknowledgement "compiled from the words of the Tannaim and Amoraim of blessed memory". Yet, although the work was endorsed by such authorities as Simon Schreiber of Cracow, Isaac Elhanan Spector of Kovno, Israel Joshua of Kutno, Zevi Hirsch Ornstein of Lvov and Samson Raphael Hirsch of Frankfurt, some scholars censured Gershon Heinokh for producing a pseudo-Talmud. Rabbi Bezalel and his colleagues on the *Bet Din* of Vilna issued a ruling forbidding to "keep the book in Jewish homes".

"The redemption will begin," wrote Rabbi Gershon, "when we will be permitted to rebuild the Temple. If we will be worthy, permission will be granted even before the ingathering of the exiles." In

1887 he published *Maamar Sefunei Temunei Hol* ("Dissertations on the Items Hidden in the Soil"), a study of the *Ptil Tekhelet* (the blue strand in the fringes of the garment described in Numbers xv. 38."And they shall put with the fringe at each corner a thread of blue"). The blue dye was derived from a mollusc called by the Talmud (Menahot 44a) *Halozon*, but so complex was the process, that for some two thousand years Jews had ceased to include the prescribed blue strand in the ritual fringes.

Accompanied by his attendant, Israel Kotzker, Rabbi Gershon studied the Italian seashore and became an expert on marine life. On the eve of Pentecost, 1888, he published his second thesis on *Ptil Tekhelet* ("Discourse on the Blue Strand") in which he claimed to have discovered *Halozon* ("sepia officinalis"). On the first day of *Hanukkah*, 1889, he began to wear the blue thread, and his Hasidim followed suit. The practice was adopted by the Hasidim of Nahman of Braclaw with a slight variation. While the Hasidim of Radzyn are content to include one blue thread among the eight prescribed by the Torah, the Hasidim of Braclaw prefer two blue strands and six white ones.

A workshop for the manufacture of the ritual fringes was established at the Rabbi's court in Radzyn. Many scholars, however, opposed the restoration of the blue thread. Among them were Rabbi Joshua of Kutno and Rabbi I. E. Spector. To Gershon Heinokh the *Tekhelet* was closely interwoven with the rebuilding of the Temple, and its introduction represented an attempt to hasten the apocalypse. The Rabbi of Radzyn studied medicine, diagnosed the illnesses of sick Hasidim and wrote prescriptions in faultless Latin. He was also a fine musician. He died in 1891, and his third tractate on the blue thread *Ein Tekhelet* was published posthumously.

His son, Mordecai Joseph Eliezer (1865–1929), was active in communal affairs. He was one of the delegates who interceded with the Russian Minister of the Interior, Peter Stolypin, with Josef Pilsudski and with the Socialist leader, Hermann Diamond. He dedicated himself to the publication of his father's voluminous writings. Nine texts were published, while fifteen remained in manuscript. Among the published works were *Tiferet Ahanohi* ("The Glory of Hanokh"), a commentary on the Zohar, and *Daltot Shaare Ha-Ir* ("The Doors of the Gates of the City") on the Talmudical tractate *Erubin*; *Sod Yesharim* ("The Secret of the Upright") discourses on the High Holy days and Festivals; *Orhot Hayim* ("The Paths of Life") and ethical will generally attributed to Eliezer b. Hyrcanus but probably written by the German rabbi of the eleventh century, Eliezer ben Isaac Ha-Gadol.

He was forthright in his opposition to autopsies. "If you are not prepared," he declared at a rabbinical conference in Warsaw, "to wage full-scale war against the mutilation of Jewish bodies, you should give up your posts as rabbis."

An extraordinary personality was the miracle worker Rabbi Yehiel Meir Lipshitz (1816–88) better known as the "*Tehillim Yid*" ("The Psalm Jew") or the "Good Jew of Gostynin". Rabbi Mendel of Kotzk regarded him as one of the Thirty-Six, the *Lamed Vav* (in each generation there are thirty-six hidden saints, whose merit sustains the world).

Yehiel Meir was a disciple of Rabbi Mendel, of Rabbi Isaac Meir of Ger and of Rabbi Abraham of Ciechanow. For forty years he served as Rabbi in Gostynin and only in 1875 did he become a Hasidic *Rebbe*. He refused to accept any monies from his followers and lived a life of penury.

The Book of Psalms was his constant companion. He believed that reciting Psalms could relieve any sorrow. "Again and again, study the Psalms," he urged upon his children, "and study the translation with the commentary of Rashi. Let them be familiar to you. Take heed to recite daily at least five chapters." The rabbi was of small stature, thin and emaciated, but he was always sensitive to his followers' troubles and, in the course of the thirteen years of his rabbinate, he helped many people.

"I have finally found your father, Rabbi Isaac," the Rabbi of Kotzk told Rabbi Jacob David. "I searched for him in the Higher Regions but could not find him. I searched for him among the disciples of the Besht. I looked for him among the *Amoraim*. Eventually I found him gazing sadly at a river. 'What are you doing here?' I asked him. 'This river is full of the tears of the children of Israel and I cannot move away from it,' he replied."

This apocryphal story aptly epitomised the outlook of Rabbi Isaac Kalish of Warka (1779–1848). A disciple of Lelov and of the Seer, he looked on all men with kindness. For a while he worked for Tamara Bergson. He participated in communal affairs. It was he who deputed the convert, Stanislaus Hoga (who later settled in England and translated Bunyan's *Pilgrim's Progress* into Hebrew), to defend the Hasidim against the accusations of the *Maskilim*.

He travelled widely to urge the Hasidic rabbis to fight with a united front to abolish the military conscription of children. Rabbi Israel of Rizhyn advised him to send Israel Binenfeld (d. 1849) of Cracow to London, to enlist the support of Sir Moses Montefiore. This was done, and in March, 1846 Sir Moses was received by the Czar. The Rabbi of

Warka also sent petitions to the Russian Minister Uvarov and to Paskevitch, Viceroy of Poland. Rabbi Isaac met Sir Moses in Lomza and urged the Englishman to support orthodox Jewry in its stand against the decrees which virtually enforced assimilation.

Rabbi Isaac's son, Rabbi Jacob David Kalish (1814–78) of Amshinov, also served the community with self-effacing dedication. Despite his inability to speak either Polish or Russian, he managed to find his way to the heads of various government departments, and even in some instances to have harsh edicts mitigated. When Jews were forbidden to wear beards, he worked with Rabbi Jacob Gezundheit, Chief Rabbi of Warsaw, to help combat the decree.

His brother Menahem Mendel Kalish of Warka (1819–68) was known as "the silent Rebbe". What other *Rebbes* achieved through discourses, he achieved through silence. For him it was a way of life. Every word was weighed. Every syllable and, indeed, every letter, was fraught with significance. He would sit among his Hasidim for a whole night without uttering a single word. And for all who shared it such a night of silence was a moving and meaningful experience. "In Warka," Hasidim would say, "God is served by thought." "It does not matter whether we study or whether we pray," the Hasidim of Warka believed, "provided that we do not provoke our Father in Heaven."

Such important rabbinic works as the voluminous responsa *Avne Nezer* on the Codes and *Egle Tal* (on the laws of the Sabbath) were written by Abraham Bornstein (1829–1910), Rabbi of Sochaczew. "I am now like a broken vessel, completely shattered" the son-in-law of Mendel of Kotzk would remark, "but when I remember my days in Kotzk my bones revive." He occupied rabbinical posts in Parczew (1863–66), Kreshnewice (1866–76) and Nasielsk (1876–83)—these were twenty restless and troubled years of persecution and misunderstanding. He could not reconcile himself to the disparity between his high ideals and the community's way of life. He was accused by his opponents of omitting the prayer for the Czar on the day of the coronation of Czar Alexander III, and the authorities threatened him with expulsion from Nasielsk. In Sochaczew he finally found peace, and there he studied and taught and wrote his books.

In 1864, he issued a proclamation denouncing the "heretical" works which were being published in both Hebrew and Yiddish. Repeatedly he stressed the importance of Torah study. "Through the merit of learning Torah, the children of Israel receive material as well as spiritual benefits." In unequivocal terms he censured the then current practice of purchasing rabbinical posts, and such leading rabbis as Abraham Mordecai of Ger and the Rabbi of Alexander agreed with him. In every situation he tended to take the traditional viewpoint. For instance, he concurred with Rabbis Joshua of Kutno and Hayim of Sanz in forbidding the baking of *Matzot* by machinery, "lest we should transgress the laws of our Fathers".

Few nineteenth-century scholars could match the versatility of Rabbi Zadok ha-Kohen Rabinowicz (1823–1900) of Lublin, prolific writer, bibliophile, Cabbalist and codifier. A child prodigy, known as the "Illui of Krinick", he had completed the study of the Talmud by the age of seventeen. He wrote forty-one books, of which twenty-one were published, demonstrating the wide span of his interests. He wrote homiletical works on the Pentateuch, responsa, a treatise on the calendar, novellas on the Talmud, a geographical gazetteer, biblical commentaries, a commentary on the Zohar and even mathematical textbooks. Like Joseph Caro (1488–1575), Zadok Ha-Kohen claimed that solutions to diverse problems often came to him in his dreams.

When his wife refused to give him a divorce, he resorted to the only other method open to him under Jewish law, *Heter Mea Rabbanim*, the dispensation granted by one hundred rabbis. It took him twelve months to gather the necessary signatures and his far-flung travels brought him into touch with many of the rabbinic and Hasidic leaders of Poland and Russia. Although he wrote a treatise, eighty-six pages long, in justification of the desired divorce, such rabbis as Isaac Meir of Ger and Hayim of Sanz refused to co-operate. "Do not without cause put a daughter of Israel to shame," pleaded Rabbi Hayim. "If you divorce her, you will remain childless." This prediction was accurate. The divorced Rabbi Zadok remarried, but the marriage was childless.

Hanokh Heinokh Ha-Kohen Levin, Rabbi of Alexander (Alexandrow), served a long "apprenticeship" and did not become *Rebbe* till the age of sixty-eight. In turn, he was disciple of the Yehudi, the Seer, Simha Bunam, Mendel of Kotzk and Isaac Meir of Ger. He was reluctant to become a *Rebbe*, and he humorously explained how he had overcome this reluctance. "I did not accept the yoke of the Rabbinate until I saw the face of my wife as black as a pot." With the death of Rabbi Isaac Meir, he could no longer refuse responsibility. Having for so long subordinated his will to the will of others, he found the crown of leadership weighty and burdensome. "Woe to the generation that has me for its leader," he sighed. Yet he was a conscientious and dedicated *Rebbe*, who established a personal rapport with every single one of his Hasidim. He made a special point on the Sabbath of handing each Hasid a goblet of wine. One of his innovations was the acceptance of *Kvitlech* (petitions) from women, which had not been the custom in Ger or Kotzk.

An ardent lover of Zion, he raised 12,000 roubles for charitable institutions in the Holy Land. He was renowned for his riddles, poems, discourses and, above all, parables. With characteristic tolerance, he defended those Hasidim who prayed not at the appointed hours, but when the spirit moved them. "In peace time," explained the Rabbi of Alexander, "soldiers exercise according to time-tables laid down in the military manuals. But in an emergency they dare not conform to the conventional pattern. Similarly, regular procedures do not apply to the Hasidim; for them every day is a battlefield and when they pray they fight, and regulations no longer apply."

"The world is like a wedding," says the Talmud (*Erubin* 54a). The *Rebbe* of Alexander interpreted this in terms of the man from a small town who came to Warsaw. He heard the sound of wedding festivities issuing from a certain house, and he assumed that the owner of the house was celebrating the wedding of a member of his family. Several days passed and the house was still filled with merriment and music. Can a man have as many sons as the days of the year, he wondered. Then his his neighbours laughingly explained that the house was a banquet hall, and every day someone else held a different celebration there. So it is with life. Men's fortunes change from day to day. The rabbi died in 1870 at the age of seventy-two.

So the town of Alexandrow (or Alexander, as the Hasidim called it) was destined to become the home of the Dancyger family, the Rabbis of Alexander. Only Ger had a larger Hasidic following in Poland than Alexander.

There were few Polish towns without one or two Alexander *Stieblech*. Whilst Ger lured the scholars, Alexander drew the *Baale Batim* ("Householders"), the merchants and the masses. Alexander Hasidim were affiliated with neither the *Mahzike Ha-dat* of Belz nor with the *Aguda* of Ger. Many were closely associated with the Mizrachi.

Founder of the dynasty, Shragai Feivel (d. 1849) had been a disciple of Jacob ben Jacob Moses of Lissa (d. 1832) the Seer, of Simha Bunam and of Isaac of Warka. When the Rabbi of Warka died, Shragai Feivel was appointed *Rebbe*. He died six months later on *Shemini Atzeret*, 1848, in Makov.

His only surviving son, Yehiel Dancyger (1828–94), acted both as

Rabbi and *Rebbe* to the Jews of Alexander. He did not give long discourses, nor did he accept *Pidyonot*. With kindness and warmth he welcomed every Hasid. Every Hasid was important to him. His prayers were interspersed with soul-searing sighs, for he often quoted the aphorism of Alfasi (1013–1103) that "when a man weeps during his prayers the stars and the planets weep with him". In his final message to his children, he implored them to pray for him and urged them to seek forgiveness every night for any misdeeds they might have committed.

The dynasty of Alexander grew in influence and prestige under the "wise Rebbe", as Yehiel's son, Yerahmiel Yisrael Isaac Dancyger (1863–1910), was called. He was also known as the *Yismah Yisrael* ("Let Israel Rejoice"), the title of his homiletical work on the Pentateuch. In a message issued in 1907, the "Wise Rebbe" urged his followers to instruct their children in moral conduct, to banish heretical books from their shelves, to keep a watchful eye on teachers, to set aside regular times for study and to refrain from idle talk during the services. "The grave sin for which we are in exile is the causeless hatred we bear one another. When we live in brotherhood and true friendship, we will be worthy of redemption."

Founder of the Biala dynasty was Rabbi Isaac Jacob Rabinowicz (1847–1905), son of Rabbi Nathan David of Sydlowiece (1814–66), a direct descendant of the Yehudi, the Holy Jew of Przysucha. Significantly, Isaac Jacob, the third son of Nathan David, was born on *Tevet* the fourteenth, and it was on *Tevet* the fourteenth, 1158 that the medieval scholar Abraham ben Meir Ibn Ezra (1092–1177) wrote *Iggeret Ha-Shabbat* ("The Letter on the Sabbath"). It was significant because the observance of the Sabbath, more than any other *Mitzvah* absorbed the heart and the soul of the Rabbi of Biala. There is hardly a discourse in which he does not touch upon some aspect of the Seventh Day, and it runs through his writings like a thread. He married Rachel Levia, daughter of Rabbi Joshua ben Sholem Leib of Ostrow (d. 1873), son of Rabbi Solomon Leib of Leczna. His father-in-law became a second father to the young Isaac Jacob and took him to meet Rabbi Israel of Rizhyn, Shalom of Belz, Moses of Kobrin and other *Zaddikim*. Isaac Jacob called his first book *Yishre Lev* ("Upright of Heart"), an acrostic of his father-in-law's name, "for most of my wisdom I derived from him". Predictably, this book deals with the significance of the Sabbath.

Isaac Jacob was barely twenty-six when he succeeded his father-in-law. Whilst thousands of followers sought his counsel, the youthful *Rebbe* sought inspiration from Rabbi Abraham, *Maggid* of Turisk. "A wise man is superior to a prophet," were the words which the *Maggid* applied to this devout disciple. The *Rebbe* of Biala followed the doctrines of Przysucha. Protestations of piety were discouraged. Action and service, charity and loving-kindness, were the measure of a man's sincerity. The *Rebbe* was known far and wide for his open heart and his open house. A special kitchen at his "court" provided meals for visiting Hasidim and for poor townsfolk. In practical proof of his wish that the poor be treated as members of his household, the rabbi himself regularly "tasted" the dishes to make sure that they were up to standard.

In the Biala tradition, Rabbi Isaac Jacob left an ethical will, which is in effect a testimony to the writer's modest, kindly character. In this will he requested his Hasidim to "notify" his father, his father-in-law and the "Holy Jew" of his death, so that his ancestors might intercede for him. "I would like you to make known by means of posters and through newspapers that I ask forgiveness of those people who pressed gifts into my reluctant hands. They regarded me as a *Zaddik*. But verily I am unworthy." He died in 1905 in Warsaw.

The fours sons of the Rabbi of Biala branched out and established their dynasties. The eldest, Nathan David of Parczew (1866–1930) married Leah Reizel, daughter of Rabbi Yehiel Jacob of Kozienice. The second son, Meir Solomon Yehudah (1868–1933) settled first in Miedzyrzez and then in Warsaw. The third son, Abraham Joshua Heschel (1875–1933) made it his life work to publish his father's writings. It was he who edited *Yishre Lev* ("Upright of Heart") and *Divre Binah* ("Words of Understanding"), commentaries on the Pentateuch, on the Passover *Haggadah* and on the Ethics of the Fathers. He made his home in Lublin and was himself the author of *Yeshuot Abraham* ("Salvation of Abraham"), a commentary on Genesis.

Most gifted of the sons of Biala, and one of the most remarkable of all the Hasidic rabbis, was Yerahmiel Zevi (1880–1906) who wed Hava, daughter of Yehudah Arie Leib of Ozarow (d. 1903), author of *Birkhat Tov* ("The Good Blessing"), a commentary on the Pentateuch. A great Talmudist, Yerahmiel Zevi was also an accomplished violinist and a painter of rare promise. His sketches reveal extraordinary insight, and his voice could stir the soul, awakening in his listeners a new awareness. He lived in Siedlce, where he was *Rebbe* for barely six months. He died at the age of twenty-six, leaving six children.

Chapter 16

The Greatness of Ger

How does a small town on the Vistula achieve fame and immortality? By becoming the Jerusalem of one of the greatest Hasidic dynasties. At least this is how it was with Ger (Gora Kalwaria) near Warsaw.

Isaac Meir Rothenburg (Alter), better known as the *Hiddushe Ha-Rim* ("Novellae of Rabbi Isaac Meir") after the title of his works, was born in 1799 in Magnuszew, near Radom, where his father, Israel, was Rabbi. He traced his ancestry as far back as to Rabbi Meir ben Barukh of Rothenburg (1215–93). He was descended from such celebrated scholars as Rabbi Joel Serkes, Rabbi Jonathan Eibeschütz and Rabbi Shapira of Cracow. At the age of nine, little Isaac Meir, on the advice of Rabbi Israel of Kozienice, became engaged to Feigele, daughter of the wealthy banker, Moses ben Yitzhak Eisig Lipshitz, known as "Reb Moses Halfan". The wedding took place in Warsaw in 1811. After three months in Kozienice, Isaac Meir settled in the flourishing Warsaw community. Some sixteen thousand Jews lived there in 1813; in 1831 the Jewish population had grown to 31,384 and the number had more than doubled by the middle of the century.

Isaac Meir studied in the Yeshiva of his relative Aryeh Leib Zinz, later rabbi of Plock and author of ten important works. Among Isaac Meir's fellow students were Abraham Landau (later Rabbi in Ciechanow) and Jacob ben Meir Gesundheit (1815–78), later Rabbi in Warsaw (1870–4). With single-minded passion Isaac Meir devoted himself to his studies, spending some eighteen hours a day at his books. To his worried wife, he exclaimed: "Do you know why your father chose me as your husband? Because of my aptitude for study. What I can absorb in two hours would take another man a whole day. Similarly, four hours of sleep are enough for me."

Isaac Meir, or "Itsche Meir", as he was popularly called, gathered around him young men of exceptional talent and studied with them. He had no desire for high office and declined many honours. His teachers gave him every encouragement. "If Hasidic preoccupations do not distract him from his studies," predicted Rabbi Akiva ben Moses Eger (1761–1837), "Isaac Meir will reach the level of Rabbi Jonathan Eibeschütz."

Like his father, Isaac Meir was a devoted follower of the *Maggid* of Kozienice. However, he also visited the Seer and the son of the *Maggid* of Kozienice, Moses Eliakim Beriah (d. 1828). But when the latter embraced him, Isaac Meir rather ungraciously exclaimed: "I do not want a rabbi who embraces me. I want a rabbi who would rend the flesh from my bones." Clearly, he needed teachers of the calibre of the Yehudi and of Rabbi Simha Bunam. Loyalty to the *Maggid*'s successor kept him in Kozienice, yet in his heart and soul, he yearned to visit the Holy Jew of Przysucha, whom he greatly revered. He went as far as to say: "When the Yehudi smokes his pipe, his thoughts are the very same thoughts that were in the mind of the High Priest officiating in the Holy of Holies, on the Day of Atonement." All his life he grieved because circumstances had prevented him from studying under the Holy Jew.

Meanwhile his erstwhile teacher, Rabbi Moses, found it hard to forgive his favourite pupil's defection to Rabbi Simha Bunam. "Isaac Meir has spoilt a Sabbath for us," was his harsh comment. "I fear that many Sabbaths will be spoilt for him." Hasidim regarded this as an ominous prediction that Isaac Meir would suffer many bereavements, which would take place on the Sabbath. However in Rabbi Simha Bunam, spiritual heir of the Yehudi, Rabbi Isaac Meir found solace for his restless soul, and he visited Przysucha no fewer than seventeen times. Mutual was the esteem between *Rebbe* and disciple. "Had he lived in the time of the *Tannaim*," remarked Simha Bunam, "Isaac Meir would have been a Tanna."

In Przysucha Isaac Meir found stimulating and compatible colleagues in Heinokh of Alexander and Mendel of Kotzk. And, equally important, he found there a way of life that was ideally suited to his scholarly temperament and inclinations. Actually, Isaac Meir arrived at Przysucha at a particularly auspicious moment. Isaac Meir was one of the five delegates who were deputed to defend their Master at the wedding at Ostilla. The doctrines of Przysucha had been misinterpreted and Przysucha devotees were estranged from their Hasidic colleagues. The outstanding scholarship of Rabbi Isaac Meir helped to dispel a great deal of this causeless hostility.

When Rabbi Simha Bunam died, Rabbi Isaac Meir transferred his allegiance to Mendel of Kotzk and played a key role in establishing the hegemony of that dynasty. In 1837, Isaac Meir's sister-in-law married Rabbi Mendel and in 1844, Isaac Meir's granddaughter (daughter of Abraham Mordecai) married Rabbi Mendel's son, Benjamin. Although Mendel of Kotzk was a demanding and sometimes capricious task-master, Isaac Meir's devotion never waned. Perhaps their earlier camaraderie, the common apprenticeship under Rabbi Simha Bunam, helped to cement the bond between the gentle scholar and the tempes-tuous *Zaddik*. In the depths of winter, Isaac Meir took his young grandson to Kotzk because, "It is worth the effort so that the child may behold a true Jew."

The Polish Insurrection of 1830–31 reduced Isaac Meir's father-in-law to poverty. For the first time Isaac Meir was beset with financial worries and faced the urgent need to earn a living. He opened a work-shop for the manufacture of *Taletsim* (prayer shawls), sold books and turned printer. He prized his independence and refused to present himself as a candidate for the rabbinate. He himself supported the candidature of the octogenarian Davidsohn and, later, the Polish patriot Dov Meisels, as Rabbis of Warsaw. It was not until 1852 that Isaac Meir was officially appointed *Dayan* at Warsaw with a fixed salary.

Rabbi Isaac Meir's personal life was beset by tragedies. He had thirteen children and outlived them all. In 1834, his sole surviving son, Abraham Mordecai, died at the age of forty. "I am not lamenting my son, who died in his prime," sobbed the bereaved father, "that is the will of God. I grieve because I am now unable to carry out the precept, 'And you shall teach them (the laws) diligently unto your children'" (Deut. vi. 7).

Rabbi Mendel of Kotzk died in 1859, and reluctantly Isaac Meir became a Hasidic *Rebbe*, first in Warsaw at *Eisengass* street, 56 and later in Ger. "Rabbi Simha Bunam led with love and Kotzk led with fear," he said. "I shall lead them with Torah." When a Hasid once complained that he had no friends, the rabbi retorted "Surely you have a *Gemara* (a volume of the Talmud) in your house?" In simple terms he set forth his objective. "I am not a *Rebbe*. I do not want money. I do not care for honour. All I want is to spend my years bringing the children of Israel nearer to their Father in Heaven."

The doctrines of Przysucha and Kotzk were combined in Ger. There was neither emphasis on miracles nor acceptance of *Pidyonot* (gifts of money). "If the people who come here do not exert themselves to help themselves," the Rabbi of Ger once exclaimed, "then the greatest *Zaddikim* of this generation will be powerless to aid them. There is an old proverb, 'If you cannot cross over, you do not cross over', but I say that the more impossible a task seems, the harder one should strive to accomplish it."

In 1841, Isaac Meir associated himself with Rabbi Hayim Davidsohn and was one of the signatories to a manifesto urging Jews to settle on the land. "Not only is there no trace in the Talmud," states the letter, "against working on the land . . . but, on the contrary, we find in the Talmud that many of the saintly Amoraim who lived outside Israel possessed estates . . . It is therefore proper that every rabbi give these words the widest publicity." Among others who associated themselves with enterprise were Rabbi Isaac of Warka and Zalman Posener.[1]

When Sir Moses Montefiore (1784–1885) visited Warsaw in May 1846, Rabbi Isaac Meir, with Rabbi Isaac of Warka, called upon the distinguished visitor at the *Angelski* Hotel in *Wierzbowa* Street. "The same day," recorded Dr. Louis Loewe, Sir Moses' secretary, "a deputation of that pre-eminently conservative class of the Hebrew community, known by the appellation of Khasseedim, paid us a visit. They wore hats, according to European fashion instead of the Polish 'czapka' or the 'mycka' which is similar to that of the Circassians. They were headed by Mr. Posener, a gentleman who had done much for the promotion of industry in Poland, and his son; and he informed Sir Moses that he would, though an old man, comply with the desire of the Government and change the Polish for the German costume. Being a man held in high esteem by the Jews, and well spoken of by the Prince, his example would have a most favourable effect upon others."[2]

There are many accounts of the encounter of Sir Moses with the Hasidim. "Behold, there is a good case to be made in favour of Enlightenment," Dr. Loewe reasoned. "Mordecai, (hero of the Book of Esther), understood the dialect of Bigtan and Teresh, two of the king's chamberlains, who sought to lay hands on King Ahasuerus (Esther ii. 21). Had not Mordecai been conversant with his native tongue, he would not have been able to discern the plot. The salvation of the Jews was due to Mordecai's linguistic ability." Isaac Meir countered this argument: "From the story of the Book of Esther one can prove that the Jews were not conversant with the foreign tongue. Had it been generally known that the Jews understood the native tongue, Bigtan and Teresh would never have spoken in the hearing of Mordecai. Mordecai, as a member of the *Sanhedrin*, was a linguist, but this did not apply to the masses." Asked Sir Moses, "If you oppose the study of secular subjects, who will be qualified to protect your rights before the Government?" "We are praying for the advent of the Messiah," replied Isaac Meir, "but until then we are well satisfied with you, honoured Sir."

This was not the only meeting between the Rabbi of Ger and the Englishman. On May 20 Sir Moses had written: "There is much to be done in Poland. I have already received the promise of many of the Hasidim to change their fur caps for hats and to adopt the German costume generally. I think this change will have a happy effect on their position and be the means of producing good will between their fellow subjects and themselves. I have received the assurance of many that they would willingly engage themselves in agriculture if they could procure land; and his Highness the Viceroy is desirous that they should do so."[3]

"With respect to the peculiar costume which most of the Israelites have been accustomed to wear for many centuries, which I had an opportunity of seeing," Sir Moses wrote to Count Kisseleff, "I can assure your Excellency that most of them have already adopted the European habit and I have not the least doubt that, in the course of time, the ancient costume will have entirely disappeared. It is erroneous to suppose that the ancient custom is enjoined by or has any foundation in religion; such is not the fact. It originated from a decree of the Government in existence three hundred years ago, when the Israelites were commanded under a most severe punishment to assume the garb, to distinguished them as members of the Jewish faith."[4]

Together with Mendel of Warka and Jacob David of Amshinov, Rabbi Isaac Meir barred secular subjects from the *Heder* curriculum. "It is impossible for the words of the Torah to enter into the hearts of the children," wrote Isaac Meir, "when their minds are full of other things." Undaunted in his struggle against compulsory assimilation, he took a firm stand on the issue of the distinctive garments worn by the Hasidim. Some rabbis were not opposed to a modification of the distinctive garments. To Mendel of Kotzk "the robes were merely a custom which could be modified". Similarly the Rabbi of Rizhyn pointed out that "our father Jacob received the blessings of Isaac when he was dressed in the garments of Esau". But Isaac Meir stood firm and was duly imprisoned by Governor Paskevitch for his defiance. So great was the indignation of the entire Jewish community that he was soon released. The Government required the Hasidim to choose between the European and the Russian way of dress. Isaac Meir preferred the latter.

During the Crimean War (1853-6) Isaac Meir prayed for the allied victory, and he remained aloof when on June 22, 1863 the Poles rose in revolt against their Russian masters.

In 1866 a serious injury brought him increasing and continuous pain. But with calm fortitude he continued his normal way of life. He died that year. His last words, "Leibele Kaddish", were interpreted to mean that his grandson Yehudah Leib should recite *Kaddish* after him and should be his successor. And so it was. Sadly Rabbi Jacob ben Isaac Gesundheit (1815-78) of Warsaw voiced the popular sentiment when he said: "The Hasidim will find another *Rebbe*, but no one can take his place."

Isaac Meir was a prolific author. Published posthumously were the *Hiddushe Ha-Rim* (novellae) on tractate *Hullin*, *Teshuvat Ha-Rim* (Responsa) on Codes. His responsa pinpoint some of the day-to-day problems that Jewry faced in the mid-nineteenth century. For instance, scholars at that time debated the permissibility of baking *Matzot* ("Unleavened bread") by machines. Isaac Meir endorsed the view of Rabbi Solomon Kluger (1783-1869) and forbade the use of machines.

The Sefat Emet

Hasidic rabbis are generally known by the towns in which they lived. But some are known by the titles of their most celebrated works. Thus Isaac Meir of Ger was often referred to as *Hiddushe Ha-Rim* and Rabbi Elimelekh of Lezajsk as the *Noam Elimelekh*, Levi Isaac of Berdichev as *Keddushat Levi*, and Leibele or Yehudah Leib, son of Abraham Mordecai (d. 1855) is known as *Sefat Emet* ("Language of Truth"), for his last discourse ended with the verse from Proverbs (xxi. 19) "The lip of truth shall be established for ever," and *Sefat Emet* became his literary pseudonym.

Yehudah Leib was born in 1847. His father died when the lad was barely eight years old. To his grandfather's great joy, Leibele studied with phenomenal ardour and diligence. "Come and see," Rabbi Isaac Meir used to say, with grandfatherly pride, "how my grandson studies Torah for its own sake."

He was nineteen years old when Isaac Meir died, and although he inherited his grandfather's position, he had no inclination at that time to become a *Rebbe*. So for the next four years he became a devoted disciple of Rabbi Heinokh Ha-Kohen of Alexander. When the *Rebbe* of Alexander died in 1870, Yehudah Leib reluctantly assumed leadership of the Hasidim of Ger, but it was the custom of the modest young rabbi to sit at the middle of the table rather than at the head, to demonstrate that all were equal in his eyes.

His father had opened a bookshop in *Krochmalna* Street, Warsaw, in order to earn a living for his family, and a tobacco shop sustained Yehudah Leib, enabling him to decline the *Pidyonot* that his Hasidim were only too willing to offer him. He lived a frugal life, content with very little, and deplored costly and elaborate celebrations. He believed in the dignity of labour and held that a rabbi who accepted money for his spiritual services forfeited his independence. The Torah was not to be studied for self-aggrandisement or material gain.

Not one minute was wasted. Yehudah Leib rose at dawn and spent the entire day in study and prayer. Even during the hours (usually between 9.30 and 11 a.m.) in which he received visitors, he would hold a volume of the Codes in his hands. "How can one give advice," he would say, "unless one refers constantly to the four parts of the *Shulhan Arukh*." "Only the *Shiurim* (Regular studies) give me strength," he asserted. Prayers were not prolonged in Ger. The *Rebbe* himself prayed in his own room, and only on the Sabbath and on Festivals did he attend the *Bet Ha-Midrash*. After the Reading of the Law, he would return to his room, where he would recite *Musaph* privately.

Meanwhile the dark clouds of persecution were gathering. The assassination of Alexander II and the accession of Alexander III brought an outburst of anti-Jewish violence, prompted by the fact that a Jewish girl, Hessia Hellmann, had been involved in the plot. In April 1881, a pogrom took place at Elisabethgrad, followed by others in Kiev, Odessa, and Warsaw later that year. In the Kiev region alone, there were pogroms in forty-eight towns. On May 1882, the infamous "May Laws" forbade Jews to settle in rural districts even within the Jewish Pale of Settlement, and prohibited them from engaging in business activity on Sundays and on Christian holidays. Former tutor of Alexander III, K. P. Pobiednostzev, Procurator of the Holy Synod, expressed the far from pious hope that one-third of Jewry would convert, another third would emigrate, and a third would die of starvation.

Matters reached a catastrophic climax with the Kishinev pogrom on April 19, 1903, the last day of Passover. It was followed by further outrages in Gomel, in what seemed to be an attempt to drown the revolution in Jewish blood. Yet many Jews were forcibly conscripted into the Russian army, where they suffered unspeakable hardships. The unfortunate youths thronged the Rabbi's court for counsel and spiritual consolation. The Rabbi worried over the thirty thousand Jewish soldiers who were fighting the Japanese (1904–5). All who wrote to him from the battlefield received personal letters expressing sympathy and encouragement.

Rabbi Yehudah Leib was against emigration. He participated in the conference convened in 1888 by the Rabbi of Grodzisk to discuss ways of strengthening the traditional educational system. The rabbi of Ger volunteered to raise one hundred thousand roubles for this purpose.[5]

Yehudah Leib died in 1905 at the age of fifty-eight, leaving such monumental works as *Sefat Emet,* a commentary on the Pentateuch, and studies on *Moed* and *Kodashim,* edited by his son-in-law Rabbi Jacob Biderman. He also left a great spiritual empire. In the lifetime of Rabbi Yehudah Leib, Ger had grown great and powerful. Not without reason did the Rabbi of Grodzisk call his illustrious contemporary "the King of Israel".

Chapter 17

Early Twentieth Century:
Storm Clouds Gather

At the end of the nineteenth century, there were six million Jews in Europe. In the Russian Empire the Jewish population had increased from 1,000,000 in 1800 to 5,189,000 in 1897. There were 811,000 Jews in Galicia, 266,000 in Rumania, 96,000 in Bukovina and 851,000 in Hungary.

Yet the Jews, a literate and law-abiding community, were "second-class" citizens. There was a total of one hundred and forty Statutes discriminating against the Jews in the twenty volumes of the Codes of Laws of the Russian Empire. The Jews were permitted to live only in an area which constituted no more than four per cent of Russia's territory. The area became known as the Pale of Settlement. By 1880, ninety-four per cent of the entire Jewish population of Russia were restricted to the Pale. Their predicament is graphically outlined in a memorandum of December 10, 1890, addressed to the Czar by the Lord Mayor of London:

"Pent up in narrow bounds within your Majesty's wide Empire, and even within those bounds, forced to reside chiefly in towns that reek and overflow with every form of poverty and wretchedness; forbidden all free movement, hedged in in every enterprise by restrictive laws; forbidden tenure of land or all concern in land, their means of livelihood have become so cramped as to render life for them well-nigh impossible.

Nor are they cramped alone in space and action. The higher education is denied them, except in limits far below due proportion of their needs and aspirations. They must not freely exercise professions, like other subjects of your Majesty, nor may they gain promotion in the army, however great their merit and their valour."[1]

The exodus from Eastern Europe of some 2,000,000 Jews began in 1881 and continued with diminishing tempo until the outbreak of the First World War. In the years 1881–90 Russian Jewish immigrants to the U.S.A. numbered 135,000. During the next decade the number doubled, averaging 30,000 a year.[2] Some Rabbinical leaders did not encourage emigration. "It is proper for you to remain in your own land and walk in the ways of the Lord."[3] From London, Chief Rabbi Nathan Adler urged his Eastern European colleagues "to preach in the Synagogues and Houses of Study to publicise the evil which is befalling our brethren who have come here, and to warn them not to come to the land of Britain, for such ascent is descent."[4]

Many Hasidic rabbis agreed with him, and Hasidim were not encouraged to uproot themselves from their familiar environment. Hence the proportion of emigrating Hasidim was comparatively small, though pogroms were a daily occurrence in the Czarist Empire. The cries of the victims of Kishinev and the shouts of their persecutors: "Kill the Jews!" "Burn their houses!" "Spare none!" echoed through a horrified but unhelpful world. Nevertheless, Hasidim feared to expose their children to the spiritual dangers of the "Godless" countries even more than they feared the violence of the murderous mobs. America to them was not only a *Goldene Medinah* ("Golden country") but also a *frei land* ("free" country—loose), free in too many ways.

The Hasidim endured the terror-raids in Russia, the Mendel Beilis ritual trial, the World War, the Russian Revolution of 1917, the pogroms of Petlura and the vicious onslaught of the Denikin Czarist army and the Black Hundreds. The situation continued to deteriorate. "Hundreds of thousands of Jews have been robbed of their last shirt; hundreds of thousands have been maltreated, wounded, humiliated; tens of thousands have been massacred. Thousands of Jewish women became the victims of the bestial instincts of savage hordes. Hundreds of thousands of Jewish women are haunted daily by one idea—that tomorrow they will no longer be able to hold their heads erect. The panic which seized on the Jewish population of these regions is without precedent in all history. . . . The Jewish masses in the Ukraine are on the verge of madness and many have actually lost their reason. These unfortunate beings, having lost all that makes life worth living, their nearest, their homes, everything they had, all means of existence, mutilated physically and broken morally, how can they solve the problem of their existence? Where are they to find shelter? How can they save the children from dying of starvation and cold and all the accompanying miseries?"⁵

During the First World War, Poland became the principal battlefield of the Eastern campaigns. Six times between 1914 and 1917 Russian armies swept through Galicia and were beaten back by the Austrians. Each campaign brought death and desolation to the local population. Grand Duke Nicholas Nikolayevitch, commander-in-chief of the Russian Army, found convenient scapegoats in the Jews. "The Jews are spies," and "The Jews are helping the Germans," were his slogans. Mass expulsions became the order of the day. Ironically, it was with relief that Polish Jewry greeted the German entry into Warsaw on August 5, 1915.

With the Bolshevik revolution and the establishment of the Union of Soviet Socialist Republics, the three million Jews in Russia obtained civil emancipation. But simultaneously the authorities instituted drastic and devastating measures designed to extinguish every spark of Jewish religious life. Jewish schools, *Hedarim* and *Yeshivot* were made illegal. Synagogues were requisitioned and converted into workers' clubs. Yiddish was recognised, but *Yiddishkeit* ("Judaism") was outlawed. At that time Rabbi Sholom Dov Baer (1860–1920), fifth rabbi of the dynasty of Lubavitch, remained in the Soviet Union and dedicated himself to the cause of *Hinukh* ("education"). He organised clandestine centres of religious instruction even in remote places and under the most undesirable conditions.

The son of Rabbi Sholom Dov Baer, Rabbi Joseph Isaac Schneerson (1880–1950), was well qualified to continue his father's manifold tasks. With the help of Jacob and Eliezer Poliskoff, he opened in Dubrovna, Mogilev, a spinning and weaving mill, which provided a livelihood for many Jewish workers. He even established a *Yeshiva* in Buchara as late as 1917. The authorities viewed with disapproval the educational and economic reforms of the sociologist rabbi, and he was imprisoned four times between 1902 and 1911. Nevertheless, in 1920, when Rabbi Joseph Isaac succeeded his father, he intensified the campaign for Jewish education throughout Russia. Neither the menace of the *Tcheka* (secret police) nor the machinations and the threats of the *Yevsektzia* (the Jewish section of the Russian Communist Party) could curb his activities. Forced to leave Rostov-on-Don, he lived for a while in Leningrad.

In 1927 he was arrested for the fifth time and thrown into the Spalierna Prison in Leningrad. Accused of "counter-revolutionary" activities, the sixth Rabbi of Lubavitch was sentenced to death, a sentence later commuted to three years of banishment to Kostroma in the Urals. Through intense political pressure applied by President Herbert Hoover of the United States and Senator William E. Borath, he was released in 1928 and permitted to live in Malachovka (near Moscow). Eventually he settled in the Latvian capital of Riga.

Rabbi Schneerson was tormented by the plight of his people in Russia, doomed to spiritual extinction. He travelled to Germany, France, the Holy Land and the United States of America, where he was received by President Hoover in Washington. In 1934, the Rabbi took up residence in Warsaw and established *Yeshivot* in Warsaw and Otwock.

Between the two World Wars, Poland was the greatest reservoir of European Jewry. The Treaty of Riga, signed in March 1921, placed the Western Ukraine and Byelorussia under Polish sovereignty. It was a large country with a population of about twenty-seven millions, of whom only about two-thirds were Poles. The rest of the population consisted of some four million Ukrainians, Germans, Byelorussians, Lithuanians and Tartars. Within the boundaries of the new Polish States were 2,500,000 of the 4,500,000 Jews who lived in the old Russian Empire. By 1939 there were 3,300,000 Jews in Poland, comprising nine and a half per cent of the total population. The Jews were the second largest minority, and they made up one-third of the total urban population. Seventy-five per cent of the Jews lived in the urban areas.

Three hundred thousand Jews lived in Warsaw, one hundred and ninety-four thousand in Lodz, fifty-five thousand in Vilna, forty-four thousand in Lublin and one hundred thousand in Lvov. Despite the liberal Constitution and the Minority Rights clauses of the Treaty of Versailles, Poland's newly acquired independence brought neither social security nor economic freedom to the Jewish community. The ink of the Versailles Treaty was hardly dry when Jewish blood began to flow. Pogroms became an everyday occurrence, and Jewish life was soon the cheapest commodity in the country.

The much-vaunted tolerance of medieval Poland vanished beyond recall as every class of Polish society embraced anti-semitism, the convenient old-new creed. During the single month of November 1918, pogroms took place in no fewer than one hundred and ten different towns and villages. The United States sent a commission in 1918, headed by Henry M. Morgenthau (1856–1946), to study the situation. This was followed by a British Government mission in September 1919, consisting of Sir Stuart Montagu Samuel (1856–1926), President of the Board of Deputies of British Jews, and Captain Peter Wright. Samuel's plea that "a genuine and not a masked equality be accorded to the Jewish population of Poland" was, of course, ignored. There were provocative municipal ordinances against ritual slaughter, *numerus clausus* (a quota system for admittance into educational institutions), ghetto benches at the universities, and innumerable economic restrictions that almost annihilated Jewish commerce.

Leading Polish statesmen preached a virulent racialist policy that anticipated the Nazi platform. In 1926 Bogulaw Miedzinski, Deputy Speaker of the Polish Seym, declared in the Diet: "Poland has room for fifty thousand Jews. The remaining three million must leave Poland." The "Cold Pogrom" policy was officially endorsed by the State, which now took over and monopolised such key industries as salt, tobacco, alcohol, matches and batteries. Inevitably Jews, constituting a large percentage of those engaged in trade and commerce, suffered most from these totalitarian sequestrations. "My Government considers that nobody in Poland should be injured," was the glib pronouncement of General Slawoj Skladkowski (1885–1962), Premier of Poland, on June 4, 1936. "An honest host does not allow anyone to be hurt in his house. Economic warfare is, of course, permitted."

The Polish masses were not content with economic boycott. Pogrom followed pogrom in sinister succession, occurring in Przytyk on March 9, 1936, in Minsk Mazowiecki, Brzesc (Brest-Litovsk) on May 13, 1937, and Czenstochowa on June 19. The Austrian *Anschluss* (March 12, 1938) gave Poland the opportunity to legislate for the denationalisation of persons who had lived outside the country for more than five years. On October 28, 1938, over 15,000 Polish Jews were made homeless and stateless. Five thousand were kept virtual prisoners in a camp at Zbaszyn (Neu Benschen) a small Polish township where they were driven across the frontier by the Germans.

More than a third of Polish Jews were Hasidim, most of them associated with the Aguda, by then an intricately organised and widespread structure wielding tremendous power. The Aguda maintained its own schools, published a daily newspaper (*Dos Yiddishe Togblatt*), ran its own publishing house (*Yeshurun*), youth organisations (*Zeire Agudat Yisrael*) and *Pirche Aguda* and even a women's division (*Bnot Agudat Yisrael*)

Hasidic Children in the State of Israel—1968

Hasidim dance in Jerusalem—1968

which numbered 25,000 members by 1939. The *Poale Agudat Yisrael* protected the interests of the working class and established, among other things, a sick fund for workers.

By 1936 the Aguda controlled one hundred and fifteen co-operatives, with a total membership of 15,825. Striving to wrest communal leadership from the assimilationists, it provided candidates for both local and parliamentary elections. Between 1927 and 1937 the Aguda controlled Polish Jewry, and two hundred and forty-two delegates represented Poland at the *Knessiah Gedolah* (Aguda World Conference) in 1929.

Agudists Rabbi Aaron Lewin (1879–1941) of Rzseszow (Reisa) and Rabbi Meir Shapira (1887–1934) were deputies in the Seym, while Jacob Trockenheim and Asher Mendelsohn represented the Aguda in the Senate. Prominent Aguda leaders, all devoted Hasidim of Ger, included Meshullam Kaminer (1861–1943), editor of the *Dos Yiddishe Togblat*, Leib From (1908–1943), co-founder (with Yehudah Leib Orlean) of the *Poale Agudat Yisrael*, Leib Mincberg (1887–1943), leader of the Jewish community of Lodz and member of the Seym; Moses Deutscher (b. 1880), leader of Cracow Jewry, and Moses Lerner (1887–1943), deputy Mayor of the Jewish community of Warsaw.

Notable among the Hasidic rabbis was Rabbi Meir Yehiel Halevi Halstock (1851–1928) of Ostrowiec. A baker's son, born in Sabin near Warsaw in 1851, he became known when still a young child as the "Vorker Illui". He had been known to study the entire Talmud in the four weeks between *Purim* and *Passover*. At the age of eighteen he was ordained by Rabbi Joshua Trunk of Kutno, Rabbi Elijah Hayim of Lodz and Rabbi Eliezer Wacks of Kalisz, who exclaimed with humility and telling rhetoric: "How can a fly with broken wings testify against an eagle who soars through the highest heaven?"

At the age of twenty-seven, Meir Yehiel became Rabbi at Skierniewice, where he spent ten peaceful years. In 1888 he moved to Ostrowiec. For forty years he fasted every day, eating only a frugal meal at night. He was proud of his father and of his humble origin. "My father of blessed memory," he would frequently recall, "used to say that the best thing is freshly baked bread." During the First World War, he was for a short time imprisoned by the Austrian authorities. When he died in 1928 at the age of seventy-seven, scores of rabbis were among the ten thousand people at his funeral. The grateful community granted a pension to his widow. His writings, collected under the title *Or Torah* ("Light of the Torah") were published posthumously.

An individualist true to the traditions of Kotzk, was the Rabbi of

Sokolow, Isaac Zelig Morgenstern (1867–1940), a great-grandson of Rabbi Mendel and son of the Zionist Rabbi Hayim Israel of Pilev. At the age of eighteen, Isaac Zelig married Hayah, daughter of a Hasid of Ger, Mordecai Shonfeld of Pinczow, and in 1897, at the age of thirty, he became Rabbi of Sokolow. He became *Rebbe* when his father died in 1905 and established a *Yeshiva Bet Yisrael*. Dr. Zygmunt Bichowski had instructed him in medicine, and like the rabbi of Radzyn, Isaac Zelig wrote prescriptions in Latin.

"Find me, if you can, two hundred Jews who have not bowed to Baal," cried Rabbi Mendel of Kotzk, who tended to pessimism. Isaac Zelig was more charitable in his judgements. As a delegate to the conference of communal leaders in St. Petersburg (Leningrad) in 1910, he came into contact with Rabbi Hayim Soloveitchik (1852–1918) and Rabbi Joseph Isaac Schneerson of Lubavitch. He joined the Aguda in 1919 and became Vice-President of the *Agudat Ha-Rabbanim* (Rabbinical Union). At the Aguda conferences he delivered stirring orations, and his discourses appeared in the Rabbinical journal *Degel Ha-Torah* ("Flag of the Torah") and *Be'er* ("Well").

Like his father, the *Rebbe* of Sokolow urged his followers to support the *Yishuv*, and he himself visited the Holy Land in 1924. Mendel, Rabbi of Wegrow, son of the Rabbi of Sokolow, was murdered by the Nazis on *Yom Kippur*, 1939. The aged father, celebrating *Succot* (The Feast of Tabernacles) had a telepathic awareness of the bitter news. The wine goblet fell from his hands. "They have killed my son," he cried. The *Rebbe* of Sokolow died in 1940 and was buried in Warsaw near the grave of Rabbi Abraham Mordecai Alter, son of Rabbi Isaac Meir of Ger.

The most powerful "court" in inter-war Poland was that of Ger. Abraham Mordecai Alter (1866–1948), Rabbi of Ger, was the "Emperor" of Hasidism, and Ger was the capital of his empire. Among his followers were outstanding Rabbinical scholars and leaders of Polish Jewry. The Rabbi's influence was far-reaching. A word from him could decide a communal election, and any cause he favoured was assured of success. It was mainly due to his astute leadership that the Aguda received the support of the Hasidic *Rebbes*.

When the Rabbi of Ger came to a town, it was in the nature of a State visit, surrounded by pomp and ceremony. Mr. (later Judge) Neville Laski, President of the Board of Deputies of British Jews (1933–40), gives an eye-witness account: "I heard much talk of the wonder-working Rabbi, who is almost worshipped by a section of the population, and I managed to obtain ocular demonstration of his popularity. I went to see his arrival from his cure at Carlsbad and was presented with a spectacle such as I had never imagined. Hundreds and hundreds of, to me, medieval-looking Jews wearing strange hats and kaftans crowded on the platform, alongside which steamed a train of the latest type, composed of wagons-lits. Excitement reigned supreme. I stood on a railway truck against a fence to obtain a better view, but soon repented, as a surging crowd, marching step by step with the Rabbi, nearly turned me and my truck into the roadway. Four police-men in front, four behind and two on either side, pushed a way, through a seething and excited mob, for a very small old man who took not the slightest notice of the crowd of admirers who had come specially to see him, and went to a motor car, in which he was whisked away preparatory to his going to his *Nachkur* (rest after treatment)."[6]

Abraham Mordecai Alter was born in 1866 and succeeded his father in 1905. Following the Kotzk tradition of spontaneity in prayer, many Hasidim had been in the habit of bypassing the appointed hours and praying whenever and wherever the spirit moved them. The accession of Rabbi Abraham Mordecai marked a return to meticulous observance of the *Shulhan Arukh*, and the emphasis was on Torah study. On Friday evening and on Sabbath between *Shaharit* (morning service) and *Musaph* (the Additional Sabbath Service) time was set aside for study. Following ancestral traditions, the Rabbi of Ger refused to accept *Pidyonot* (donations) from his followers, lest he become dependent on the gifts of man.

Like his grandfather, Abraham Mordecai had a deep sense of com-munal responsibility. At the Bad-Homburg Conference in 1909, he helped pave the way for the founding of the Aguda, and he attended the three Agudist conferences of 1923, 1929, and 1937. He supported the orthodox publications *Der Yid* ("The Jew") and *Dos Yidishe Togblat* ("The Jewish Daily Paper"). "Long have I wanted a newspaper true to the Jewish spirit," wrote the *Rebbe*, "where free thinking and indecency would have no place. How many of you have come to me weeping, seeing your sons and daughters turn from us and flee else-where because they read wicked books and newspapers which poison the body and the soul? Now I appeal to you: Let this understanding not appear trivial in your eyes, because with only a few pennies a day you can help this paper grow and benefit the community. I appeal particularly to my own followers." In a discourse before the blowing of the *Shofar* in 1931 he urged his followers to avoid reading newspapers published by heretics, and to support Agudist publications. He supported, too, the *Bet Jacob* movement and the Warsaw *Metivta*.

A dedicated bibliophile, the rabbi of Ger had a library of over five thousand volumes, among them early editions and *incunabula*. He encouraged the publication of such manuscripts as the "Meiri" (Menahem ben Solomon of Perpignan 1249–1306) on tractates *Succot* and *Erubin*, as well as the work *Etz Ha-Daat Tov* ("Tree of Good Knowledge"), on Psalms by Rabbi Hayim Vital. Especially warm was his welcome to young people. "In Ger there are ten thousand Hasidim who eat on the Day of Atonement," was the startling statement which meant that ten thousand boys too young to fast were visiting Ger for the High Holy Days.

The Rabbi of Alexander also attracted a vast multitude. Rabbi Isaac Menahem Mendel Dancyger (1880–1942) stood at the helm for eighteen years, founding *Yeshivot* both at Alexander and Lodz. Like his father Samuel Zevi (d. 1924), author of *Tipheret Shmuel* ("The Glory of Samuel"), he stressed *Torah*, *Tephillah* (prayer) and service to fellow men. Just as Warsaw was the stronghold of Ger, so Lodz, "the Manchester of Poland", was the capital of Alexander Hasidim, and Lodz alone had no fewer than thirty-five Alexander *Stieblech*. There were few towns in Poland which did not have such a *Stiebel*.

Considerable rivalry existed between the followers of Ger and Alexander. Ger represented the power of the Aguda, and Belz supported the *Mahzike Ha-Dat*, while the Rabbis of Alexander stood aloof from political parties. Alexander was the third force in Hasidic Poland. Alexander however, took no organised part in civic or national elections leaving its followers free to follow their own political trends. Many were closely associated with the work of Mizrachi.[7]

Paradoxically enough, although more than a third of Warsaw's Jewish population were Hasidim, the principal Rabbis of the city were *Mitnagdim*; among them: Solomon Lipshitz, Rabbi Hayim Davidsohn, Dov Berush Meisels and Abraham Weinberg. Up to the First World War there were no Hasidic Rabbis at all in Warsaw, for the *Rebbes* generally avoided the big cities. They preferred remote hamlets, where they could sequester themselves with their Hasidim. The First World War, however, brought a number of Rabbis to Warsaw, and soon the capital of Poland became the home of over fifty *Zaddikim*.

One of the most prominent Rabbis was the Rabbi of Novominsk, Alter Yisrael Shimon Perlow (1874–1933), scion of the dynasties of

Ostilla, Kaidanov, Czernobiel, Karlin and Berdichev. His father, Jacob (1847–1902),[8] had been brought up in the home of Rabbi Solomon Hayim Perlow of Kaidanov, and he married Hava Hayye Perl, daughter of Rabbi Leibish of Proskurow. "Go to Poland, raise a family and establish a dynasty," Rabbi Isaac ben Mordecai of Neschitz (1789–1868) counselled the young man, and Jacob obeyed. He set up his "court" in Minsk-Mazowieck, where he made many "converts" and won wide recognition. Here he built a *Yeshiva* where many young men lived and studied, and a great Synagogue which held over five hundred worshippers. This was a showpiece *hof* (court), complete with its own gardens, orchards, stables and horses.

Rabbi Abraham Isaac Kook, later Chief Rabbi of the Holy Land, described Rabbi Jacob as "unique in his generation". On his death in 1902, his eldest son, Alter Yisrael Shimon, then aged twenty-eight, took over the leadership of the Hasidim of Novominsk. He married Feige Dinah, daughter of Rabbi Baruch Meir Twersky of Azarnitz, Russia, the seventh direct descendant of the Besht.

In 1917, the Rabbi settled in Warsaw. To his home at 10, *Franciszkanska* Street, came Hasidim of all "denominations", and non-Hasidim visited him too. He knew the whole *Mishnah* by heart, and every day he rehearsed twenty-three chapters. On the Sabbath he spoke only Hebrew, the Holy Tongue. Crowds thronged to his famous Sabbath discourses, remarkable for their length as well as their profundity. The passion with which he preached and the intensity with which he prayed, the kindliness with which he received every individual and the wisdom of his counsel, spread his fame far and wide.

Hillel Zeitlin used to say: "Whenever I felt depressed and needed to repent I visited the Rabbi of Novominsk." Once heard, the melodies of the Rabbi of Novominsk were never forgotten. They were expressions of his soaring soul, a revelation that awed and elevated his listeners. His prayers before the reader's desk on the High Holidays, particularly at *Neila* (the concluding service on the Day of Atonement) were highlights in the lives of the Hasidim.

Faithfully the *Rebbe* of Novominsk ministered to his people. Every day he set aside several hours to receive petitioners. From Warsaw and from the provinces people flocked to him for guidance, for comfort and for inspiration. With infinite patience he would listen and give practical painstaking advice. He was associated with the Agudist Rabbinical Council, and he was on cordial terms with all his Hasidic colleagues. The Rabbi of Ger was a devoted friend who rarely passed

Warsaw without visiting him. "Go to the Rabbi of Novominsk," the Rabbi of Ger advised many of his followers.

From his famous forefathers the Rabbi of Novominsk inherited a remarkable legacy: from Rabbi Shlomo Hayim of Kaidanov, the ability to lose himself in prayer; from Rabbi Levi Isaac of Berdichev, love of humanity; from Rabbi Phinehas of Koretz, love of music; and from his father, a phenomenal memory. He died in 1933, leaving twelve children and ten manuscripts on Torah and Cabbalah. Many of these manuscripts were destroyed in the Holocaust. *Tipheret Ish* ("The Glory of *Ish* (Man)", i.e. an acrostic of the Hebrew name Alter Yisrael Shimon), a commentary on the Passover *Haggadah*, was published posthumously.

The brother of Alter Yisrael Shimon, Solomon Hayim Perlow (1860–1943) married the daughter of Rabbi Joshua Heshel of Bolechow. He was the author of a commentary on the Prayer Book (*Siddur Kehilat Shlomoh*) published in 1907 and a 1,781-page anthology of Hasidic commentary on the Psalms entitled *Mikdash Shlomoh* (published in Bilgorai in 1937). Rifka Reizel, twin sister of the Novominsker *Rebbe*, married Rabbi Mordecai Heshel (1866–1918), the Rabbi of Pelcovizna, son of the Rabbi of Medzibozh.

The son of the *Rebbe* of Radzyn, Rabbi Samuel Solomon (1908–42) left Warsaw in 1928 and returned to Radzyn. With fatherly solicitude he cared for the young students in his charge, introducing many innovations into the somewhat stereotyped Yeshiva routine. His students were spared the indignities of the rota system whereby they ate in a different household every day. In the Yeshiva of Radzyn, named *Sod Yesharim* ("The Secret of the Upright"), over two hundred students lived in comparative comfort.

The dynasty of Radzyn had been founded by the "Miracle worker" Rabbi Aryeh Guterman (1792–1877), who played a significant role in Polish life. Guterman's wealthy grandson, Rabbi Aaron Menahem Mendel (1842–1934) owned twenty-one houses. Educator, organiser and social worker, he founded the *Shomer Shabbat Society* ("Sabbath Observance") and *Tomhei Assurim* ("Prisoners' Aid Committee") and was President of the *Rabbi Meir Baal Ha-Nes Foundation*, the traditional charity boxes in the Diaspora which raised funds for the poor Jews in the Holy Land. In 1928, Rabbi Aaron Menahem Mendel journeyed there to settle a dispute over the distribution of these funds.

In Lublin too, arose famous Hasidic rabbis such as Rabbi Solomon Eiger, son of Rabbi Abraham, author of *Shevet Yehudah* ("The Rod of

Judah") (d. 1914). At 30 *Lubertowski* Street lived Rabbi Abraham Heshel Rabinowicz. At 27 *Lubertowski* Street lived Rabbi Moses Mordecai Twersky (d. 1943), son of Rabbi Leib of Trisk, who married a daughter of Rabbi Jacob of Novominsk. After the Russian Revolution, Lublin became the centre of the Hasidim of Braclaw, who gathered at the *Yeshivat Hahme Lublin* of Rabbi Meir Shapira. "I am a *Rebbe* without Hasidim. You are Hasidim without a *Rebbe*. Let us, therefore, join forces," he facetiously suggested.

Poland, the home of Torah study, was not at first the home of Hasidic *Yeshivot*. During the nineteenth century, *Mitnagdic* Lithuania had the monopoly and the "voice of the Torah went forth out of Mir and the word of the Lord from Slabodka". Hasidic *bahurim* (young men) studied in the *Stieblech* and the *Bate Midrashim* ("Houses of Study") of the *Rebbes*. In the inter-war years, however, Polish *Rebbes* began to establish their own *Yeshivot*, and their young followers were spared the difficult choice between inadequate study in the homely atmosphere of the *Stiebel* and a thorough Talmudic grounding in the alien setting of a *Mitnagdic Yeshiva*, such as Mir, Baranowicze, Radin or Ponovez in Lithuania.

During his residence in Otwock (1927–29), Rabbi Joseph Isaac Schneerson founded a number of *Tomhei Tmimim* ("Supporters of the Godly") *Yeshivot*. Meanwhile, Rabbi Solomon Henoh Hakohen Rabinowicz (b. 1882) of Radomsk, son of Rabbi Ezekiel, author of *Knesset Yehezkel* ("Gathering of Ezekiel") was establishing the *Keter Torah* ("Crown of the Torah") *Yeshivot*, and soon there were thirty-six branches in Poland and Galicia. Although many rabbis followed the *Rebbe* of Radomsk, he regarded himself as a Hasid of Czortkov. The Rabbi of Radomsk was a man of substance who owned a glass factory as well as houses in Sosnowice, Berlin and Warsaw. He had one of the finest libraries in Poland and was the author of *Tiferet Shlomoh* ("The Glory of Solomon"), homilies on the Pentateuch and the Festivals.

The successor-designate of the Rabbi of Radomsk was his first cousin and son-in-law, Moses David Ha-Kohen Rabinowicz (b. 1906), a disciple of Rabbi Dov Berish Weidenfeld of Chebin and the author of *Zivhei Kohen* ("The Sacrifices of the Priest"). Three times a day he lectured to one hundred and fifty students in the *Kibbutz Gavuo* ("Academy for Higher Study") in Sosnowiec. Under his direction the *Yeshivot* of Radomsk established high standards, particularly in the famous *Keter Torah* colleges of Lodz, Bendin, Radomsk, Piotrkow and Czenstochowa. The Rabbi himself supplied half the expenses of the

Yeshivot and the remainder was subscribed by his Hasidim. No provision was made, however, for the Rabbinical Diploma, for emphasis was on study for the sake of study and not for certification. *Gemara* (*Talmud*) and *Tosaphot* (critical notes on the Talmud by French and German scholars) were the main subjects of the concentrated curriculum. Under the influence of Rabbi Israel Meir Kahan, the *Hafetz Hayim*, particular attention was paid to *Kodashim* (the Fifth Order of the *Mishnah* dealing with Temple rituals). Students and teachers were not necessarily Hasidim of Radomsk. The principal of the Yeshiva of Radomsk in Sosnowiec was Joseph Lask, a Hasid of Ger.

"Nowadays, Yeshiva students should not live in shacks and eat like beggars," declared Rabbi Meir Shapira. "I will build a palace for them." At Lublin, one-time seat of the medieval council of the Four Lands, Shapira erected his "palace" under heavy verbal fire. "Wasteful" and "untimely" were among the terms used by his critics. Yet the dynamic Rabbi Meir overcame every obstacle and crushed the opposition.

The foundation stone was laid on *Lag B'Omer* in 1924, in the presence of fifty thousand people, including the Rabbis of Ger and Czortkov. In the next four years Rabbi Shapira travelled to Germany, France, England and America raising funds for this building. In the United States he spent over thirteen months and made two hundred and forty-two speeches. The Yeshiva was consecrated on *Rosh Hodesh Sivan*, 1930 in the presence of the *Rebbes* of Ger and Czortkov. It was one of the finest buildings in pre-war Poland; it rose six storeys high with one hundred and twenty rooms, a huge auditorium, stately lecture halls, a library of some forty thousand books, and even a model of the Temple to aid the study of *Kodashim*.

Candidates were carefully screened and only the most brilliant could meet the high entrance requirements. For instance, each had to know by heart two hundred pages of the Talmud. Among concessions granted by the State to *Yeshivat Hahme Lublin* students was that of buying railway tickets at half-price like regular university students. When Shapiro died at the age of forty-seven, such men as Rabbi Solomon Eiger, Joseph Koningsberg and Moses Friedmann of Boyan maintained the high academic standards.

What Ger was to Poland, Belz (Belza) was to Galicia. "The whole world," Belzer Hasidim were wont to say, "journeys to Belz." The Rabbis of Belz underlined sincerity and simplicity as fundamentals of the good life. Rabbi Issahar Dov (1854–1927), second son of Rabbi Joshua Rokeah, was a staunch upholder of tradition. In October 1922,

Count Galecki, Governor of Lvov, backed by several orthodox supporters of the assimilationist camp, urged the Rabbi of Belz to direct the Jews to vote against the Minority Block. Unequivocally, the Rabbi of Belz refused. In 1927, Rabbi Aaron (b. 1880), named after Rabbi Aaron of Karlin, succeeded to his father's chair.

Next in importance to Belz was the dynasty of Bobov (Bobowa). Like his father Solomon, Rabbi Benzion Halberstamm (1874–1941) was a noted composer who created many melodies. To this day his Friday night *niggun* (Melody) *Yah-Ribbon* ("God of the World") is chanted in Jewish homes. He was one of the two hundred rabbis at the 1927 Lvov conference which resolved to urge the Jews to vote only for lists which were loyal to the State, a move against the National Minority Block (An electoral block with other national minorities, Ukrainians, White Russians and Germans). Like the Rabbi of Ger, he was actively engaged in education, and established the *Etz Hayim* ("Tree of Life") Yeshiva, which eventually developed forty-six branches throughout Galicia. A special society, *Tomhe Tmimim* ("Upholders of the Perfect"), attended to the material needs of the students.

There were sizeable Hasidic groups outside Poland. Moses Teitelbaum of Ujhely (Ohel) made Hasidism popular in Hungary. His work *Yismah Moshe* ("Let Moses Rejoice") is one of the classics of Hasidic literature. He befriended the Hungarian patriot Louis Kossuth (1802–94). To the *Rebbe* of Ohel, interpretations of the Torah were revealed in dreams. Even greater was the following of his son Eliezer Nisan Teitelbaum (d. 1855).

Munkacs was the home of Rabbi Shlomoh Shapira (1832–94), the founder of the Munkacs Hasidic dynasty, who was descended from a family of scholars from Speyer, Germany. Shlomoh, who was born at Ribatic near Premyslan, was the son of Rabbi Eliezer Shapira of Lancut. Shlomoh was a disciple of Rabbi Zevi Elimelekh Shapira, author of *Bene Issachar* ("The Children of Issachar"), Rabbi at Munkacs and subsequently at Dynov. Shlomoh visited the Hasidic Rabbis of Ropcyzce, Rymanov, Rizhyn and Belz. He held rabbinical posts at Sassov, Strizov (1857–82), and in 1882 he succeeded Rabbi Hayim Sopher as Rabbi in Munkacs. He wrote a work of responsa called *Shem Shlomoh* ("Name of Solomon").

Under his son, Zevi Hirsch, Munkacs became a great centre of Hasidism. Zevi Hirsch was a disciple of Rabbi Hayim Halberstamm of Sanz and of Rabbi Ezekiel of Shinove. Zevi Hirsch was one of the greatest *Halakhic* luminaries of Hasidism. He wrote a monumental work, *Darke Teshuvah* ("Way of Repentance"), on *Yoreh Deah*. Among his other noted works were *Zevi Tiferet* and *Be'er-lehai-roi* ("The Well of the Living One who seeth me") on the *Zohar*. He played a prominent part as a rabbi and *Rosh Yeshiva* ("Head of Yeshiva") and was the uncompromising spokesman of the Hasidim in Hungary and Galicia. No problem defied his analysis. His masterly responsa reflected Jewish life in all its ramifications. The greatest Talmudic authorities enthusiastically welcomed his works. He died on the fifteenth of *Tishri* in the year 1914.

His son Hayim Eliezer (1868–1937) was an outstanding scholar. Among Hayim Eliezer's works were responsa, *Minhat Eliezer* ("The Offering of Eliezer"), in four parts. He was a great opponent of both political Zionism and the *Agudat Yisrael*. Few escaped his censure. In the parliamentary election of 1935, he made the following appeal to his followers: "I am writing to you concerning the elections for Parliament, a subject on which no Jew may remain silent, though many say, either out of ignorance or a desire to deceive that the voting has nothing to do with the question of Jewish religion ... Every Jew, young or old, who voices such an opinion in favour of the Zionist list for Parliament errs grievously by abetting the sinners."[9]

He had a bitter controversy with Rabbi Issahar Dov Rokeah of Belz. The issues involved were due more to differences in temperament than to religious opinions held by the two rivals. This was a clash of two forceful personalities. They were both difficult and dogmatic, and neither was of a conciliatory disposition.

Influential, too, was the dynasty of Vishnitz, which was founded by Menahem Mendel Hager, son of Rabbi Hayim of Vishnitz in Bukovina. Rabbi Hager was the head of a *Yeshiva Kolel Vishnitz and Marmaros* Rabbi Barukh Hager (1845–93), author of *Imre Barukh* ("The Words of Baruch"), and his eight sons all extended Hasidic influence.

His eldest son, Israel Hager (1860–1935), was ordained by Rabbi Shalom of Bezan and established a Yeshiva *Bet Israel* ("The House of Israel").

Rabbi Isaac Weiss of Spinka, son of Joseph Meir, a descendant of Isaac Taub, had thousands of followers throughout Hungary. In Unterland, the lower part of Hungary, and in Marmaros there were large groups of Hasidim. A Hasidic Jew even became the Vice-President of the Central Orthodox Bureau.[10]

During the First World War, between 200,000 and 300,000 Jews found refuge in Austria, 77,000 of them in Vienna.[11] Prominent among them was Rabbi Israel Friedman (1858–1933) of Husiatyn, author of *Tiferet Israel* ("The Glory of Israel"). He advocated the establishment of *Torah Melacha* schools, where study of the Torah could be combined with craft-training. His son Nahum Mordecai (d. 1946), from his home in *Heinestrasse*, Vienna, wielded great influence. The other Hasidic Rabbis who lived in Vienna were Rabbi Abraham Jacob Friedmann of Sadagora, Rabbi Mordecai Shlomoh Friedmann of Boyan, Rabbi Mordecai Shragai Friedmann of Husiatyn, Rabbi Mordecai Sholem Joseph Friedmann of Sadagora-Przemysl and Rabbi Isaac Meir Heschel of Kopyezyne (1864–1933). His son Abraham Joshua Heschel remained in Vienna until 1933. There, together with Akiva Schreiber, he founded the *Shomer Shabbath* organisation to stimulate Sabbath observance. The Ninth and the Second Districts of the capital of Austria resounded with the songs and discourses of the Hasidim.

Chapter 18

In the Shadow of Death

With the outbreak of the Second World War on September 1, 1939, the fate of Eastern European Jewry was sealed. The Jewish leaders called upon the community to "defeat the intentions of Hitler to make Poland a country of slaves". The Rabbis of Sochaszew, Alexander and Ger urged their Hasidim to subscribe generously to the Polish Air Defence Loan. "The fate of Jewry," wrote the *Rebbe* of Ger, "is bound up with the fate of the State." Physically as well as financially, Polish Jews, including the Hasidim, played an active role in defence measures. Old and young, some of them with dangling *peyot* ("earlocks") and long *kapotes*, dug trenches, even on the Sabbath, in view of the imminence of war. However, the partially mobilised Polish army was no match for the superior armaments of the enemy. Under the Nazi blitzkrieg and the Russian invasion, Polish resistance was over in a month. The Jews were helpless as systematic persecution started in the towns and the villages, the first steps towards the Nazi objective of genocide.

The population of Warsaw multiplied rapidly as Jews were transferred from provincial towns and as refugees flowed in from outlying areas. In the six years between 1939 and 1945 the culture of millennia perished in a blood blaze such as the world has never seen; Poland became a central cemetery for the great Jewish communities of Europe. By the time that a Ghetto was established on October 16, 1940 there were, in that confined area, between 450,000 and 500,000 Jews. The three years of agony that followed actually brought a revival of Hasidism. Many Polish Hasidic Rabbis had found refuge in Warsaw and even *Maskilim* would come to them for comfort and inspiration.

In the valley of the shadow of death they sang their melodies and served their Maker as best they could. There was not enough food for

Shirayim, but nothing could extinguish the indomitable optimism of Hasidism.

Chaim A. Kaplin, in his *Scroll of Agony*, records:[1] "Even though we are now undergoing terrible tribulation and the sun has grown dark for us at noon, we have not lost our hope that a ray of light will surely come. Our existence as a people will not be destroyed. Individuals will be destroyed, but the Jewish community will live on . . . Hasidim were even dancing, as is their pious custom. Someone told me that on the night of the holiday (*Succot*), he met a large group of zealous Hasidim on Mila Street, and they sang festive songs in chorus and in public, followed by a large crowd of curious people and sightseers. Joy and revelry in poverty-stricken Mila Street. When they sang, they reached such a state of ecstasy that they could not stop until some heretic approached them shouting: 'Jews, to safeguard your life is a positive Biblical command; it is a time of danger for us. Stop this.' Only then did they become quiet. Some of them replied in their ecstasy, 'We are not afraid of the murderer'."

In the *Judenrat*, the Jewish Community Council (at 26 *Grzybowska* Street), set up by the Nazis under the chairmanship of Adam Chernikov, Hasidic leaders were represented. Among them were Isaac Meir Levin (b. 1894), President of the Aguda in Poland (later Minister of Social Welfare in Israel, 1949–52), Dov Shapira, Simeon Stockmaker and Eizig Ackerman. These overburdened men did their utmost to lighten the yoke of their brothers. By a decree of the Chairman of the Council of January 20, 1941, the Sabbath was recognised as an official day of rest. A public soup kitchen for students was opened in the *Bet Jacob* school on *Nalewki* Street. To the end, Meshullam Kaminer worked on a traditional Yiddish translation of the Bible and Alexander Zusya Friedmann (b. 1897) organised an underground network of schools and study courses for young and old, so that the "Torah should not be forgotten in Israel."

On July 22, 1942, on the eve of the Fast of *Ab*, deportations began, and the daily number of deportations from the Ghetto to Treblinka reached ten thousand by October, 1942. Within fifty-five days 350,000 Jews had been deported to such demoniac death factories as Treblinka, Majdanek, Oswiecim (Auschwitz), Sobibor, Chelm and a dozen other infamous destinations. In the Schults shoemaking factory at 44–46 *Novolipki* Street, the Hasidic manager Abraham Handel (now in Tel Aviv), sheltered many Rabbis. Among the illustrious employees were Sholom Rabinowicz, son of Rabbi Hayim Meir of Neustadt, Moses

Bezalel Alter, son of Yehudah Leib, Abraham Alter, Rabbi of Pabianice, David Halberstamm, Rabbi of Sosnowiec, Rabbi Kalonymous Shapira of Piaseczno, author of *Hovot Ha-Talmidim* ("The Duties of the Disciples"), Alexander Zusya Friedmann and Rabbi Joseph Perlow of Novominsk.

A survivor has drawn a vivid picture of this strange workshop: "Here you see sitting at the wood blocks mending shoes (the work mostly consisted of pulling out nails with pliers) the Koziglower Rabbi, Aryeh Frumer, the former *Rosh Yeshivah* (Principal) of *Yeshivat Hahme Lublin* . . . From time to time he addresses a word to the Rabbi of Piaseczno . . . *Gemarot* (Talmudical passages) and Biblical texts are quoted and the names of Maimonides and Rabbi Jacob ben Asher are mentioned, and who now cares about the S.S. men, about the *Volksdeutsch* supervisor or about hunger and misery and persecution and the fear of death! Now they are soaring in higher regions. They are not in the shop at 46 *Novolipki* Street, where they were sitting, but in the lofty halls."[2]

Such Hasidic leaders as Rabbi Moses David Rabinowicz, son-in-law of the Rabbi of Radomsk, worked for a time for the *Hesed Shel Emet* (Pinkert) Burial Society. Others were active in *Toz* (the Society for the Protection of Health among the Jews) or the *Judenrat*, which employed five thousand people. The Rabbis of Ger, Bobov, Lubavitch and a few others, narrowly escaped the Holocaust, but most of the Hasidic Rabbis in Poland, a total of well over two hundred, perished with their families and followers in the action which began on July 22, 1942 on the eve of *Tisha B'Ab*. The Jewish historian Ringelblum records: "Most of the rabbis were shot during the raids. The long beards and the sidelocks aroused the hatred of the Germans, and many a rabbi paid with his life for his great courage in sticking to his beard and sidelocks."[3]

They died the death of martyrs under circumstances recalling only too closely Jewish heroism in the days of the Maccabees. Rabbi Ezekiel Halevy Halstock, son of the Rabbi of Ostrowice, died together with his seven sons proclaiming the Jewish declaration of faith, "Hear O Israel, the Lord our God, the Lord is One." In Treblinka perished the Rabbi of Alexander, Isaac Menahem Mendel Dancyger, together with his seven sons-in-law, Rabbi Moses Bezalel, brother of the Rabbi of Ger, Rabbi Hayim Yerahmiel Taub, the Rabbi of Zwolin, and the Rabbi of Grodzisk: Rabbi Israel Shapira, too, met his Maker there in 1942, with the words of *Ani Maamin* ("I believe with a perfect faith in the coming of the Messiah.")

Rabbi Benjamin Paltiel Morgenstern (b. 1895) of Sokolow, as well as Rabbi Isaac Weiss of Spinka (d. 1944) and Menahem Mendel Hager, were murdered in Auschwitz. Every crematorium had its Hasidic victims. Rabbi Elimelekh Aryeh ha-Kohen Rabinowicz, brother of the Rabbi of Radomsk, died in Mauthausen. Rabbi Moses of Boyan (b. 1891), the spiritual head of the *Yeshivat Hahme Lublin*, died in 1943 at Belzec.

Rabbi Moses Mordecai Twersky was murdered in the Kempnitz forest in 1943. In Lvov on that Friday, *Rosh Hodesh Ab*, in 1941, Rabbi Benzion Halberstamm (b. 1884) shared the fate of many of his followers. Many of the sages, fragile and aged, utterly defenceless, met their heavily armed assailants with death-defying valour. Rabbi Shlomo Henokh Rabinowicz of Radomsk resisted the deportation. "I know you have come to kill me," he told the Nazis. "I am ready to die. But I will die here in my own home. I will not enter your gas wagons." He was shot in his house at 30 *Novolipki* Street, together with his son-in-law, one Sabbath in 1942, and was buried in the sepulchre of the Rabbi of Novominsk. The Rabbi of Radzyn, Samuel Solomon, urged his Hasidim in the Ghetto of Wlodawa (near Lublin) to fight back, to escape to the forests and to join the partisans, and vehemently he denounced the Jewish collaborators: "Whoever treads the lintels of the *Judenrat* (the Jewish Council appointed by the Nazis) will forfeit both worlds, for they are aiding the Nazis in their extermination of the Jews." The poet Isaac Katznelson (1866–1944) wrote in tribute "The Song concerning the Radzyner".

And so Rabbi Isaac, Rabbi Abraham and Rabbi Berl, brothers of the Rodzitzer *Rebbe*, Rabbi Kalmish Finkler, the Rovner *Rebbe*, Aaron Patshenik (b. 1899), son of Rabbi "Itzikel", the Brezener *Rebbe*, joined the partisans. Among the heroines was Perele Perlow, wife of the Koidonover *Rebbe* and daughter of the Biala *Rebbe*, Yerahmiel Zevi of Siedlice. With her husband she escaped from Baranowicze to Vilna, and there she established a synagogue and a religious institute for women. From the valiant Koidonover *Rebbetzin* the women and girls of the Ghetto drew comfort and strength in those black hours.

With dignity and with faith, the Hasidim went to their death. Hillel b. Aaron Eliezer Zeitlin (1872–1943), Cabbalist, philosopher, journalist, exercised tremendous influence over the Jewish intelligentsia. Born in Kormo, in White Russia, he settled in Homel in the early 1890s. An ardent Zionist, he supported the Jewish Territorial Organisation (which aimed at finding a suitable site, not necessarily in Palestine, for Jewish settlement on an autonomous basis). For a time he lived in Vilna, then this "Litvak from the land of the Litvaks" ("Lithuanian from the land of Lithuania"), made his home in Warsaw. At ease in Hebrew and in Yiddish, he wrote many monographs which were both learned and lucid. His controversial articles in the Yiddish paper, *Der Moment*, ranged from the *Tanya* of Rabbi Shneur Zalman of Liady to the stories of Rabbi Nahman of Braclaw, from the Seym elections to anti-semitism.

An impassioned writer who preached religion, a one-man party with a highly individualistic philosophy, Zeitlin was regarded as a heretic by the ultra-orthodox and a hypocrite by the *Maskilim*. Yet to his home at 60 *Zyska* Street, Warsaw, flocked Hasidim, *Mitnagdim*, writers, politicians, Agudists, Bundists and Zionists to listen and to learn from this modern "prophet". He was no demagogue. He spoke quietly, eyes closed, apparently oblivious to the people around him. Yet every public appearance brought eager crowds to hear him.

On the road to Treblinka, Hillel Zeitlin heard the footsteps of the Messiah. He went to meet him on the Eve of *Rosh Hashanah*, 1943, wearing *Tallit* and *Tephillin* and reciting passages from the *Zohar*, engaging on the fringes of earthly hell in mystical, esoteric speculation. This, personified, was the indestructible soul of Polish Jewry.

Survivors relate how the frail young Rabbi Joseph Perlow of Novominsk (then thirty years old) wandered around Bergen-Belsen comforting the sick and suffering prisoners. So fragile in physique that even the Nazis exempted him from forced labour. He was so indomitable in spirit that he regularly gave away his own meagre allocation of food. In Bergen-Belsen he died on April 16, 1945, the morning after its liberation by the British Second Army under General Sir Miles Dempsey. Courage was not the exclusive prerogative of the young. The eighty-two-year-old rabbi of Warsaw, Isaac Meir Kanal, deliberately provoked a Nazi by snatching his revolver and was shot immediately. But he attained his goal, which was, records an eye-witness, "to be buried according to the Jewish ritual".[4] Rabbi Heinoh Levin of Bendin offered his portion in the world to come for a glass of water, so that he could recite his last prayers in a state of purity.

The Hasid Menahem Ziemba played a key role in the last days of the Warsaw Ghetto. Menahem was born in 1882 in Praga, a suburb of Warsaw. His father, Eleazar Lippa, died when the boy was barely nine years old, and he was brought up by his grandfather Abraham. An ailing child, Menahem possessed a phenomenal memory and a most incisive mind. At eighteen he married Mindele, daughter of Hayim Isaiah Zederman, a wealthy iron merchant. Relieved of financial worries, the young husband could now dedicate twenty hours a day to his studies. And each day for five or six hours he shared his Talmudical "discoveries" with a small group of students, believing that the master should not prepare his lectures in advance, since it was more profitable for the students to participate in the preparations.

The death of his father-in-law compelled Menahem to attend to business, but even ironmongery did not distract him from his studies. Moreover, he did not study in a vacuum, but kept in touch with the intellectual giants of the era. Talmudist Rabbi Meir Simha Ha-Kohen of Dvinsk referred to him as a "beautiful vessel". In 1919, Menahem Ziemba published his work *Zera Abraham* ("The Seed of Abraham") and two years later *Tozo'ot Hayim* ("Offsprings of Life"), a compendium on the "Thirty-Nine Categories of Labour" prohibited on the Sabbath. For his work on Maimonides (*Mahzeh La-Melech*—"Visions of the King") a novella on *Yad Ha-Hazaka*, he was awarded a literary prize by the Warsaw municipality.

In 1930, he contributed to the periodical *Degel Ha-Torah* ("The Banner of the Torah"), edited by Rabbi Menahem Kasher, director of the *Metivta* Yeshiva in Warsaw. When Kasher left for the United States, Ziemba himself published the last two issues. Every Sabbath evening he delivered a Midrashic discourse, and every day, from noon until 2 p.m. he gave a *Shiur* (discourse) to selected young men. He received many "calls" to distant pulpits. When Joseph Hayim Zonnenfield died, Moses Blau was deputed to offer Ziemba a rabbinical post in Jerusalem, but Ziemba refused to leave his beloved Warsaw. To the end he remained a devoted disciple of Ger, and the Rabbi of Ger loved him dearly. "Come, let us ask our Menahem," he would say.

Ziemba was the author of twenty published works. Among unpublished manuscripts destroyed in the Holocaust were a four volume set of responsa, a two-thousand page commentary on the Palestinian Talmud, *Menahem Yerushalayim* ("Comforter of Jerusalem") and a work on Maimonides. When he lost his son, Yehudah, at the age of eighteen, he wrote *Gur Aryeh Yehudah* ("Judah is a Lion's Whelp") in memoriam. In 1935, Ziemba was elected to the *Vaad ha-Rabbanim* and in Warsaw, where he worked closely with Rabbis Jacob Meir Biderman and Abraham Weinberg. During the Nazi occupation, Ziemba, together with David Szapira and Samson Stockmacher of the Rabbinical Council, were the spokesmen of traditional Judaism in the Ghetto. At the memorable Council of War on January 14, 1943, Ziemba spoke out with characteristic fire:

"Of necessity we must resist the enemy on all fronts . . . We shall no longer obey his orders. Henceforth we must refuse to wend our way to the *Umschlagplatz*, which is but a blind and a snare, a veritable stepping-stone on the road to mass annihilation . . . Had we lived up to our so-called status of a 'people endowed with wisdom and understanding' we would have discerned the enemy's plot to destroy us as a whole, root and branch, and would have put into operation all media of information in order to arouse the conscience of the world. As it is now, we have no choice but to resist. We are prohibited by Jewish law from betraying others, nor may we deliver ourselves into the hands of the arch-enemy . . . Our much-vaunted prudence—not to be identified with a genuine wisdom and true understanding—blurred our vision and turned out to be more devastating than folly and stupidity. To paraphrase the words of our Sages, Korah of old accentuated his innate aptitude for provisions to such an extent that it blurred his vision and in the end it was his folly that brought his ultimate doom. At the present, however, when we are faced by an arch-foe, whose unparalleled ruthlessness and total barbarism knows no bounds, *Halakhah* demands that we fight and resist to the very end with unequalled determination and valour, for the sake of the Sanctification of the Divine Name."[5]

Ziemba was murdered in 1943 while crossing *Kupiecka* Street.

The Yeshiva of Lublin shared the fate of Polish Jewry. The *Deutsche Jugendzeitung*, in February 1940, gives a painfully detailed account of the wanton destruction of this Hasidic citadel of learning. "It was a matter of special pride to us," exults the Nazi narrator, "to destroy this Talmudic Academy, known as the greatest in Poland. We threw out of the building the large Talmudic library and brought it to the market place. There we kindled a fire under the books. The conflagration lasted twenty hours. The Jews of Lublin stood about weeping bitterly. We could hardly hear ourselves speak over the sound of lamentations. We called out a military band and the triumphant cries of the soldiers drowned the noise of the Jewish wailing."[6]

The revolt of the Warsaw Ghetto began on the first night of Passover, April 19 and continued until May 16, 1943.

Soon the streets of Warsaw: *Novolipki, Nalewki, Franciszkan, Mila,*

Muranowski, once citadels of Hasidism, were a pile of rubble nearly a square mile in area. The loss suffered during the war by the Jews of Poland, who numbered 3,300,000 in August 1939, was reckoned at between 2,350,000 and 3,000,000 persons. As the Holocaust raged, the lights of Hasidism were dimmed and a deathly pall descended. Sages by the score perished with the Holy Scrolls in their hands and holy words on their lips. The Jewish quarters of Warsaw, Lodz, Lublin, Otwock, Ger and Alexander, once citadels of piety and learning, were dust and ashes, physical symbols of the almost total destruction of Hasidism in Eastern Europe.

Chapter 19

The Hasidic Way of Life

Hasidism is one of the "martyr movements" of history. Like new religious sects throughout the ages, Hasidim were at first persecuted, their principles distorted and their practices maligned. Learned Talmudists put aside the calm deliberation that cloaked their every utterance, precipitously condemning the movement and excommunicating its followers. In one instance, the protagonists of *Jüdische Wissenschaft* ("Science of Judaism") sided with Hasidism's bitter opponents, the *Mitnagdim*, and were equally irrational in their condemnation. Anti-Hasidic texts abounded. Joseph Perl wrote *Megale Temirin* ("Revealer of Secrets") and *Bohan Zaddik* ("The Test of the Righteous") and had a number of followers. Israel Lobel wrote *Taavat Zaddikim* ("The Lust of the Righteous") and *Sepher ha-Vikuah* ("The Book of Debates"). David Markov produced *Zemir Aritzim Veharbot Zurim* ("The Discomfiture of the Wicked") and *Sheber Poshim* ("Destruction of the Sinners"). "They could not understand," comments Dr. Shalom Spiegel, "the awkward simplicity, the crude depth of the clumsy attempt to stammer the ineffable. They saw merely the repellent exterior, and, because they rejected the irrational and unaesthetic, they viewed the entire Hasidic movement as an aberration and a snare, a quackery, or at least, self-delusion."[1]

By the second half of the nineteenth century a number of *Maskilim*, gifted with deeper insight, began to express different sentiments. The German social philosopher and precursor of Zionism, Moses Hess (1812–75), rather grudgingly gives Hasidism its due in *Rome and Jerusalem*, published in 1862. "Although the Hasidim are without a social organisation they live in socialistic fashion. The house of the rich man is always open to the poor, and the latter is as much at home there as he is at his own home. They seem to have taken as their motto the saying in *Abot*, 'He who says what is mine is thine, is a saint' . . . A sect which practises such self-abnegation and whose members are capable of such religious enthusiasm, must have for its foundation something more than mere crudeness and ignorance."

More positively the essayist Eliezer Zevi Zweifel (1815–88) wrote in *Shalom Al Yisrael* ("Peace on Israel") in defence of the life and works of the Besht and demonstrated that Hasidism is deeply rooted in mysticism.

Historian Heinrich Graetz (1817–91) illuminates many an obscure period in Jewish history, but plainly he himself was groping in the dark when he dealt with the movement that was making such headway in his own lifetime. According to him, "the new sect, a daughter of darkness, was born in gloom, and even today proceeds stealthily on its mysterious way . . . as ugly as the name, Besht was the form of the founder of the order that he called into existence". Showing an astonishing disregard for historical accuracy, he castigates Dov Baer, the *Maggid* of Mezhirichi: "Among his intimates were expert spies, worthy of serving in the secret police. They discovered many secrets and told them to their leader; thus he was enabled to assume an appearance of omniscience."[2] So the master historian showed himself remarkably inept in his interpretation of this signal contribution to Jewish life and thought.

Not until the end of the nineteenth and the beginning of the twentieth century did Hasidism really receive a realistic evaluation. In his *History of the Jews in Russia and Poland*, Simon Dubnow (1860–1941) was able to paint a more objective picture based on a non-hostile study of the facts. This is how he describes a journey through Poland: "The train has taken me through Zlotchow, Zbarzh and other historical places in Hasidic history. In the forests that we passed I saw a vision, the Besht, as he was praying amidst nature and gathering medical herbs, or the shades of Michal of Zlotchow, Wolf of Zbarzh and others."[3]

In his *History of Hasidism*, the only work he wrote in Hebrew, Dubnow attempts an assessment. In his preface to the Yiddish edition he writes: "I had to gather the building material all by myself, digging for sand and clay, making the bricks and then erecting the building according to a definite architectural plan. I used the entire Hasidic literature, both learned and legendary material, and I attempted to find some system in the maze of the various Hasidic currents and tried to reveal the kernel of truth present in the native folk tales."[4] Yet he lists only one hundred and ninety-four works in his Hasidic bibliography, insisting that the creative period of Hasidism ended in 1815. Despite this objectivity, he asserts that "the Besht began by dabbling in magic." In the eyes of Moritz Steinschneider (1816–1907), father of "Jewish bibliography", Hasidism was a "malady of Judaism".[5]

But the time came for the historians and writers to enter "the Pardes", the garden of Hasidism, and they assigned the movement an honourable position in the chronicles of religious revivals.

To Samuel Abba Horodetzky (1871–1957) in his works, *Ha-Hasidut Ve Ha-hasidim*, a collection of essays from the Besht to Rabbi Israel of Ryzhin, Hasidism is a revolt against the severe legalism of the Rabbinate. "Legal and practical Judaism is hemmed in within the 'four ells of the Halakhah'. This is the God of Rabbi Akiba who derived numerous Laws from every letter and iota of the Torah," writes Horodetzky. "He is the God of Maimonides, of Joseph Caro, of Isserles and the God of the Gaon of Vilna. It is the Cabbalah which supplied Judaism with poetic feeling and complete devotion to God."

Isaac Leib Peretz (1852–1915) popularised Hasidism in the first decade of the twentieth century, and the Yiddish novelist and playwright Sholem Asch (1880–1957), in his novel *Der Thillim Yid* (Salvation), gives a glowing account of Hasidism. Micah Joseph Berdichevsky (1865–1921), Geshom (Gerhard) Scholem (b. 1897), Hillel Zeitlin (1872–1943) and Eliezer Steinmann (b. 1892) made notable contributions, and Hasidism was now seen from a startling new perspective.

"We must admit," writes "Ahad Ha-Am" (pseudonym of Asher Ginsberg, 1856–1927), "that if we want to find original Hebrew literature today we must turn to the literature of Hasidism; there rather than in the literature of the *Haskalah* one occasionally encounters (in addition to much that is purely fanciful) true profundity of thought which bears the mark of the original Jewish genius."[6] Philosopher Martin Buber (1878–1965), who had grown up in the home of his grandfather Solomon Buber (1827–1906), researched in depth the form and content of Hasidism and found it surprisingly relevant to our time. The summer months he spent in the towns of Sadagora, Czortkov, citadels of Hasidism. It was Buber who brought Hasidism to the attention of the world at large. For Buber, religion was a dialogue between God and man, and in Hasidism the dialogue was particularly meaningful. He found truth and beauty in the stories and his *Tales of Rabbi Nachman*, *The Legends of the Baal Shem* and the *Tales of the Hasidim* brought the essence of Hasidism home to millions. It was "Cabbalah transformed into Ethos." "The Hasidic movement" writes Buber, in his work *The Origin and Meaning of Hasidism*, "takes over from the Cabbalah only what it needs for the theological foundation of an enthusiastic but not over-exalted life in responsibility—responsibility of a single individual for the piece of the world entrusted to him." All Buber's philosophical writings are impregnated with the traditions of Hasidism.

In Hasidism there was no chasm between theory and practice. The life of the Hasid was regarded as the best exposition of Hasidism, for the Besht was a revivalist rather than a revolutionary. His objective was to revitalise the Jewish religion and the Jewish people, to make the "crooked straight and the rough places smooth". Unlike the Essenes, the Hasidim did not believe in asceticism or in detachment from the turmoil of the material world.

The Hasidic sky was composed of many planets, each set in its appointed place, each revolving in its own orbit and each contributing to the brilliant light that floodlit the Jewish world. Upon the foundations laid by the Besht many superstructures were erected. There were marked differences in the philosophies of Rizhyn and Kotzk, Sochaczew and Sadagora, Ger and Lubavitch, yet all were united in common fellowship.

Under the wings of the Besht, all could shelter—the scholar and the unlearned alike. But though Hasidism uplifts the poor, it neither glorifies poverty nor denigrates wealth. It simply eliminates the barriers between man and man, and between man and his Maker. Much is expected of the Hasid. He is required to fulfil himself, to perfect himself, as his own personal contribution to the redemption of the world. Hasidism recognises no aristocracy, neither the aristocracy of wealth, nor the aristocracy of learning. All are children of the living God. All men are equal, and no man is more equal than his neighbour. Hasidim translate the concept, "All Israel is united in fellowship" into every phase of human relationship. "Let no man think himself better than his neighbour," said the Besht, "for each serves God according to the understanding which God gave him."

How does one define a Hasid? Hasidism has no "articles of faith", nor does it demand adherence to a formal code. A Hasid is known, not by the beliefs that he holds, but by the life that he leads. Faith in the *Zaddik*, joy, humility, devotion (*Kavanah*) and enthusiasm (*Hitlahavut*) are signposts along the Hasidic pathway. Hasidism attaches importance to every word, to every thought and to every act. For every Jew is a co-worker with the Almighty in the renewal of creation.

In the Bible, *Hasid* connotes a man of piety, and the term is even applied to the Deity. "The Lord is righteous in all His ways and gracious (*Hasid*) in all His works," sings the Psalmist (Ps. cxlv. 17). "Let the saints (*Hasidim*) exult in glory; let them sing for joy upon their beds. Let the high praises of God be in their mouth, and a two-edged sword in their hand" (Ps. cxlix. 5).

"Hasid" is frequently used in this sense in rabbinic literature. According to Hillel, "an ignorant man cannot be a Hasid" (Abot. ii. 6). Rabbi Jose ha-Kohen is termed a Hasid (Abot. ii. 11), because he obeyed the spirit, rather than merely the letter of the law. "The former Hasidim," says the *Mishnah*,[7] "would spend a long time meditating before prayer." "A foolish Hasid," says the Talmud,[8] "is one who sees a woman drowning in the river and says: 'I am forbidden to look at a woman, so how can I save her?'"

In the second century B.C.E., there are references in the Talmud and in the Books of the Maccabees to the sect of the "Hasideans" (from the Greek transliteration of the Hebrew Hasidim). These valiant defenders of the Law fought Antiochus IV "Epiphanes" (reigned 175–163 B.C.E.), at first refusing to defend themselves on the Sabbath. Later they allied themselves with the Hasmoneans and then they merged with either the Pharisees or the Essenes. In the thirteenth century, the *Hasidei Ashkenaz* ("the pious men of Germany") group produced such personalities as Judah ben Samuel he-Hasid of Regensburg (d. 1217), and his disciple Eleazar ben Judah of Worms.[9] During the eighteenth century a number of small groups arose who were known as Hasidim.

The concept of the *Zaddik* did not originate with the Besht. Noah is termed "a man righteous (*Zaddik*) and whole-hearted in his generation" (Gen. vi. 9). "The Zaddick," says the prophet Habbakuk (ii. 4), "shall live by his faith." The Book of Psalms lists the attributes of the *Zaddik*, and the Book of Job depicts his sufferings. "Great is the power of the *Zaddik*," says the Talmud "for God decrees and the *Zaddik* annuls."[10]

Developing this concept even further, Hasidism produced a type of leader unique in the Jewish religious hierarchy. The *Zaddik* is teacher, counsellor, and confessor, to whom the Hasid could unburden his heart. He is a friend in this world and an advocate in the world to come, giving life new meaning, new colour and new hope. He is not an official of the *Kahal*. He is neither elected nor appointed by the community. Unlike the Rabbi (*Rav*), he requires no ordination, and unlike the priest (*Kohen*), his office is not necessarily hereditary.

The *Zaddik* was not self-sufficient. He looked to his followers for inspiration, just as they looked to him for guidance. Although he reached for the skies, he was mindful of his earthly commitments. "The Zaddik," writes Buber,[11] "lifts up the holy sparks from the depth of earthliness and removes the stains from the souls of men." According to the Besht, the Zaddik is the messenger of the Shekhinah. "The will of the Zaddik," declared the Maggid, reflects the will of God."[12]

"The Zaddik strengthens his Hasid in the hours of doubting, but does not open his eyes to the truth. He only helps him to conquer and reconquer the truth for himself. He develops the Hasid's own ability to pray. He teachers him how to give the words of prayer the right direction and he joins his own prayer to that of his disciple, thereby increasing the power of the prayer and lending it wings."

Heavy are the burdens of the Zaddik. "His heart," declared the Maggid, "is flooded with the lifeblood of others and weighed down with the sorrows of his people." "For what sin," he sighs, "have I become renowned?" For renown brings the Zaddik even weightier responsibilities. When the time came, runs the legend, for the appearance of Rabbi Levi Isaac of Berdichev, Satan writhed in anguish, lest the sage redeem the House of Israel. But Satan's fears were allayed. He was told that Levi Isaac would become a Rebbe and would be so enmeshed in communal matters that Satan would still have ample scope for his activities. Yet the Hasidic leaders were not without misgivings about the "cult of the Zaddik", as detractors called it. "I can foresee," prophesied the Besht, "that before the advent of the Messiah, rabbis will sprout forth like the grass of the field, delaying the redemption because the conflicting loyalties of their followers will divide the community and bring about causeless strife."

There was no clear-cut rule regarding succession. Dov Baer of Mezhirichi succeeded the Besht. Zevi Hirsch of Rymanov (d. 1846), a tailor's apprentice, succeeded his master, Rabbi Menahem Mendel. As a rule, however, son followed father, and thus the dynasties were perpetuated. Inevitably, quarrels occasionally broke out between the followers of different Rebbes and, to the amusement of Mitnagdim and Maskilim alike, these controversies sometimes degenerated into unseemly squabbles.

The life style of the Zaddikim varied considerably. The Besht could not sleep unless all the money in his house had been distributed among the poor. Similarly, many of the great rabbis endured abject poverty, refusing to accept the "gifts of flesh and blood". On the other hand, there were Zaddikim, like the Rabbis of Rizhyn and Sadagora, who lived in luxury with servants to attend their palatial residences and fine horses in their stables. It is said that Rabbi David Talna (Talnoye) sat on a golden throne, inscribed with the words "David, King of Israel". Rabbi Abraham of Turisk possessed a rare *Menorah*, wrought in gold and silver, over which skilled craftsmen had worked for many years.

Hasidism are often accused of disparaging study, but such an accusation is without foundation. Rabbi Dov Baer and Rabbi Shneur Zalman were among the greatest Talmudists of their generation, and in the nineteenth and twentieth centuries many Hasidic rabbis in Poland, Galicia and Hungary were acknowledged Princes of the Torah. The Holy Jew, Mendel of Kotzk, Isaac Meir of Ger, Abraham of Sochaczew, Jechiel Meir Halevy, Menahem Mendel of Lubavitch, Zadok Kohen of Lublin, Zevi Hirsch Shapira of Munkacs, were outstanding scholars.

Miracles did not cease with the end of the Biblical era. Such celebrated sages of the Talmudic era as Honi Ha-Meagel and Hanina ben Dosa were said to perform miracles, and this power was ascribed to a number of medieval rabbis. However, the wonder-working aspect of Hasidism was invariably over-emphasised. Many Hasidic leaders did not believe in miracles, and this sizeable and significant category included the Rabbis of Przysucha, Kotzk, Izbica, and Lubavitch. On the other hand, Hasidim firmly believed that the Besht, the Seer of Lublin, Rabbi Jacob of Radzymin, Rabbi Hayim Meir Yehiel of Moglienice and Rabbi Dov Baer of Radozyce were indeed miracle workers, and a wealth of legends was woven around their supernatural activities.

It is known that the Besht distributed *Kamayot* ("Amulets") and two scribes were kept busy writing them. Amulets were popular in ancient times and are referred to in the *Mishnah* and *Tosephta*.[13] The amulet was simply a strip of paper or parchment about two inches by ten in size, inscribed with one or two verses from the Bible. For the most part the successors of the Besht discontinued this practice.

Dear to the Besht was the custom of observing *Tikkun Hazot* (midnight service) which had been practised by the sixteenth century Cabbalists. Apart from Elimelekh of Lezajsk and Aaron of Karlin, few *Zaddikim* recited these mournful elegies over the destruction of the Temple.

"It is a man's duty," says the Talmud[14] "to pay his respects to his teacher on festivals, on New Moons and on the Sabbath." A visit to the *Rebbe* was a major event in the life of the Hasid. "Those who travel to the *Rebbe*," says Rabbi Nahman of Braclaw, "are recompensed.

Although they may not receive Torah from him, they are nevertheless rewarded for their efforts." According to Rabbi Uri of Strelisk, a Hasid is obliged to travel to the *Rebbe*, even though he must forgo a certain amount of Torah study and prayer in order to make the journey."[15]

"Court" affairs were governed by the *Gabbai*, who acted as liaison between the rabbi and his followers. Usually each visitor presented a *Kvittel* ("Note"). Usually the petitions were related to basic human needs: recovery from sickness, longing for a child, the need for finding a suitable mate for one's children, the difficulty of earning a livelihood. The Hasid wrote his name and the name of his mother on the petition. Accompanying the *Kvittel* was a *Pidyon* ("redemption money"), which varied according to his finances. It was usual to give a sum corresponding to the numerical value of the Hebrew word *Hai* ("life", i.e. eighteen). Hasidim would even place *Kvittlech* at the graves of their *Rebbes*.

The Hasidic leaders would ceremoniously *fir Tish* ("conduct a table"), and the Hasidim would share a symbolic meal with their *Rebbe*. The master would utter *Divre Torah* ("Words of Torah") and the Hasidim would sing joyous melodies in fiery fellowship. Watching the *Rebbe* was as important as listening to him. Every gesture was observed and analysed. It was the Hasid's privilege to share *Shirayim* ("remnants") of the rabbi's food. The rabbi would merely taste a dish and then pass it down the table, a custom that can be traced back to antiquity. "He who leaves no bread on the table (at the end of a meal) will never see a sign of blessing," warns the Talmud.[16] The Palestinian Talmud records that Rabbi Johanan bar Napaha would gather up the morsels left over from the previous night's meal and eat them, saying "Let my portion be among those who were here (in the Synagogue) yesterday."[17]

Hasidism developed the idea further, maintaining that the *Zaddik* sanctified the food, setting free the imprisoned *Nizozot* ("Sparks") and and restoring them to their source.

It was a special privilege for a Hasid to spend the Sabbath with his *Rebbe*. In preparation, he would visit the *Mikveh* ("Ritual Bath"). The *Zaddik* would wear his finest garments, usually a *kapote* of silk or velvet. Many *Zaddikim* would don a *Tallit* during the Evening Service that ushered in the Sabbath. Some would utter a benediction over spices before the *Kiddush* on Friday night, because the Talmud relates that on the Eve of Sabbath, before sunset, Rabbi Simon ben Yohai and his son saw an old man bearing two bundles of myrtle. "What are these for?" they asked him. "They are in honour of the Sabbath" he replied.[18]

In Lurian style, the Hasidim would set twelve twisted loaves on the table at every Sabbath meal, a visual reminder of the "twelve cakes" that were set out in the Sanctuary (Lev. xxiv. 4). During the Reading of the Law the most important *Mitzvah*, apart from the *Kohen* and *Levi* portions, was *Shishi* (the sixth portion) which corresponded to the Cabbalistic symbol *Yesod*. The *Zaddik*, the foundation (*Yesod*) of the world, was customarily honoured with *Shishi*.

Shalosh Seudot, the Third Meal, was the highlight of the Sabbath. The menu rarely consisted of more than fish and bread. But the sparse meal was supplemented by spiritual fare. In the gathering dusk the Rabbi spoke in illuminating phrases and the Hasidim sang such mystical melodies such as *Atkinu Seudata* or Luria's *Bene Hekhala*. Together they swayed and danced in an ecstasy that transcended the barriers of time and place. After *Habdalah* many rabbis chanted the prayer poem of Rabbi Levi Isaac of Berdichev *"Gott fun Avruhom"* ("God of Abraham"). Both the *Rebbe* and his Hasidim were reluctant to let the honoured guest depart and prolonged the day as much as possible. At the conclusion of the Sabbath they celebrated the *Melaveh Malkah* ("Accompanying the Queen"), chanting hymns and relating Hasidic tales.

The Hasidic centre was the *Stiebel*, the Yiddish word for the little room which served as both place of worship and house of study. Hasidic rabbis would establish branches, *Stieblech*, in the various towns in which their followers resided. In Poland, most towns had several such Stieblech, probably a Gerer, an Alexander, and a Belzer *Stiebel*. Here the Hasidim would commune with God as well as with each other, discussing the depth of the rabbi's discourses and the manifold facets of his personality.

The *Shibhei Ha-Besht*, an anthology of legends concerning the Baal Shem Tov, was published in Kopyss in 1815. Many treasuries of Hasidic fables followed. It was believed that relating stories of *Zaddikim* was equivalent to reciting prayers.

Prayer was the pivotal point. *Kavanah* ("devotion") and *Hitlahavut* ("fervour") were essential, and the intimate atmosphere of the *Stiebel* encouraged uninhibited outpourings of the soul. The Besht and Rabbi Levi Isaac of Berdichev worshipped with blazing intensity. For Rabbi Uri of Strelisk, known as the "Seraph", prayer was so devastating an experience, that he regularly took the precaution of preparing his "Last Will and Testament" before attending the Synagogue. The Besht attributed his powers to the intensity of his prayers rather than to the extent of his studies. Hasidim believed that prayer could achieve the impossible, and could even change the order of nature.

Yet *Zaddikim* like the Rabbis of Rizhyn and Sadagora were seemingly calm and dispassionate when they stood in prayer. "There are *Zaddikim*," it was said, "who serve God with all their limbs, and there are *Zaddikim* who fear God so much that they are too terrified to move as much as a muscle during the service." In the words of Rabbi Nahum of Czernobiel: "We behold many people engaged in study and prayer . . . they raise their voices . . . they clap their hands, they jump to their feet. Many ignorant people imagine that this constitutes prayer. The truth is not so. It is fitting that a man should pray in awe and dread."

Total involvement generally characterised Hasidic worship. For the Psalmist says (xxxv. 10): "All my bones shall say, Lord, who is like unto thee." Inevitably their opponents mocked these manifestations: "They (the Hasidim) rise to offer prayers of thanksgiving and praise, intermingled with songs and whistles, twisting their lips and twinkling their eyes, frisking and whooping."

The Hasidim adopted the Lurian liturgy, *Nusah Ari*. Rabbi Dov Baer favoured the Lurian liturgy and he was supported by many authorities.[19] In his prayer book published in Shklow in 1803, Rabbi Shneur Zalman made substantial changes in the liturgy, and *Habad* Hasidim use this text. The Hasidim generally omitted *Piyutim* (liturgical poems), but recited special introductions to various prayers, composed by Rabbis like Elimelekh of Lezajsk.

"Permissible pleasures" were not scorned. At a *Siyyum* (completion of the study of a tractate of the Talmud), on the anniversary of the *Zaddik*'s death, on *Purim* and *Simhat Torah*, at weddings and similar festivities, Hasidim would gulp spirits in careful measure, and wish each other *Lehayim* ("For Life"), and thus "banish grief from the heart".

Asked why the Hasidim drank whisky after the service, whereas the *Mitnagdim* usually studied a chapter of the Mishnah, Rabbi Israel of Rizhyn replied: "The *Mitnagdim* pray frigidly, without enthusiasm or emotion. They appear almost lifeless. After their prayers they study the Mishnah—an appropriate subject when one mourns the dead. But the prayers of the Hasidim are alive, and living people need a drink." The Hasidim called this *Tikkun*, ("Repair"), for by creating harmony in this way they were smoothing out some of the disharmonies in the cosmos.

Hasidim followed the established educational patterns. At a very early age sons were sent to the *Heder*. Secular subjects had no place in the curriculum, and Hebrew grammar and the study of the Bible were neglected. "Verily, grammar is useful," admits Rabbi Menahem Mendel of Vitebsk. "I know that our great ones studied it, but what can we do, now that the godless have taken possession of it?" At first the Hasidim did not send their sons to the *Yeshivot*, and the young men would study in the *Bet Ha-Midrash*. But, by the twentieth century, Hasidim had established their own *Yeshivot*, such as the *Metivta*, set up in 1919 under Rabbi Meir Don Plotski, Rabbi of Ostrowiec. Hasidic youngsters, reluctant to travel to far-off institutions, converged upon this local fountainhead of scholarship. Candidates had to be over thirteen and able to master unaided one page of the Talmud and *Tosaphot* (commentaries compiled in the twelfth and thirteenth centuries). Unlike other *Yeshivot*, which concentrated wholly on Talmudical studies, the *Metivta* devoted two hours a day to Polish language, mathematics and history. This revolutionary departure did not go unchallenged. Rabbi Hayim Eliezer Shapira of Munkacs termed it "heresy".

In the inter-war years, many Hasidic *Yeshivot* sprang up, and today they flourish in Israel, England and the United States.

Hasidim still wear the distinctive attire favoured by their ancestors. Proudly they wear the *Kapote*, the *Yarmulka* (skull cap), the *Streimel* (fur hat) and the *Gartel* (girdle). They button their coats from right to left. Any innovation in dress is regarded as *Hukkat Ha-Goy* (imitating the Gentiles). Even wearing a collar and tie was regarded by some Hasidim as the beginning of heresy. Like the Cabbalists, they do not countenance the trimming (even with scissors) of beard and side-locks.

Many rituals distinguish Hasidim from their fellow Jews. Some Hasidim don two pairs of *Tephillin* each morning. For *Rabbenu Tam* disagreed with Rashi as to the order of the texts on the four parchments, and so two versions of *Tephillin* are available. To satisfy both celebrated authorities, devout Hasidim use both. On *Hol Ha-Moed*, however, they do not put on *Tephillin* at all. On Passover they eat only *Matzah Shemura*, (unleavened bread) made from flour that had been supervised from the moment the wheat was harvested. Mendel of Kotzk would drink five cups of wine at the *Seder* celebration instead of the customary four. Special verses are recited before the sounding of the *Shophar* on the New Year, and when the *Shophar* is sounded the congregation recite the *Musaph Amidah*. Hasidim have *Hakafot* (processional circuits around the *Almemar* with Scrolls of the Law) on *Shemini Atzeret* as well as on *Simhat Torah*.

Eventually the *Mitnagdim* joined forces with the Hasidim in the strenuous and ceaseless battle against *Haskalah*. The warning of the *Mitnaged* Rabbi Moses Sopher (1763–1839) of Pressburg, "Touch not the works of Dessau (Mendelssohn)" was echoed by all Hasidic leaders. A refusal to compromise ensured the continuance of traditional Judaism and kept the flames burning in the darkest days.

Chapter 20

A Renaissance of Joy and Song

Music and dance have always been important in Judaism. When Elisha wished to prophesy, he demanded: "Now bring me a minstrel" (II Kings iii. 15). Half of the one hundred and fifty Psalms in the Book of Psalms were designed to be sung with instrumental accompaniment, and the Temple musicians were organised into twenty-four guilds according to the instruments they played. The Bible records the victory dances with which Miriam and the Israelite maidens celebrated the defeat of Pharaoh's host. David and Saul returning from battle were met with "timbrels and joy" (I. Sam. xviii. 6), and David danced in holy ecstasy before the Ark of the Lord (II. Sam. vi. 14–16).

Dances figured in the rituals of the Temple. The Talmud describes the picturesque torch dances in which the leading citizens participated. "Whosoever has not witnessed the joy of the Festival of Water Drawing" (during *Succot*), comment the Sages, "has seen no joy in his life."

With the destruction of the Temple, instrumental music was no longer used to accompany the liturgy, although the tradition of singing the Psalms and some of the prayers was transferred to the Synagogue. By the ninth century the musical accents, called in Hebrew *Teamim* (literally "tastes") or *Neginot* ("notes") were generally accepted. Cantillation of the Torah and *Haftorah* was now according to marks placed above and below the Hebrew text. For it was held that the Torah and the Books of the Prophets must be chanted according to their appointed melodies because these melodies were handed down to Moses on Mount Sinai.[1]

During the Middle Ages the Jews paid little attention to music, having other matters on their minds. "The exile," laments the sixteenth-century scholar Leone da Modena, "dispersion over the face of the

A Hasidic boy at the Western Wall in 1968

globe, the incredible persecution that has afflicted us, all these have inevitably caused us to neglect the arts and the sciences . . . Therefore we have today been obliged to borrow the music of our neighbours and to adapt our religious chants from it." By the sixteenth century the *Baal Tefilah* ("Master of Prayer") had been replaced by a Cantor sometimes accompanied by a choir. Salomone Rossi of Venice (1587–1628) officiated in Ferrara with a choir of eight voices. But it was not until the nineteenth century that *Hazanut*, the art of "liturgical singing", was really developed to the full.

Hasidism brought about a veritable renaissance of Jewish music. For the Masters of Mysticism, melody was rich with mystical meaning, and the Zohar often elaborates on this theme. "In the highest heavens," says the Zohar, "there is a certain Temple with gates that can be opened only by the power of song." The Zohar explains that all creation sings glorious songs of praise to the Creator. All the prophets, save only Moses, "father of the prophets", used melody to heighten their receptiveness to divine inspiration.[2]

The Cabbalists of Safed, among them Isaac Luria, Solomon Alkabetz and Israel Najara, created many notable melodies that have echoed through the ages, which throb with faith, joy, yearning and hope. For they fervently believed that only when they were joyous, did the Divine Presence dwell among them.

"Serve the Lord with joy," was the vibrant theme that surged through Hasidism. "No child can be born except through joy. By the same token," reasoned the Besht, "if a man wishes his prayers to bear fruit, he must offer them with joy."[3] The most important aspect of a *Mitzvah* (good deed) is the joyfulness with which it is carried out. The Divine Presence is the antithesis of melancholy. Sadness emanates from the *Kelipot* ("Shells of sin"), but from the Godhead radiates joy. The path to the Realm of Repentance passes first through the Sphere of Song. To every day, the Besht applied the verse, "Thou shalt be altogether joyful" (Deut. xvi. 15), which the Torah applies to the Festival of Tabernacles. He believed that there could be no absolute evil because in every occurrence there was an element of good, in every judgement there was mercy. . . ."

"A poor man," the Besht related, "once came before his king with weeping and bitter lamentation. Out of compassion the king gave him a few coins. Then another petitioner came in. He, too, was in great need. However, he smiled cheerfully and made his request in a pleasant, merry manner. The king's mood brightened, and he gladly presented the second petitioner with lavish gifts." Echoes are found in Hasidic melodies of military marches and of Russian, Polish, Viennese, Moldavian, Walachian and Rumanian tunes. For the singer refines the song. "Even in the songs of the non-Jew," maintained the Besht, "there are sparks of the Divine."

The dance, too, was revived by the Hasidim. It was no longer confined to the *Mitzvah Tanz*, "the handkerchief dance" performed at weddings by close kinsfolk of the bride and groom. It became a form of self-expression and "sacred service" complementary to the song. Among the Hasidim the dance reached the highest level of religious enthusiasm, even to the point of self-oblivion. Hands as well as feet were caught up in the passion of the dance. This was no social pastime, no mere "poetry in motion", no auto-intoxication. This was religious ecstasy that lifted the participants out of themselves and out of their surroundings into the highest heavens. The Hasid danced on festivals, on the Sabbath, on the anniversaries of a *Zaddik*'s death. And the dance itself was a prayer, a mystical experience, a passionate outpouring of love for the Creator and His works.

"My dancing," remarked Rabbi Leib, son of Rabbi Abraham, "the Angel", "was more important to God than all my praying." When Rabbi Levi Isaac danced on *Simhat Torah* "all the upper worlds were hushed into silence, and even the Ministering Angels held their breath and stopped their daily songs of praise before the Holy One, Blessed be He, and never was there in heaven such a great spiritual delight".[4] The Rabbi of Shpola composed many *niggunim*. One of them is a dialogue in which the Almighty enquires of His children: "Where have you been? Why have you forsaken me? Dear children, please return home. I feel forlorn without you." Each verse is sung in Hebrew, in Yiddish, and in Russian.

In the Middle Ages, cantors were criticised on all sides. They were censured for prolonging the service unduly and for mispronouncing the text. Rabbi Joseph of Polnoy tabulates many of their alleged offences:[5] "Our souls are sick with listening to *Hazanim*, for in every fine and pious community the plague has spread. They sin and cause others to sin. When they prolong their melodies without end, the people gossip in the Synagogue, interrupting the silence of prayer at times when it is forbidden to interrupt. How can he shamelessly stand up as the advocate, the messenger of the congregation, the intermediary between Israel and our Father in heaven, before the great and awful King, the root and source of all worlds?"

Yet the Cantor's role was all-important. Rabbi Phinehas of Korzec said of the *Maharil*, Rabbi Jacob b. Moses Ha-Levi Mölln (1360–1427) that he reached spiritual heights because he was a *Shaliah Zibbur* (a congregational reader) and sang well. "The Hasidim narrowed the gulf between Reader and congregation, for all worshippers were urged to participate." Sincerity and spontaneity were of more consequence than mere harmony. "All the worlds," writes the *Maggid*, "are nourished by the songs of Israel, the sacred songs to God: and even as in days of old, when the Holy Temple stood, the songs of the Levites in their sacred service of worship would ascend upwards and the worlds were stimulated and nourished by them, so God today should be worshipped in joy, in song and in lyrical praise."[6]

The synagogal melodies were dear to the Besht, and he loved to officiate at the Reader's desk. It was his custom to read the *Musaph* (Additional Service) on the New Year, and on the Day of Atonement he would recite *Neilah* (the concluding service). The *Maggid* did not himself act as Reader for his Hasidim. His reader was Rabbi Jehudah Leib Kohen, author of a Torah commentary, *Or Ha-Ganuz* ("Hidden Light"). The *Maggid* composed a number of melodies.

Hasidic music was in many ways unique. Songs were handed down from father to son. Often simple folk melodies became vehicles for awesome concepts.

Rabbi Yitzhak Eisik (1751–1828) of Kalov (Nagy Kallon), North Hungary, adopted a shepherd's love song. "Rose, rose how far away you are" (*Ros, ros, wie weit bist du*), Forest, forest, how large you are (*Wald, wald, wie gross bist du*). Would that the rose were not so far, that the forest were not so large (*Wolt die ros nit aso weit gewen, wolt der wald nit aso gross gewen*)." The Rabbi of Kalev substituted *Shekhinah* ("Divine Presence") for rose and *Galut* ("exile") for "forest", and he created a song that has inspired and consoled generations of Hasidim.

Prayers and *Zemirot* ("Sabbath melodies") were, of course, composed in Hebrew. But many of the Hasidic lyricists gave expression to their hopes and longings in Yiddish.

Every dynasty had its own favourite tunes, which became almost "signature tunes". From the melody that a Hasid hummed, it was often possible to identify the school to which he belonged. "Every Israelite has a portion in the World to Come, and the main delight in the World to Come will be derived from melody," declared the poet of Hasidism, Nahman of Braclaw. "The only way to detach oneself from the world and to approach the Almighty is through song and praise." "Through songs," he maintained, "calamities can be averted. Music emanates from the prophetic spirit and has the power to elevate and inspire."[7] It was Rabbi Nahman who interpreted the verse in Genesis (xliii. 2). "Take of the choice fruits (*Zimrat*) of the land in your vessels and carry down to the man a present," to mean "take of the songs of the land."

"Every branch of wisdom in the world has its own specific melody," Rabbi Nahman explained in his characteristically cryptic manner, "and it is from that melody that wisdom itself is derived. Even Epicurean philosophy has tunes of its own. Moreover, all learning has a melody in accordance with its nature and rank: the loftier the learning, the more sublime is the tune pertaining to it, and thus it ascends even higher and higher until it reaches the primal point of creation which is the beginning of the Divine emanation." To Nahman everything was a song. "Winter is like conception, like birth. In the winter all vegetation is dead, when summer comes all awakes to life." "When a man prays in the field all nature aids him and adds power to his prayers." Rabbi Nathan, his disciple, confessed that when he heard Rabbi Nahman singing he felt compensated for all his suffering. Rabbi Nahman held, moreover, that "the root of all blessings is to be attained only through dances." Hence Hasidim used to say: "Whosoever has not seen the Rabbi of Braclaw dancing, has not seen true goodness."

Habad also established its own musical traditions. The founder of the dynasty, Shneur Zalman, himself a gifted singer, believed that only step by step could one ascend to the highest of spiritual heights. There are certain stages: *Hishtaphut Ha-Nephesh* ("outpouring of the soul"), *Hitorerut* ("spiritual awakening"), *Hitpaalut* ("ecstasy"). And at each stage music could help. The first Rabbi of Lubavitch composed what became known as the Rabbi's Song (*Der Rebbe's Niggun*). This is the anthem of *Habad* chanted only on special festive occasions, such as on the nineteenth of *Kislev* (the day when Shneur Zalman was released from prison). This pensive song consists of four bars which correspond to the four Cabbalistic regions: *Beriah* ("creation of the plant world"), *Yezirah* ("living beings"), *Asiyah* (making or creating of man) and *Azilut* ("emanations").

In many cases words were superfluous. Shneur Zalman once said to one of his followers: "I realise that you have not quite grasped the import of my discourse. So I will sing you a song." Shneur Zalman sang and the Hasid listened. "Now I understand what you wish to teach," responded the Hasid with warmth and intelligence. "I feel an intense longing to be united with the Lord."[8]

Similarly, Hasidim relate that Shneur Zalman once visited Shklow, a city renowned for its scholars and militant *Mitnagdim*. There the *Rebbe* met a rather hostile group and to conventional queries he could only return conventional answers. So he raised his voice in song. So moved were his listeners, that it seemed to them that their questions were answered and their problems were solved.

The orchestra and choir of Rabbi Dov Baer, son of Rabbi Shneur Zalman, won great renown, and his court was the training ground of many famous *Hazanim*. "First, it is necessary," explains Dov Baer in his "Tract on Ecstasy" (*Kunteres Ha-Hitpaalut*) "to understand the nature of the ecstasy produced by melody. This is in the category of spontaneous ecstasy only produced involuntarily without one's desiring it and without any effort of will. This is an ecstasy that is felt, and yet the one who experiences it is not himself aware of it, because it does not result from an intention of the self to produce ecstasy, but is produced automatically and comes of its own accord without it being known to him."[9]

Although all Hasidim agreed on the importance of melody, in the nineteenth century there were marked differences in attitude. The Karliner Hasidim's melody and dance were on the same level as study and meditation. The Seer of Lublin would sing some of the prayers and would listen with great pleasure to the mellifluous tones of his reader, Rabbi Feivish, for "when Rabbi Feivish sings, 'All of them are beloved, pure and mighty', (part of the morning service); the Holy One Blessed be He says to His heavenly hosts, 'Let us go down and contemplate the virtues of mortal man and you will be abashed.'"

The Seer employed a "court jester", or "*Badhan*", Mordecai Rakover, who with extemporised quips and rhyming jests, merrily lampooned the guests at weddings and other festivities. The words *L'el asher Shovat* ("To the God who rested from all His works"), were set by the Seer to a melody which he had heard in the "Heavenly spheres". In Przysucha, Kotzk and Ger however, music played a subsidiary role and the emphasis was on study. Nevertheless, Isaac Meir of Ger remarked: "Were I blessed with a sweet and beautiful voice, I would sing a new hymn for You every day. For as the world is created anew every day, new songs are created with it." Different types of melody were favoured by various groups of Hasidim, for there was nothing stereotyped or regimented about Hasidic life. Some liked sentimental lyrics, while others preferred exuberant, rollicking rhythms.

At the court of Rabbi Hayim of Sanz resided a number of cantors, and outstanding among them was Rabbi Abush Meir. Rabbi Hayim had no ear for "modern" *Hazanim*. "Their melodies do not come," he said, "from the Temple of music but from the notes themselves." The Rabbi of Belz attached great religious significance to the dance. "I cannot tell you the reason for dancing on *Simhat Torah*," he said, "but I can tell you that all the prayers that did not ascend to God during the whole of the year will ascend to him on this day through these dances."

Both Kuzmir (Kazimierz) and Modzitz occupy high places in the history of Hasidic musicology. What *Habad* did for the philosophy of Hasidism, Modzitz did for its music. Founder of the dynasty was Rabbi Ezekiel of Kuzmir (1806–56). He was born in Plonsk, son of Zevi Hirsch, one of the disciples of the Besht. His father was probably murdered by the Cossacks. Ezekiel lived for a while in Warka and visited a number of Hasidic leaders. The Seer said of him: "His face resembles the face of Abraham our Father." Rabbi Ezekiel became the patron of Hasidic music in Poland. Like his master, the Seer, Rabbi Ezekiel employed a *Badhan* ("Jester") and a choir. Commenting on the verse of Deut. xxii. 4, "Thou shalt surely help to lift him up again," which refers to an animal which has fallen by the wayside, Rabbi Ezekiel explained that a man was duty bound to help the singer by joining in the song. He would say: "I do not feel any delight in the Sabbath unless it brings forth a new melody." He died in 1856 at the age of fifty. His commentary on the Pentateuch, *Nehmod Mizahav* ("More precious than gold"), contains many references to song and dance.

Rabbi Ezekiel left four sons. One of them, Rabbi David Zevi of Neustadt, founder of the Yablona dynasty, followed the traditions of Kotzk and paid little attention to music. The family tradition was maintained by Samuel Elijah of Zwolyn (1818–88) who was gifted with a fine voice as well as a fine mind. "The law of God is perfect," he declared, "therefore melody, too, must be perfect. Great responsibilities rest upon the singer. He has to prepare and purify himself most carefully. Nor should he deviate one iota from the song, lest he transgresses the precept, 'Thou shalt not add unto the word which I command you, neither shall ye diminish from it'" (Deut. iv. 2).

All five sons of Rabbi Samuel Elijah were music-lovers. The eldest, Rabbi Moses Aaron (1837–1918), succeeded his father, but made his home in Nubi Debar. Another son, Rabbi Hayim Yerahmiel Taub, studied under Rabbi Joab-Joshua Weingarten of Kinsk, and eventually settled in Warsaw, at 16 *Pavia* Street. He composed many subtle melodies. His father, Samuel Elijah, was his musical mentor, and would lead the prayers during the High Holidays. Samuel Elijah remarked that throughout the year he was sustained by the pleasure he had derived from his son's prayers on the Days of Awe. The inspired cantor rarely concluded *Musaph* (the additional Service) before 5.30 p.m., for he was apt to lose all sense of time when he sang before his Heavenly Father.

Rabbi Jacob Taub of Radom, second son of Rabbi Samuel Elijah, was a gifted musician, and his father-in-law Rabbi Leib Epstein of Ozarow (d. 1914) also took great delight in music. Both enjoyed officiating as cantors for the congregation.

The baton of Rabbi Ezekiel, however, fell to Rabbi Israel (b. 1849). Even as a young child, he had been musically inclined. At the age of fourteen he married the daughter of one of the most oustanding *Baale Tephilot* (cantors) of Poland, Hayim Saul Freedman of Ozarow, and for the next fifteen years he lived with his parents-in-law, devoting all his time to intensive study.

In his work *Divre Yisrael* ("Words of Israel"), Rabbi Israel devotes a lengthy excursus to music. "They say," he writes, "that the Temple of Song is adjacent to the Temple of Repentance. I say that the Temple of Music is the Temple of Repentance." From the melodies a man favoured, the rabbi could discern his character. He likened the seven tones of the scale to the seven moral spheres in the Cabbalistic theory of creation and to the seven days of the week. "There are two phrases in liturgy 'Lord of wonders, who chooses song and psalm,' and 'King of the Universe who hast chosen us from all the nations and given us Thy law.'" "I do not know," reflected Rabbi Israel, "which phrase is of greater significance."

For twenty years Rabbi Israel lived in Modzitz, attracting followers from far and wide. In 1913 he fell dangerously ill. "Through the merit of your songs by which you have redeemed thousands of Jewish souls," Rabbi Menahem Kalisz of Amshinov assured him, "the Almighty will grant you a speedy recovery." That same year one of his legs was amputated in Berlin. Pain did not extinguish his fiery spirit, nor crush the music from his soul. On the operating table he composed a soaring song called *Ezkeroh* "I will remember and pour my soul within me" (Psalm xlii. 5), and what the "Rabbi's Song" was to Hasidim of Lubavitch, *Ezkeroh* became to the Hasidim of Modzitz. The doctors marvelled at the composure of their venerable patient. "In the next room," the surgeon, Professor James Adolf Israel (1848–1926) remarked, "I have a patient who is a Cabinet Minister. He moans and complains constantly. I said to him, 'You ought to be ashamed of yourself. I have here an aged rabbi, and whenever he is in pain he sings'." In 1914 Rabbi Israel settled in Warsaw, and he died seven years later.

Next in the line of the Modzitzer melody-makers was Rabbi Israel's son, Rabbi Saul Yedidiah Eliezer Taub, who was born in 1887 at Ozarow. He was Rabbi in Rakov from 1918 to 1922, and in 1929 he settled in Otwock, near Warsaw. Rabbi Taub received no formal grounding in the rudiments of musical theory, yet there was music in his veins. *Maskilim*, as well as Hasidim, cantors from all over Poland, music-lovers Jewish and Gentile, flocked to Otwock to listen to the compositions of this untutored genius. What other rabbis achieved through scholarship, Rabbi Taub achieved through music, drawing many to *Hasidism*. More than a thousand people sat at his table every Sabbath at *Shalosh Seudot* to hear his Torah discourses and his melodies. He is said to have composed more than seven hundred of them.

When the Second World War broke out, he was among the eleven thousand Polish refugees who fled to Vilna. He narrowly escaped the Holocaust, journeying via Siberia and Japan to the United States. He arrived in New York in 1940, where he published the third part of his father's commentary on Leviticus, *Divre Yisrael*. Rabbi Taub could not resist the call of the Holy Land, which he had visited in 1925, 1935 and 1938. There he settled in 1947, but he was not destined to live there for very long. He died on November 29, 1947, on the day the United Nations passed a resolution prescribing the partition of Palestine into an Arab State and a Jewish State and the internationalisation of Jerusalem. He was the last person to be buried on the Mount of Olives in 1947.

The dynasty of Bobov (Bobowa), founded by Rabbi Benzion Halberstamm and today headed by Rabbi Solomon Halberstamm of New York, is renowned for its musical creativity. The composition of Hasidic melodies was not confined to Poland. The melodies of Vishnitz, a dynasty established by Rabbi Kopel Hasid and his son Rabbi Menahem Mendel Hager in Kosov, near Stanislaw, echoed through Hungary, Rumania and Czechoslovakia.

Even in the valley of the shadow of death, even as they trod the fearsome paths that led to the crematoria, where a multitude of Hasidim perished, even there, song sustained them. It was then that Rabbi Azriel Pastag, a Hasid of Rabbi Taub, composed a triumphant melody that was a passionate affirmation of undying faith. "I believe," he sang, and hundreds of thousands sang with him, "with perfect faith in the coming of the Messiah, and though he tarry, yet will I wait daily for his coming." This was the faith for which the Hasidim lived and this was the faith for which they gave their lives in Sanctification of God's Name.

Echoes of Hasidic music are still heard today. The most prominent of the nineteenth- and twentieth-century *Hazanim*, such as David Brod Shtresliker (1883–1948), Nissan Spivak or Nissi Belzer (1824–1906), Jacob Margowski (known as Zedel Rovner), and a host of others, were all brought up in Hasidic homes. Hasidic music has influenced synagogal music, and the songs and dances of modern Israel are greatly indebted to Hasidism. The steady output of long-playing albums of Hasidic song and dance is audible evidence of the timelessness of the Hasidic melodies, which poignantly express the strivings of the Jewish soul.

Chapter 21

Lady Rabbis and Rabbinic Daughters

Popular misconception puts the Hasidic woman in her place—the kitchen and the nursery—assigning to her the sole function of producing and serving an ever-increasing family. This is a falsification of the facts. The fact is that the *Hasida*, as she was called, occupied an honoured position in the Hasidic world.[1] Often it was the wife who converted the husband, for Hasidism attracted women, and they reacted with sensitivity and appreciation to the basic principles of the movement. They read Hasidic anecdotes (printed in Yiddish) as avidly as their twentieth-century counterparts devour romantic novels.

The Besht never forgot the devotion of his own wife, Hannah. Despite her brother's opposition, Hannah had married Israel when the hidden Master appeared to be a poor ignorant peasant, and their abiding love had weathered many hardships. Israel loved her deeply and after she died, he did not remarry. "Heaven has departed with her," he grieved. "I thought that a storm would sweep me up to Heaven like the prophet Elijah, but now that I am only half a body, that is no longer possible." In his last Testament, *Tzavaat Ribash*, he urged Hasidim to honour their wives.

The Besht adored his only daughter Udel, who accompanied him on many of his journeys. To her he applied the verse in Deuteronomy xxxiii. 2 "At his right hand was a fiery Law unto them", for the first letters of the Hebrew words *Esh Dat Lamo* make up the name Udel.

When the Besht visited Satanov, he perceived a great spiritual light, and found that this radiance emanated from a woman. "Shame on you!" he rebuked the leaders of the community. "Through a woman have I seen the light." He believed that women's prayers were particularly efficacious. The Besht liked to tell how a certain community had once proclaimed a public fast in order to ward off some imminent disaster. The whole community, men and women, young and old, assembled in the Synagogue. Weeping before the Ark and trembling with terror, the Rabbi prayed for hours. Yet neither the piety of the Rabbi nor the prayers of the elders, could force the Gates of Heaven. They opened at the cry from the heart of a simple woman, a humble mother in Israel. "Master of the Universe! Thou art a merciful father and thou hast many children," she pleaded. "I am a mother of five children and when but one child suffers I cry out and my heart goes out to it. Surely, Thou art more compassionate than I am. Even if Thy heart were made of stone, it should melt at the agonising cry of Thy children. O God, listen to them and save them."

When one of his followers, Jonah Spradlaver, complained to the Besht of his Yente's strange behaviour, the Master reassured him. "She has seeing eyes and hearing ears," he enigmatically announced, bestowing upon her the title "Prophetess". Yet husbands were not always gratified by the spiritual prowess of their wives.

Hasidic writers tried increasingly to raise the prestige of women in Jewish life. It is said that the wife of one of his opponents met Rabbi Levi Isaac of Berdichev in the street and poured out a pail of water over his head. Rabbi Levi Isaac went to the Synagogue and prayed: "O Lord, God of Israel, do not punish the good woman. She must have done this at her husband's command, and she is therefore to be commended as a loyal wife."

To lighten the burden of the widow was a major *Mitzvah* and in such situations Hasidic rabbis did not stand on their dignity. Rabbi Hayim Halberstamm was once walking through the market place, when he noticed a widow behind her fruit stall bitterly bewailing the lack of customers. Without further ado, Rabbi Hayim took her place at the stand and shouted: "Buy fine apples, a gulden a dozen." The news that the *Zaddik* had turned salesman spread through the market, and people rushed to buy from the Holy man. The poor widow made a fine profit that day.

Not since the Bible times that brought forth the "Four Matriarchs" and the "Seven Prophetesses" (*Megillah* 14a), has Jewry produced women as outstanding as those who emerged in the heyday of Hasidism. Rabbi Leib Sarah's (1710–91) was however, the only Hasidic personality whose name was always associated with that of his mother. He is also the subject of more stories than any other *Zaddik* save the Besht, for he travelled ceaselessly, rescuing and redeeming fellow Jews. A woman of rare beauty, Sarah, the mother of Leib, had married an elderly scholar in order to escape the unwelcome attentions of the local Squire's son. Presumably, her reward was her illustrious son and the way in which her name was linked with his.

Feige, daughter of Udel, was said to be endowed with "divine spirit", which her son Rabbi Nahman of Braclaw seemed to inherit. Like the daughters of Rashi, Merish, daughter of Rabbi Elimelekh of Lezajsk, was renowned for her scholarship. Hasidim would go to hear her learned discourses and to receive her blessings; Freida, eldest daughter of Rabbi Shneur Zalman, was honoured by *Habad* Hasidim. She collected her father's aphorisms and wrote a number of remarkable manuscripts on a variety of subjects.

Even the study of Cabbalah did not satisfy the spiritual aspirations of certain Hasidic women. Perele, eldest daughter of Rabbi Israel of Kozienice and wife of Rabbi Ezra Zelig Shapira, Rabbi of Magnuszew (d. 1849), wore *Tzitzit* ("ritual fringes"), fasted on Mondays and Thursdays, and received petitions from her followers. She lived a life of poverty, promptly distributing among the needy all the money that she received from the Hasidim. "The *Shekhinah* rests upon her," acknowledged Rabbi Elimelekh of Lezajsk, and her own father urged his Hasidim to visit her.

Rachel, daughter of Rabbi Abraham Joshua Heschel of Opatow (1745–1825), was equally renowned. Her father, an ardent believer in her powers, declared: "She has a holy spark." She accompanied him on many journeys, and he consulted her constantly. Most of the Hasidim of Apt paid court to the daughter as well as to the father, for they believed that she, too, could accomplish great things.

Rebecca, wife of Rabbi Simha Bunam, was known for her hospitality and her kindliness. Her home in Przysucha was a second home to all her husband's disciples and many of them later became the leading lights of Hasidism. After the death of her husband and her son, she devoted herself to charitable causes. Travelling from place to place, she held out a helping hand to all who were in need. Often she appealed to her husband's disciples and her appeals were always heeded. The "miracles" wrought by Rebecca were acts of loving-kindness.

"The rabbi of Belz and his wife," it was said, "were like Adam and Eve before they sinned in the Garden of Eden." Shalom consulted his wife, Malka, on almost every problem, and his example was followed by his Hasidim. Once, when a man complained of a painful leg, she advised him to light a candle every day in the Synagogue. He did so, and made a complete recovery. To her awed husband she explained:

"It is written in Psalms (cix. 105) 'Thy word is a lamp unto my feet.'"
"Lord of the World! If I had the strength to waken her, would I not
have done so by now?" exclaimed Rabbi Shalom, when she died. "I
am simply not able to do it. But you, Lord of the World! You have
the power to awaken the dead. Why do you not awaken Israel?"

The adage "Like mother, like daughter," certainly applied to Belz.
Malka's daughter, Eidele, married Rabbi Isaac Rubin of Sokolov (d.
1876), a son of Rabbi Asher of Ropczyce. Interestingly enough, Rabbi
Isaac had been reluctant to become a *Rebbe*, whereas his wife inclined to
the role. She delivered discourses, distributed *Shirayim* and generally
conducted herself like a *Rebbe*. "All Eidele needs is a rabbi's hat,"
remarked her father, fondly.

Similarly, Sarah, the daughter of Rabbi Joshua Heshel Teumin
Frankel, made a name for herself among the Hasidim. She was born in
1838 in Tarnopol. Her father died when she was only three months
old and she was brought up by Rabbi Josele, the "good Jew" of
Neustadt, who later married her to his grandson, Rabbi Hayim Samuel
Horowitz Strenfeld. When her husband died in 1916, Sarah more or
less took his place. A system of regular contributions was instituted to
support her, and this money she distributed among the poor. Her
sayings were wise and her parables so apt, that even rabbis sought her
counsels and her blessings. She fasted regularly and asceticism was her
way of life. Yet it proved to be no barrier to longevity. She died in
1937 at the age of ninety-nine.

In the same way, "Malkale the Triskerin", as she was called, daughter
of Rabbi Abraham of Trisk (1806–89), conducted *Tish* ("public meals"),
distributed *Shirayim* and twice a day received petitions from Hasidim.
She insisted moreover, on being present when Hasidim visited her
father, the *Maggid*.

Another celebrated woman in Rabbinic learning and piety was
Hannah Havah, daughter of Rabbi Mordecai Twersky (1770–1837) of
Czernobiel, who, according to her father's testimony, was endowed
"with the Holy Spirit from the womb and from birth". He deemed
her equal in piety to his sons, "the eight candles of the Menorah". Her
aphorisms and parables spread her fame through Poland. Tenderly and
tirelessly, she dealt with the women who flocked to her for guidance.
She emphasised the importance of correct and careful education and
urged her followers to be charitable in every way.

The most famous of all the Hasidic women was Hannah Rachel
(1805–92), only child of Monesh Werbemacher, who became known

as the "Maid of Ludmir". The limited education that was then provided for girls did not satisfy little Hannah Rachel. She studied the *Midrash*, the *Aggada* and many books of *Musar*. She was betrothed at an early age, but the betrothal brought her little happiness. A warm-hearted and affectionate child, she was forced to live a lonely and friendless existence. There was no one to share her thoughts. Sometimes surges of exultation lifted her spirit, but more often she fell prey to moods of prolonged melancholy. Then she found comfort only at the grave of her mother, where she poured out all her longings and inner desires. On one of her regular visits to the cemetery, she fell asleep by the graveside. When she awoke, it was midnight. The weird shapes and shadows looming large in the deserted "House of Life," filled her with terror. Half-dazed, she began to run and stumbled into a half-filled grave. This shock disrupted her already fragile constitution. She became very ill, and for a while she hovered between life and death. When she finally recovered, she startled her father with this announcement: "I have just returned from the Heavenly Court, where I received a new and sublime soul." Indeed, the new Hannah Rachel was different. She donned *Tzitzit*, wrapped herself in a *Tallit* and, like Michal, daughter of King Saul (I. Sam. xiv. 49–50) she put on *Tephillin*. When her father died, she recited *Kaddish* for him. Inevitably, the betrothal was annulled.

Financially well provided for by her father, the learned lady spent her time in secluded meditation. A synagogue was built with an adjoining apartment for her. Every Sabbath at *Shalosh Seudot* ("the third meal") the door of her room would be opened. Heard but not seen the Maid of Ludmir would deliver erudite discourses to which men of piety and learning listened eagerly and appreciatively, for scholars and rabbis were among the numerous Hasidim of the Maid of Ludmir. Finally, at the age of forty, she succumbed to the persuasive tongue of Rabbi Mordecai of Czernobiel and agreed to wed the Talmudical scholar that the Rabbi of Czernobiel warmly recommended. However, her influence waned after the marriage and she emigrated to the Holy Land.

There the Maid entered a mystical partnership with a Cabbalist, and both resolved to hasten the coming of the Messiah. After prolonged and elaborate preparations, a time and place were set for the enactment of the great drama. The Maid of Ludmir arrived punctually at the appointed site, a cave outside Jerusalem, and waited anxiously but in vain. For the Cabbalist collaborator had been inexplicably detained by a venerable sage, the ubiquitous prophet Elijah in disguise, whose role it was to prevent the hatching of the apocalyptic plot. The Messianic era was not due yet and could not be precipitated.

The women on the Hasidic "roll of honour" who were "rabbis" and "wonder workers", students of the Cabbalah and Talmudists, were of course exceptions. The majority of Hasidic women were themselves unlettered, yet they were often largely responsible for the erudition of their husbands and sons. Often they maintained and sustained the family, relieving their husbands of material cares, so that they could devote themselves exclusively to matters of the mind and the soul. The lives of the wives were difficult and often dangerous. Feige, wife of Rabbi Isaac of Ger, was a vendor of cloth. Yohebed, wife of Rabbi Yehuda Leib of Ger, became a sugar-merchant. The wife of Rabbi Jacob of Radzymin turned travelling pedlar, wandering from village to village with her wares. Perele, wife of Rabbi Nathan David of Szydlowiec, supervised an estate, and Hannah Deborah, wife of Rabbi Zadok Kohen of Lublin, dealt in clothes.

An important role was played by Tamarel Bergson, wife of Baer Smulevitch and ancestress of the French philosopher, Henri Bergson. What Beatrice de Luna (Gracia Mendes), 1510–69, did for the *Sephardim* in the sixteenth century, Tamarel did for the Hasidim three hundred years later. She employed a number of young men who later became *Rebbes*. She herself was a devoted *Hasida* of Rabbi Isaac of Warka, Rabbi Mendel of Kotzk and Rabbi Isaac Meir of Ger. Her generosity was proverbial and she helped countless Hasidim to extricate themselves from material misfortunes.

The Hasidim were unyielding in their opposition to *Haskalah*. No secular subject was allowed to penetrate the walls of the Yeshiva. No Yeshiva student dared to read openly the works of Judah Löb Gordon (1830–92) or Shalom Jacob Abramowitsch (1836–1917). *Ahavat Zion* ("The Love of Zion") and *Ayit Tzavua* ("The Painted Hawk") by Abraham Mapu (1808–67) could be perused only in secret. But the Hasidic fathers were more lenient with their daughters, who read whatever they wished, but were denied any formal education. Though Glückel of Hameln writes in her memoirs of *Heder* education for girls, this was certainly not the norm. For the most part, the intellectual thirst of the women in Eastern Europe was confined to the *Tz'enah U'Reenah* ("Go Forth and See") by Jacob ben Isaac Ashkenazi of Janow (a sixteenth-century Yiddish version of the Pentateuch interlaced with tales, interpretive comment and romantic fiction).

By the beginning of the twentieth century, however, the mood had changed. Many Hasidic parents now encouraged their daughters to study, and gloried in the not inconsiderable intellectual attainments of these eager and perceptive young women. In small Polish towns, private tutors were in great demand, and music, Polish and French were favourite subjects. In the larger towns, many girls attended such Jewish schools as the *Tarbut* (under the auspices of the Zionists) and *Zisho* (the Central Yiddish School Organisation). Paradoxically enough, the daughters of Hasidic families were often forbidden to enroll at *Tarbut* or *Zisho* institutions, while they were permitted to attend the gentile *Gymnasium*. Some even completed the curriculum of "eight classes" and matriculated.

A secular education was of more than academic use to these women. Often they, as breadwinners, needed to deal intelligently with the non-Jewish world. Yet many fathers came to regret the liberalism that had allowed them to expose their young daughters to the new horizons that opened for them in the gymnasia. The *Tz'enah U'Reenah* was discarded in favour of *Pan Tadeusz*, by the Polish poet Adam Mickiewicz (1798-1855). Matchmakers and parentally arranged marriages were no longer accepted with docility. Many now regarded the Yeshiva *bahur* (student) as unworldly and parochial. New knowledge gave them new ideas. Often newly emancipated young women fled from fatherly reproofs with husbands of their own choosing.

Certainly, it was not easy for an educated girl to find fulfilment in her own home, for the menfolk lived in a world of their own. This is how Sarah Schenirer, founder of the *Bet Jacob* Schools, described the scene:[2] "And as we pass through the *Elul* days, the trains which run to the little *Shtedlach* (towns), where the Rebbes live, are crowded. Thousands of Hasidim are on their way to them to spend the *Yomim Noraim* ("Solemn Holy Days") with the *Rebbe*. Every day sees new crowds of old men and young men in the Hasidic garb, eager to secure a place in the train, eager to spend the holiest days in the year in the atmosphere of their *Rebbe*, to be able to extract from it as much holiness as possible. Fathers and sons travel, and those who can afford it make this journey several times a year. Thus they are drawn to Ger, to Belz, to Alexander, to Bobov, to all those places that had been made citadels of concerted religious life, dominated by the leading figure of a *Rebbe*'s personality.

"And we stay at home, the wives, the daughters and the little ones. We have an empty *Yom Tov*. It is bare of Jewish intellectual content.

The women have never learned anything about the spiritual meaning of our festivals. The mother goes to the Synagogue, but the services echo faintly into the fenced and boarded-off galleries where the women sit out of sight. There is much crying by the elderly women. The young girls look at them as though they belonged to a different century. Youth and the desire to live a full life shoot up violently in the strong-willed young personalities. Outside the *shul* the young girls stand chattering; they walk away from the *shul* where their mothers pour out their vague and heavy feelings. They leave behind them the wailing of the older generation and follow the urge for freedom and self-expression. Further and further away from *shul* they go, further away to the dancing, tempting light of a fleeting joy."[2]

Sarah's father was a merchant and a Hasid of Belz. During the First World War, she lived in Vienna and was influenced by Rabbi Dr. Flesch. "I listened intently to Dr. Flesch's inspiring sermon," Sarah recalled. "The Rabbi painted a vivid picture of Judith, the heroine of Jewish history. He held her image up as an example to the girls and women of our days and urged them to walk in the footsteps of the illustrious women of ancient times . . . I said to myself: 'How I wish that the women of Cracow might know who we are and who our ancestors were.'"[3]

The first *Bet Jacob* school for girls was founded in Cracow under the guidance of Sarah Schenirer in 1917. The name *Bet Jacob* alludes to the verse: "O house of Jacob come ye and let us walk in the light of the Lord." Under Schenirer, propagandist and pedagogue, the movement flourished, and by 1924 there were nineteen schools with two thousand students. In 1937-8 there were in Poland two hundred and forty-eight *Bet Jacob* Schools with an enrolment of 35,585 students. The *Bet Jacob* Schools were acknowledged by the *Knessia Gedola* ("The Great Assembly"), of the Aguda to be "the best solution for the education of girls". The *Keren Ha-Torah* (the special Aguda fund established by German-Jewish Orthodoxy for Torah institutions) gave financial support. Moral support came from the Rabbi of Belz and Rabbi Israel Kahan (1835-1933), the author of *Hafetz Hayim* ("Desiring Life").

The curriculum of the *Bet Jacob* schools was heavily weighted in favour of Judaic studies. Each student was obliged to learn fifty Psalms by heart and to become thoroughly acquainted with Jewish law and liturgy, but secular subjects were also studied. To meet the ever-increasing demand for instructors, the *Bet Jacob* Teachers' Seminary was built in Cracow in 1925 at a cost of sixty thousand dollars.

Bet Jacob graduates formed themselves into an Association, and many became the backbone of the Aguda women's movement known as *Bnot Agudat Yisrael* and *N'shei Agudat Yisrael*, which numbered 20,000 in 1937.

Typical of the approving attitude of the Hasidic *Rebbes* was the stand taken by Abraham Mordecai Alter, the Rabbi of Ger. "It is a sacred duty to work nowadays for the *Bet Jacob* movement," he wrote. "The future mothers of Israel are being educated in the true traditional spirit of the Torah and are receiving a sound all-round schooling."

Openly and appreciatively, Hasidic writers and *Rebbes* acknowledge the vital role of women in Jewish life. It did not matter that they had neither the time nor the opportunity for esoteric study or spiritual achievements. No wonder women responded with such instant warmth to Hasidism. Its appeal was emotional, its tenets deeply rooted in reality. In Hasidism the mundane day-to-day routine acquired a new dimension and a new nobility.

Chapter 22

"If I Forget Thee, O Jerusalem"

"If I forget thee, O Jerusalem, let my right hand forget her cunning," wept the Jews by the alien waters of Babylon. "Let my tongue cleave to the roof of my mouth, if I remember thee not" (Ps. cxxxvii. 5–6). Throughout their long and bitter exile, they kept alive the memory of their ancient homeland, and for the Cabbalists it was particularly precious, "Happy is he who is fortunate enough to dwell in the Holy Land," says the Zohar.[1] "He causes the dew to fall upon the earth."

Three times the Besht set out for the Holy Land, on one occasion reaching as far as Istanbul, but each time "Heaven held him back,"[2] for the fusion of the Holy Man and the Holy Land would precipitate the coming of the Messiah. In vain the Besht yearned to fulfil the *Mitzvah* of living in the Land of Israel and of planting the seeds of Hasidism in the hallowed soil. Although the Master was not destined to accomplish this task himself, his aims were achieved through his pupils and associates.

In 1746 Rabbi Abraham Gershon Kutower, the brother-in-law of the Besht, a learned Talmudist and Cabbalist, emigrated to Israel. Rabbi Jonathan Eibeschütz spoke of Rabbi Gershon with the utmost reverence.[3] At first, Rabbi Gershon had not recognised the hidden greatness of his sister's husband, but later he became a devoted follower of the Besht. Rabbi Gershon arrived in Jerusalem on the eve of New Year and was warmly welcomed by both the *Sephardim* and the *Ashkenazim*. He settled first in Hebron and later in Jerusalem. The Besht often wrote to him and occasionally sent funds.

In one letter the Besht counsels: "Let the words of *Musar* (ethics), which I have spoken to you always be in your mind."[4] For the Besht, distance was no obstacle. "One Friday night, during the service," said the Besht, "I searched for Rabbi Gershon throughout Palestine and could not find him anywhere. But the next morning I found him."

Rabbi Gershon explained that he had spent that particular Sabbath at Acre, worshipping on Friday night in a Synagogue which was technically outside the boundary of Israel. "Pray for me," the Besht wrote to his brother-in-law, "Pray that I may be worthy to join the inheritance of the Lord, for the Almighty knows that I have not given up hope of going to the Land of Israel."[5]

The adoption by the Hasidim of the *Nusah Ari* ("the Lurian liturgy") forged another link with the Holy Land. But many Hasidim yearned for a more personal attachment and sought to settle there.

Like the second century *Tanna*, Nahum of Gimzo, Rabbi Nahman of Horodenka accepted every misfortune with *gam zu letovah* ("This, too, is for the best"), for his faith was as "strong as a pillar of iron".[6] He accompanied the Besht on many travels. "I have afflicted my soul and I have immersed myself in ritual baths, but I could not rid myself of alien thoughts until I became attached to the Besht." Together with Rabbi Menahem Mendel of Przemyslany (d. 1772), Nahman set out for the Holy Land. The voyage was difficult and dangerous. When the ship tossed on the stormy seas, Rabbi Nahman exclaimed: "Lord of the Universe, if it has been decreed by Thy Heavenly Court that we should perish, this Holy Congregation, jointly with the *Shekhinah*, declare that we decline to accept the decree. We demand its prompt annulment." The passengers landed safely on *Tishri* 12, 1764. Rabbi Nahman and Rabbi Menahem Mendel lived in Tiberias and Safed.

"*Eretz Yisrael* is an exalted land," wrote Rabbi Jacob Joseph of Polnoy, "and the Holy One, Blessed be He, hath given it to Israel as a perpetual gift. It is reserved exclusively and entirely for them."[7] Rabbi Jacob Joseph made careful preparations for his pilgrimage, and the Besht gave him a letter to deliver personally to his brother-in-law. However, for reasons unknown to us the journey was never made and the letter was never delivered. Later Rabbi Jacob Joseph published it in his book *Porat Joseph* under the heading: "This is the epistle which the Besht gave me to hand to Rabbi Gershon."

According to Rabbi Phinehas of Korzec, it was unnatural for a man not to yearn for the Holy Land. Commenting on Moses's prayer: "Let me go over, I pray Thee, and see the good Land" (Deut. iii. 25), Rabbi Phinehas commented: "Moses said to God: 'I do not wish to be as the ten spies who brought back an unfavourable and gloomy report. I wish to see only the 'good of Eretz Yisrael'."[8] In 1790, Rabbi Phinehas left Ostrog for Israel, but he died in mid-journey at Shepetovka in 1790 or 1791.

In 1777, three hundred Hasidim left Galati in Rumania under the leadership of Rabbi Menahem Mendel of Vitebsk (1730–88), Rabbi Abraham Ha-Kohen of Kalisk (Kalishki) and Rabbi Israel Polotzker. Five months later, after many hardships, they reached their destination. "At last the day has come for which we have waited with such impatience," wrote one of the leaders. "How happy we are in the Holy Land, the delight of our hearts, the joy of our thoughts is the land which is sanctified by different types of sanctity."[9]

Although the Hasidim were received with great friendliness by the Jewish communities, the arrival of so large a group of newcomers created economic problems. Their funds soon petered out and they naturally had no means of earning a living. "Even a man with the heart of a lion melts when he beholds infants begging for bread." So Rabbi Menahem Mendel enlisted the support of his followers in Russia. He sent Rabbi Israel of Polotzk to raise funds for the *Halukah* (literally "Division"), as the collections made abroad for the support of the *Yishuv* ('Settlement') in the Holy Land came to be called. Rabbi Israel was the forerunner of many *Meshulahim* or *Shadarim* ("emissaries") who repeatedly visited Hasidic centres in Eastern Europe for this purpose.

"It is your responsibility," writes Rabbi Israel to the heads of the Jewish community in Russia, "to build up the house of our God, and it is incumbent upon Jewry to support the settlement in the Holy Land . . . Hasten to perform this great *Mitzvah* and to sustain the children of Israel, feeding the hungry and clothing the naked, in order that they, who live on the holy soil, may pray for the scattered community of Israel in exile." His appeal was not unheeded. With the help of Rabbi Shneur Zalman, a fund (*Maamadot*) was set up and considerable sums were collected. Rabbi Israel however, did not return to Israel. As he was passing Pastov, the burial place of Rabbi Abraham "the Angel", he seemed to hear a summons. "Abraham is calling me," he said. "He wants me to be buried by his side." Abraham's request was granted.

When Rabbi Hayim of Krasny (d. 1793), son-in-law of Rabbi Zeev Wolf (d. 1800) of Zhitomir, was shipwrecked en route, he regarded the incident as a mark of divine displeasure and forbade the inscription of titles on his tombstone because "I have not been deemed worthy of visiting Eretz Yisrael."

Although Rabbi Shneur Zalman, founder of *Habad*, could not abandon his followers, he actively helped to support the *Yishuv*. He arranged for systematic collections and regularly dispatched funds. Similarly, Rabbi Israel of Kosienice actively encouraged fund-raising for this pious endeavour.

Not since Judah Ha-Levi (c. 1075–1141), that "fiery pillar of sweet song", to whom Jerusalem was the "city of the world", had Zion had as lyrical a lover as the poet of Hasidism, Rabbi Nahman of Braclaw. The emotions that Judah Ha-Levi expressed in his "Songs of Zion", Rabbi Nahman voiced in the pithy aphorisms for which he was renowned. Like Judah Ha-Levi, he travelled widely through the Holy Land but, unlike the poet, he did not visit Jerusalem. Minutely, he described his visits to Elijah's Cave on Mount Carmel, to the tomb of Rabbi Simeon ben Yohai at Meron and to the grave of his grandfather Rabbi Nahman of Horodenka. Returning home, he composed many prayers.

"O Lord God, who is merciful and gracious, slow to anger and abundant in truth and mercy," he prayed. "In Thy great mercy make me and the children of Israel worthy that our hearts may yearn for the Land of Israel, the foundation of our Holy Faith, the land which the Lord has chosen for His people . . . Grant me the strength and resolution that I should fulfil this craving of my heart . . . Thou alone knowest how great is my need of the land because of the distraction, confusion and imperfection which beset my life and remove me far from thee."[10]

Although relatively few of the great Hasidic masters were actually able to make the journey to the Holy Land, most of them made the journey in spirit, for again and again they stressed the mystic significance of Zion. Rabbi Levi Isaac of Berdichev loved the land of Israel as dearly as he loved the people of Israel. "When the Jews dwell there securely in the Land of Israel," he declared, "then the country is inhabited. But when the Israelites are in exile, then the country is regarded as a wilderness, even though it may be inhabited by other nations. For the land of Israel belongs to the people of Israel. And only they can possess it."

Prophetically, Rabbi Solomon of Lutsk, disciple of the *Maggid* of Mezhirichi, linked the future of the land with the revival of Hebrew as a living language. In his *Divrat Shlomoh* "Words of Solomon" (printed in 1859) he writes: "It is essential that the people living there should use the Holy Tongue, the language in which the Universe was created. If they do not speak the Holy Tongue, then the land does not really belong to them and they can easily be banished."[11]

Throughout the nineteenth century, the links between Hasidism and

Eretz Yisrael were maintained, and a steady stream of pious pioneers exchanged comfortable homes for the rigours of a Spartan existence. When Jacob Samson, the Rabbi of Shepetovka, visited his friend Benjamin Wolf Zbarzh[12] (d. 1822) in Tiberias, he saw the Rabbi's wife labouring over the wash-tub. "Rabbi, this linen is not mine!" she exclaimed. "I am washing it for others and I am not being paid for the task. But I feel no regrets. No sacrifice is too great for the privilege of living here."[13]

The Seer of Lublin urged Jews to refuse to accept the prevailing conditions. He urged them to repossess the Land. Only then was there hope that Israel would be redeemed. Rabbi Simha Bunam compared the love of Israel for the Land of Israel with the love of a bride for her bridegroom. When the Messiah came, the "marriage" would be consummated. The first visit to the Holy Land of Sir Moses Montefiore fired the imagination of the Hasidim. Rabbi Simha Bunam reputedly asked why Montefiore was not attempting to purchase the Holy Land from the Turks. He was asked, "What use is the purchase of this territory before the arrival of the Messiah?" "When the land passes out of the hands of the Arabs into Jewish hands," replied Rabbi Simha Bunam, "the Messiah will come immediately."[14]

Rabbi David of Lelov, disciple of the Yehudi, urged his eldest son Moses (1778–1850) to visit the Holy Land and there to hasten the redemption. Moses's father-in-law, the Yehudi, also encouraged the young man to undertake the journey. The father bequeathed property to his sons Avigdor and Nehemiah but left nothing to Moses because "a house is ready for you in Jerusalem, the Holy City". In 1843, Moses sought to fulfil his father's wish. "When with the help of the Almighty, I will arrive safely in the Holy Land, I will go directly to the Western Wall in Jerusalem," promised Moses "There will I lift up my voice like a trumpet and I will bring the Messiah."

Personal and pecuniary problems, however, stood in his way. His wife, Rebekah Rachel, opposed the journey, and none of her husband's colleagues could move her. Summoned to a special gathering to discuss the matter, she stood in the doorway and cried: "Have respect for the daughter of the Holy Jew." Rabbi Moses travelled through Poland with his disciples, and Rabbi Solomon of Radomsko to raise money for the trip. He left Rumania in 1850 with his children, ten disciples and two attendants. His wife remained behind. He celebrated the High Holidays on the high seas and a *Succah* ("Booth") was erected on the boat.

The voyage took two months. When he finally arrived in Jerusalem, he was exhausted and in rapidly failing health. Since he no longer had the strength to walk to the Western Wall, he begged his sons to carry him there. "I must be at the Western Wall this very day," he told them. On the way, Arabs attacked the little group and Rabbi Moses did not reach the wall. He died seventy-two days after arriving in the Holy Land. Yet his last wish was fulfilled, and he was buried near the grave of the prophet Zechariah in Jerusalem.[15]

Through the strenuous endeavours of Rabbi Isaac Meir of Ger, 40,000 roubles were raised for the *Yishuv* between 1838 and 1840. During the Polish Rebellion in 1863, Isaac Meir commented: "We see how the Poles are sacrificing themselves to liberate their country from the hands of the foreigners. What are we doing to regain our land?" He had grave foreboding about the future of the Jews in Europe.

The publication, in 1862, of *Derishat Zion* ("Quest of Zion") by Rabbi Zevi Hirsch Kalischer (1795–1874) gave impetus to the *Hibat Zion* ("Lovers of Zion") movement. Under the leadership of Leon Pinsker (1831–91), Moses Leib Lilienblum (1843–1910) and Judah Leo Levanda, *Hibat Zion* societies were formed in Russia, Austria and Germany. With the help of Baron de Rothschild (1854–1934) of Paris, several settlements were established in the Holy Land.

As a rule, Hasidim did not join the *Hibat Zion* movement, but there were such notable exceptions as Elijah Gutmacher (1796–1875) of Gratz. Rabbi Hayim of Pilev (1870–1906), a grandson of Rabbi Mendel of Kotzk, formed *Agudat Ha-Elef* ("the group of the thousand"), aimed at settling a thousand Hasidim in the Holy Land. In collaboration with Rabbi Isaac Jacob Reines (1839–1915) and Rabbi Samuel Mohilever (1824–98), Rabbi Hayim wrote a booklet, *Shelom Yerushalayim* ("Peace of Jerusalem"), which demonstrated that every Jew was duty bound to participate in the rebuilding of the Holy Land.

In a letter to Rabbi Hayim, Rabbi Yehudah Leib of Ger writes: "Certainly he upon whom the fear of Heaven rests takes it upon himself to fulfil the Commandments of Tithes and *Maaser* for he, who knows that members of his family will not object to them, need not be afraid. It will be reckoned as a *Mitzvah*. Although the *Aliyah* is not considered for its own sake, nevertheless we can say that eventually it will turn out to be for its own sake."[16] Like Rabbi Hayim Eliezer Wacks of Kalisz, Rabbi Yehudah Leib urged that Hasidim import Palestinian *etrogim*.

While the Jewish world at large was growing increasingly enthusiastic over the possible restoration of the Jewish home through political means, Hasidim did not generally share this enthusiasm. For the battle still raged between Hasidism and *Haskalah*. The Hasidim associated *Haskalah* with assimilation and even apostasy. And many of the *Maskilim* carried the flag of Zionism. Moreover, repossession of the promised land at this stage was regarded as tantamount to interference with the Divine order of things.

Dr. Theodor Herzl (1860–1904), father of political Zionism, was anxious to enlist the support of the Hasidim. In his diary under May 8, 1896 he recorded: "The Hasid Aaron Marcus (1843–1916) of Podgorze (Galicia) again writes me a very fine letter, in which he holds out the possibility that the three million Hasidim of Poland will join my movement. I answer that the participation of the Orthodox will be welcome, but that no theocracy will be created."[17]

Three years later, Herzl pleaded passionately for the co-operation of Rabbi Yehudah Leib of Ger. "In the name of thousands of Jews whose existence, threatened by hostile neighbours," writes Herzl to the Rabbi of Ger, "grows daily more difficult; in the name of the starving multitudes who engage in all kinds of occupations to feed their children: in the name of the thousands of refugees who flee from Russia, Rumania, Galicia to America, Africa and Australia, where the danger of assimilation awaits them, and finally in the name of God and the Torah, we urge the honourable rabbi to tell us openly the sins which we have committed by espousing Zionism."[18]

The Zionist leader kept in touch with Rabbi Yehudah Menahem Ha-Levi of Przemysl (1862–1920), rabbi of Botosain, Rumania, "who offered to negotiate with the wonder rabbi, Moses Friedmann of Czortkov. I sent a letter in which I invited Friedmann to send me his son."[19] Herzl met the Rabbi's son and Aaron Marcus joined them in trying to persuade the *Rebbe* to call a conference of rabbis to promote the aims of Zionism. In Herzl's entry under November 10, 1897 he writes:[20] "A man from Jerusalem named Back came to see me. He is travelling round Europe in order to found an agrarian bank for Palestine—a vest pocket Jewish company, evidently his vest pocket. He claims to be under the patronage of the Galician wonder rabbi, Friedmann." Herzl also met another Hasidic Rabbi. "One of the most curious figures I have just encountered," writes Herzl,[21] "is the Rymanover *Rebbe* Horowitz, son-in-law of the wonder rabbi there. He came to see me, accompanied by his secretary."

Rabbi Abraham of Sochaczew urged Jews to settle in the Holy Land providing they could, for this is the fulfilment of a *Mitzvah* which is equal to the sum of all the *Mitzvot*. Moreover, there is no limit to the reward of those who participate to redeem the land.[22] To Rabbi Israel of Pilev he wrote: "I have examined the contents of your little book and I have derived much pleasure from it, for with sweet and pleasant phrases it fills the heart with love of the Holy land . . . It is proper to purchase an estate in *Eretz Yisrael* . . . I, too, want to do this." In 1898, he sent his son and his son-in-law to purchase land from the Turkish overlords, but the transaction was not completed.

Fund-raising alone did not satisfy the rabbis of the dynasty of Warka (founded by Rabbi Isaac Warka). Rabbi Simha Bunam Kalish, son of Rabbi Isaac, took his wife and five children to the Holy Land in the winter of 1887. Like all Russian tourists, he had a thirty day permit. When it expired he was arrested and imprisoned for five days until the community secured his release. He was permitted to stay for three months and then had to return home. Twenty years later, in 1906, he came back to Jerusalem and there he remained. He died in 1907 and was buried in Tiberias next to Menahem Mendel of Vitebsk.

For Rabbi Meir Yehiel of Ostrowiec, the poor of the Holy Land took precedence over the poor in his home town, and he diligently collected monies for them. He used to say: "I am from the Land of Israel, but we were exiled because of our sins and now I live in Ostrowiec. Similarly, whenever a Jew is asked: 'Where do you come from? he should reply, 'I come from the Holy Land, but now I live temporarily in exile.'"

Without exception, Hasidic rabbis agreed that it was a sacred and important task to support the poor of the Holy Land. Rabbi Israel of Rizhyn became a Turkish citizen and on his passport were the words "a native of Jerusalem". In 1843, Nissan Back of Jerusalem told him that the Czar of Russia was planning to buy a site near the Western Wall to erect a monastery. Quickly the Rabbi raised the money that enabled Back to acquire that strategic piece of land. According to legend, when the Czar heard that he had been outmanœuvred by the Rizhyner, he exclaimed: "That Jew always blocks my path." A beautiful synagogue, *Tiferet Yisrael* or *Bet Ha-knesset* of Nissan Back was built and opened in 1873 and served as a rallying centre for the Hasidim of Rizhyn.

Rabbi Israel was not impressed with the events of 1848, "Annus Mirabilis", (the National Revolutions of 1848–50). "There will come a time," he ominously predicted, "when the nations will drive us out of their lands. How shameful that after our too long drawn-out exile, the redemption should take place under such circumstances."[23]

A century before the Balfour Declaration, the Rabbi of Rizhyn foretold: "As in the time of Ezra, a Government will again arise that will permit the Jews to return to the land of their fathers." He was worldly enough to realise that a country cannot be built up by the settlement of a few celebrities. "If I go to Israel," he said, "they will ask me why I did not bring my people with me? What answer can I give them?"

Rabbi Israel's son, Abraham Jacob Friedmann of Sadagora, wrote to Sir Moses Montefiore asking him to persuade the Czar to allow collections for the Holy Land "without fear or dread".[24]

Chapter 23

The Return to Zion

"The land of Israel for the people of Israel founded on the Torah." This was the platform of the *Mizrachi* (lit. *"Merkaz Ruhani*—spiritual centre") organisation set up in 1902 in Vilna by Rabbi Jacob Isaac Reines of Lida. By 1937, the *Mizrachi* had branches in most Polish towns and operated a network of schools, youth groups and related organisations. But few Hasidim were involved with the *Mizrachi*, and the urgent need for "solutions to contemporary problems in the spirit of the Torah" led to the Kattowitz Conference and the birth of the *Agudat Israel* ("Union of Israel") in 1912. Within a decade the Aguda had become the political arm of the Hasidim.

Assembled at Kattowitz, in Upper Silesia, on May 27, 1912 were over two hundred communal leaders, laymen and Rabbis, *Mitnagdim* and Hasidim, brought there by a wide diversity of motives. Jacob Rosenheim (1870–1965), Vice-President of *Die Freie Vereinigung für die Interessen des Orthodoxen Judentums* ("Free Association for the Interests of Orthodox Judaism"), founded by Rabbi Samson Raphael Hirsch in 1855, yearned to unite the unorganised Orthodox masses of Eastern Europe. Others, like Rabbi Abraham Mordecai Alter of Ger, felt that only a Torah-entrenched citadel could hold back the tidal waves of assimilation, the anti-religious ideology of the secularists and the nationalism of the Zionists.

Although Rosenheim, the movement's founder and lifelong guide, maintained that this was not going to be "an organisation like other organisations", the Aguda ultimately adopted the whole familiar complex of institutional accoutrements: constitution, general council, executive committee, acting committee, a Rabbinical Council (*Moetzet Gedole Ha-Torah*) with an executive of eleven members and even a press bureau.

Soon there were sizeable Aguda groups in Budapest, Amsterdam and Vienna. Nominally its headquarters remained in Frankfurt until 1935, but its heart and soul were lodged in Hasidic Poland. During the inter-war years, nearly a third of Polish Jewry, most of them Hasidim, were associated with the Aguda. Moreover, in an intricate and often devious manner, the Aguda did play party politics. Isaac Breuer (1883–1946), one of the founders, believed that "political Zionism seeks to exchange the *Galut* of Israel for the *Galut* of the nations", a belief that coloured the Aguda attitude. Admittedly anti-Zionist, the Aguda, in poignant paradox, was also passionately pro-Zion. Its programme stated: "It shall be the purpose of Agudat Israel to resolve all Jewish problems in the spirit of the Torah, both in *Galut* and in *Eretz Yisrael*. . . The colonisation of the Holy Land, in the spirit of the Torah, shall be directed towards creating a source of spirituality for the Jewish people." It established a *Keren Ha-Yishuv* (Settlement Fund) and a *Keren Eretz Yisrael* (Palestine Fund) to establish training camps in Poland and to acquire territory in the Holy Land. The Jewish Agency for Palestine agreed to issue six to seven per cent of its immigration certificates to Aguda members. However, for most Agudists, love of Zion remained a purely spiritual passion, and only a few translated the ancient yearning into reality.

Between the two world wars, most of the Hasidic Rabbis were associated with the work of the Aguda. Their attitude to Zionism was negative, and they did not co-operate with the Jewish Agency, believing that "to restore Palestine without a firm religious basis would be to establish the very worst possible form of darkness".

The Balfour Declaration issued in November, 1917 by Mr. A. J. (later Lord) Balfour, the Foreign Secretary of Great Britain, to Lord Rothschild regarding the "establishment in Palestine of a national home for Jewish people" and the promise of the British Government "to use their best endeavours to facilitate the achievement of this object" spurred many Hasidim to action. In Austria, even before the end of the First World War, a number of Hasidic Rabbis had already established a society, *Yishuv Eretz Yisrael*, under the leadership of Rabbi Hayim Meir Shapira (b. 1864) of Drohobycz. Their manifesto in the Hebrew periodical *Ha-Tzephirah* ("The Dawn"), in 1918 urged orthodox Jews to help rebuild the Holy Land. "Our programme is the programme of Ezra and Nehemiah, to establish settlements in the Holy Land in the spirit of the Torah." Among the signatories was Shalom Hayim Friedmann of Sadagora. Rabbi Shapira even participated in the twelfth Zionist Congress at Carlsbad in 1921. Eventually *Yishuv Eretz Yisrael* merged with the *Mizrachi*.

It was Isaac Gerstenkorn, a Hasid of the Rabbi of Skierniewice who in 1924 founded the townlet of Bnei Berak on the borders of Ramat Gan, a garden suburb of Tel Aviv. Various districts sprang up and Bnei Berak became a thriving Torah centre.

The first major attempt by Hasidim to establish an agricultural settlement was made in 1925 by Rabbi Ezekiel of Yablona, a descendant of Rabbi Taub of Kazimierz. "I would rather be a labourer in the Land of Israel," his father Rabbi Jacob had remarked, "than a *Rebbe* in the Diaspora." Together with Rabbi Isaiah (d. 1967), son of Rabbi Elimelekh Shapira of Grodzisk (d. 1945), and Rabbi Eliezer of Kozienice, the Rabbi of Yablona formed a society called *Nahlat Yaacob* ("Inheritance of Jacob") "to enable everyone to buy land by spreading the payments over five years." Later *Nahlat Yaacob* merged with a similar association *Avodat Yisrael* ("Service of Israel") founded by the *Rebbe* of Kozienice.

Towards the end of 1925, the Yablona Rabbi and twelve of his followers established *Kfar Hasidim*, "the village of the Hasidim", on the banks of the River Kishon.

With astonishment and approval, Dr. Chaim Weizmann (1873–1952) describes in his autobiography an encounter with these unusual pioneers: "On the way to Nahalal we passed a hill crowned with a newly erected barracks, around which clustered a number of people who looked like recently arrived refugees. They made a striking group. We discovered that they were Hasidim who, led by their Rabbi (the Rabbi of Yablon), had landed in Palestine only a few days before. Many of them had since then been compelled to sleep in the open, which, in spite of the light rains still to be expected in April, they were finding a wonderful experience. Balfour (Lord Arthur James Balfour, 1848–1930), alighted from the car and went into the barracks to receive the blessings of the Rabbi. I told him that if he would come again in a year or two he would find quite a different picture; he would find these people established on their own land, content, and looking like peasants descended from generations of peasants."[1]

The Jewish National Fund allotted them six thousand dunams near Nahalal, and soon there were one hundred and ten families living there. Their industry and courage "aroused general admiration and served to bridge the wide gap that existed between their outlook and that of the workers".[2]

The 1937 Aguda Conference at Marienbad discussed the proposal of the Peel Commission (the Royal Commission set up by the British Government in 1936 under Viscount Peel), that the Holy Land be partitioned into two sovereign States, one Jewish and the other Arab, with historic and strategic sites remaining under British jurisdiction. In forceful opposition, Rabbi Abraham Mordecai Alter of Ger quoted Joel iv. 2, "I will gather all the nations and I will bring them down into the valley of Jehosophat; and I will enter into judgement with them there for My people and My heritage Israel, whom they have scattered among the nations and divided My land."

The Rabbi of Ger visited the Holy Land six times. His first visit in 1921 lasted for twenty-eight days. Then he wrote: "I am pleased to note that it is possible to conduct oneself in the Holy Land in the way of our fathers and forefathers. Whomsoever the Almighty has blessed can undoubtedly make a living there and lead a true Torah life without difficulty . . . I visited the High Commissioner, Eliezer Samuel (later Viscount Samuel, 1870–1963), and he assured me that he would give every help to the religious settlers." Returning to Poland, he urged his followers to invest their money in the Holy Land.

Three years later he returned with Rabbi Isaac Zelig of Sokolov, his brother-in-law Hirsch Heinoh Levin, Rabbi of Bendin, and a number of wealthy followers from Lodz. This time he visited Jerusalem, Safed, Hebron and Tiberias, as well as Tel Aviv. After seven weeks he returned to Poland. In the home of industrialist Tovia Bialer, the *Rebbe* said: "If but five hundred well-to-do Hasidim would emigrate to the Holy Land they would capture the country materially and spiritually. You should leave Lodz and settle there." With the guidance of the Rabbi of Ger a Yeshiva, *Sefat Emet*, was founded in Jerusalem in 1925 under the direction of Rabbi Mendel Kasher.

The third visit via Trieste and Alexandria took place in 1927. When the *Rebbe* visited the Cave of Machpelah (the traditional burial place of the Patriarchs) at Hebron, the guard was willing (at that time the Jews were not permitted beyond the twelfth step) to allow the venerable visitor to enter the Cave. But the *Rebbe* declined to take advantage of such special privileges. "All the children of Israel are the children of a king," he said. "I do not wish to ascend higher than other members of the community." The *Rebbe*'s rapport with Rabbi Abraham Isaac Kook, Chief Rabbi of the Holy Land, aroused the antagonism of the orthodox extremists, and a zealot, Meir Heller Semnitzer, wrote so hostile a pamphlet that both he and the printer of the pamphlet were excommunicated by loyal Hasidim of Ger.

The fourth visit took place in the winter of 1932, and the *Rebbe*'s overland journey through Vienna and Istanbul aroused the interest of world Jewry. "I want to know and to see," the rabbi said, "the different ways that lead to the Holy Land." As he was returning to Poland, a violent storm sprang up. "This is because we are leaving the Holy Land," sighed the *Rebbe*.

The fifth pilgrimage took place just before *Rosh Hashanah*, 1936, and lasted for eight months. By now the *Rebbe* regarded himself as a resident in the Holy Land and he no longer observed *Yom Tov Sheni* (the Second Day of the Festival observed in the Diaspora).[3]

In 1928 a Hasidic rabbi inadvertently caused an unpleasant incident in Jerusalem. Rabbi Aaron Menahem Mendel Gutterman, the Rabbi of Radzymin, during a visit earlier that year, had set a simple canvas screen at the Western Wall to separate men and women worshippers. The Muslim authorities complained this violated the rules that regulated Jewish access to the site. The British police inspector, Douglas Duff, on duty there, instructed the man in charge of arrangements for the High Holy Day Services to remove the screen and he agreed to do so. Next morning, however, the screen was still in place. While the congregation was in the midst of solemn Day of Atonement ritual, police moved in to remove the offending screen. Enraged at this desecration of the Festival, the worshippers attempted to stop the police and a number of Jews were injured in the ensuing turmoil.

The affair became a *cause célèbre* and the subject of a British White Paper. An international commission, appointed in 1930 by the League of Nations, barred benches, chairs and screens from the Wall.

After the War

Sixty members of the family of Rabbi Abraham Mordecai Alter of Ger perished in Nazi Europe. His son-in-law, Isaac Meir Alter, was shot before his eyes. Together with his son, Israel, and his son-in-law, Isaac Meir Levin (Chairman of the Agudat Israel Executive), the *Rebbe* left Warsaw in 1940, reaching Italy a few days before it entered the war. The Hasidim of Ger urged their leader to settle in the United States. "I am unable to start a new exile," he replied. So area *Geulah* in Jerusalem saw a revival of some of the glory that was Ger. The *Rebbe* died on *Shavuot* (Pentecost) 1948, and Dr. Isaac Herzog, then Chief Rabbi of Israel, proclaimed in eulogy: "On Shavuot the Torah was given and on Shavuot the Torah was taken away." As the *Har*

A Lubavitch Hasid, London

The New Lubavitch Centre—London

Kfar Habad, Yeshiva—Main Building

Hazeitim (Mount of Olives) was then in Arab hands, the Rabbi was buried in the courtyard of the *Sefat Emet* Yeshiva in Jerusalem.

Today his son Rabbi Israel (b. 1897) has the greatest following of all the *Rebbes*. He has expanded the Yeshiva *Sefat Emet* in Jerusalem and built a Yeshiva *Hiddushe Ha-Rim* in Tel Aviv which was consecrated on *Sivan* ninth, 1969. Ten *Mosdot* with a total of one thousand disciples have been established in various parts of the country. Ger also controls a *Kollel*, a Talmud Torah, and a Yeshiva *Ketanah*. A Yeshiva *Kol Yaacov* has been established in Kfar Atta, near Haifa. The annual budget of all the Gerer *Mosdot* combined amounts to half a million Israeli pounds. The movement is headed by Rabbi Phinehas Menahem Alter, the younger brother of the Rabbi of Ger.

Relatively few Hasidic rabbis reside in Jerusalem. The Holy City, paradoxically enough, has never been the home of many Hasidic rabbis. Among the few who lived there was the Sochaczewer *Rebbe*, Hanoch Heinoch Bornstein (d. 1966), who arrived there in 1923 and set up a number of *Stieblech*. Hungarian Rabbi Joseph Meir Cahana of Spinka (b. 1910) heads the Yeshiva *Imre Joseph* ("Words of Joseph") and Meir Kalisz of Amshinov and Johanan Twersky of Talno. In his *Bet Ha-Midrash* in *Rehov Joseph ben Mattathiah*, Rabbi Yehiel Joshua Rabinowicz (b. 1895) carries on the traditions of Biala and Przysucha. After living in Siedlice until the outbreak of the war, he eluded the Nazis by fleeing to Siberia. After long and arduous wanderings, he arrived in Israel in 1947. After a brief stay in Tel Aviv, he settled in Jerusalem. Devout and unworldly, Rabbi Yehiel Joshua is known as a "miracle worker" and a "great servant of the Lord". He has reprinted some of the Hasidic writings of his grandfather, Rabbi Isaac Jacob of Biala, and has established a Yeshiva *Or Kedoshim* ("Light of the Holy Ones") in Bnei Brak.

At sixty-three *Rehov Ahad Ha-Am*, Tel Aviv, was the residence of Rabbi Aaron Rokeah (1886–1957) of Belz. For three perilous years the *Rebbe* had lived precariously in Nazi Europe, moving from Przemysl to Vishnitz, to Cracow and to Budapest. He even changed his name, first to Singer then to Twersky to confuse the Germans who pursued him so relentlessly.[3] After a brief stay in Haifa he settled in Tel Aviv with his brother, formerly Rabbi of Bilgoraj, and his beadle David Shapira. From Antwerp, from Manchester, from New York and from Lugano, Hasidim would travel to see him. He impressed all sections of the Yishuv with his great attachment to the Land, and his personal example stimulated a wave of Hasidic immigrants from many countries who travelled far in order to see their *Rebbe* in *Eretz Yisrael*. The Rebbe divided his time between Tel Aviv and Jerusalem, where he spent the summer months. On one occasion, when the Jordanians complained to the U.N. Armistice Commission about heavy military traffic on Israeli territory, it transpired that the alleged military convoy consisted of an escort of two hundred and thirty-four civilian vehicles filled with Hasidim of the Rabbi of Belz accompanying him to Jerusalem.

During the Sinai Campaign (October 28 to November 3, 1956), the Rabbi fasted for three days in a marathon prayer for an Israeli victory. He spent all his time alone in his room appealing to the Creator on behalf of the "Israeli army fighting against seven armies." When he finally emerged, he declared: "My sons, we have won with the help of the Almighty". He died in 1957 and, after an interregnum of nine years, was succeeded by Rabbi Issahar Dov (Beril) Rokeah (b. 1948), his brother's son. The youthful *Rebbe*'s marriage in 1966 to Sarah, daughter of Rabbi Moses Hager of *Kiryat Vishnitz*, was the most publicised and picturesque Jewish wedding of the year, attended by thousands of Hasidim from all over the world. Young *Rebbe* Issahar Dov made his home in Jerusalem, where there is a great modern Belz Yeshiva. His former residence in Tel Aviv has been converted into a Yeshiva.

Among the many Rabbis in Tel Aviv are Moses Yehiel Halevy Epstein of Ozarow (b. 1890) author of a monumental work in 17 volumes known as *Esh Dat* ("the Fiery Law"); Rabbi Moses Mordecai Biderman of Lelov (b. 1888); Rabbi Jacob Joseph Halperin of Waslovy in Rumania; Rabbi Samuel Elijah Taub of Modzitz; Rabbi Isaac Friedmann of Bohush (b. 1900); Rabbi Isaac Friedmann of Husyatin; Rabbi Abraham Joshua Heschel Weinberg of Slonym (b. 1898) and Mordecai Sholem Joseph of Sadagora.

Bnei Brak, citadel of learning and site of many *Yeshivot*, has attracted such prominent Hasidic rabbis as Rabbi Hayim Mordecai Rosenbaum (b. 1904) of Nadvorna, Abraham Eiger (b. 1916) of Lublin, Rabbi Jehudah Moses Dancyger (b. 1898) of Alexander and Rabbi Zusya Twersky of Lelov.

Notable among the Hasidic settlements is *Kfar Habad*, five miles from Tel Aviv, established in 1949 by the Rabbi of Lubavitch, Joseph Isaac Schneersohn, for the survivors of the death camps. Lubavitch has a long history of active affiliation with the Land of Israel. In 1823, Dov Baer had established a colony in Hebron. In 1840, Rabbi Menahem

Mendel, the *Tzemah Zedek*, sent over 15,000 roubles to found Synagogues in Jerusalem, Safed, Tiberias, and organised collections to support indigent Lubavitch settlers. His son, Shneur Zalman, kept in close touch with Menahem Mendel Ussishkin (1863–1941), the Zionist, who founded the *Bilu* (initials of *Bet Yaakov Lekhu ve-nelkhah* "O House of Jacob, come ye and let us go," Is. ii. 5), the first modern Zionist pioneering movement, in 1882 and strongly supported *Aliyah*.[4]

Kafar Habad (*Kfar Safriah Habad*) is a self-sufficient settlement, where Hasidim turned farmers breed livestock and poultry. It includes a Talmud Torah, a Yeshiva, a printing and agricultural school and a carpentry workshop. In the winter of 1956, five students were murdered by Arab terrorists and a special memorial institute called *Yad Hamisha* ("Memorial for the Five") was set up in their honour. *Kiryat Vishnitz* (near Bnei Brak), is the one hundred and thirty dunam settlement established by Rumanian Rabbi Hayim Meir Yehiel Hager (d. 1969). It has a diamond polishing plant, industrial workshops, streamlined commercial bakeries, and a Yeshiva *Bet Yisrael Udameshek Eliezer* attended by many students, under the guidance of Moses Joshua Hager. Other institutions include a Yeshiva *Ketana*, a junior Yeshiva, *Kolel Avrahim* (High School for Talmudists), a girls' school, and an old age home. The *Kirya's* annual budget is 900,000 Israeli pounds. Rabbi Hayim Meir's brother, Rabbi Barukh Hager (d. 1967) created a Hasidic milieu in Haifa (*Hadar Ha-Carmel*). In *Ramat Vishnitz* he built a *Kolel Avrahim* (an Academy for advanced Talmudists) and a children's home.

An interesting fairly recent development is the Hasidic *Aliyah* from the United States. One of the leaders of this Exodus from the New World was Rabbi Yekutiel Jehudah, son of Zevi Halberstamm (b. 1904), Rabbi of Klausenburg, whose wife and eleven children were murdered by the Nazis. He established *Shikun Kiryat Zanz*, near Nathania, mainly for settlers from the United States. Founded on a one hundred and nine dunam plot in 1956, it now has a population of over two thousand. "I survived the Holocaust," explains the builder-rabbi, "only in order that I might help rebuild the Land of Israel." *Kiryat Zanz*, too, has its own Yeshiva, a school for girls, a kindergarten and a diamond factory.

The Rabbi of Bobov, Ben Zion Halberstamm, was killed in Lvov in 1941. His son, Rabbi Solomon Halberstamm, found refuge in the United States. In December, 1959 he founded the small town of Bobov near Bat Yam and also established a Yeshiva, *Bnei Ziyyon*, near Jerusalem.

In March 1963, Rabbi Hannaniah Yom Tob Lippe Teitelbaum (1906–64) of Sasov, a descendant of *Yismah Moshe*, founder of Hasidism in Hungary, set up near Ramat Gan a settlement called *Kiryat Yismah Moshe* ("Let Moses rejoice"). He married a cousin, the daughter of his uncle, Rabbi Joel Teitelbaum of Satmar, uniting two distinguished dynasties. And even the Rabbi of Satmar (of New York), despite his opposition to Zionism, is developing in Bnei Brak a settlement called *Kiryat Joel*.

The passionate love of the Hasidim for the Holy Land today finds creative and tangible expression. The largest gathering of Hasidim is to be found in the United States, but Israel has the second largest group, numbering well over fifty thousand. Jerusalem, Tel Aviv and Bnei Brak are the contemporary counterparts of Ger, Satmar and Belz. In no other country are there so many prolific writers on the history of Hasidism, and literally hundreds of volumes have been brought out in the last decades.

Now that the re-established Jewish State is a miraculous *fait accompli*, many Hasidim are among its staunchest supporters, working as well as praying for its welfare and security.

Chapter 24

Defenders of the Faith

Out of the ashes, phoenix-like, a new Hasidism has arisen. Pietists in long, silken *Kapotes* (a long overcoat) and streaming side-curls add colour and character to Jewish life in London, New York and Jerusalem. Proudly they identify themselves as Hasidim of Ger, Belz, Bobov, Lubavitch and Satmar, euphonious names that linger lovingly upon the lips. These are the contemporary Defenders of the Faith, who have replanted the traditions of their fathers in lands of freedom.

Over one hundred and twenty thousand Russian and Polish Jews settled in England between 1870 and the beginning of the First World War. By 1914, London had a Jewish population of some one hundred and fifty thousand. Of these about two-thirds were immigrants from Eastern Europe who had settled there during the last two decades. Among them were a small number of Hasidim worshipping in countless *Hevrot* ("Societies") they had formed in the East End of London. In 1887, these small congregations were welded by Mr. Samuel Montagu, M.P. (first Lord Swaythling, 1832–1911) into the Federation of Synagogues. Among them were the *Jerusalem Shul* in Union Street and the *Hevrat Agudat Ahim Nusah Ari*, at 58 Hanbury Street, which later moved to 18 New Court, Fashion Street.

In the Anglo-Jewish press Hasidism was misunderstood and misrepresented.[1] The first sympathetic interpretation of Hasidism in England was made by Solomon Schechter (1850–1915). On November 13, 1887, he delivered to the Jews' College Literary Society a lecture that stressed the simple grandeur and nobility of Hasidic teaching. This actually represented a change of heart on Schechter's part for Schechter (whose background was Hasidic) had been sharply satirical on the subject in an earlier work, *Letters by Hasidim*.[2]

Israel Zangwill (1864–1918) followed in Schechter's footsteps. In his

Children of the Ghetto published in 1892, Zangwill writes: "In the eighteenth century Israel Baal Shem, the Master of the Name, retired to the mountains to meditate on philosophical truths. He arrived at a creed of cheerful and even stoical acceptance of the Cosmos in all its aspects and a conviction that the incense of an enjoyed pipe was grateful to the Creator. But it is the inevitable misfortune of religious founders to work apocryphal miracles and to raise up an army of disciples who squeeze the teaching of their master into their own mental moulds and are ready to die for the resultant distortion . . . The Baal Shem was succeeded by an army of thaumaturgists, and the wonder-working Rabbis who are in touch with all the spirits of the air enjoy the revenue of princes and the reverence of Popes."[3]

Six years later in his book *The Dreamers of the Ghetto*, Zangwill includes Israel Baal Shem among those Jews who were saturated with the idealistic spirit of the race and who rebelled against the drab existence of their people. "The Baal Shem came," says Zangwill, "to teach man the true life and the true worship . . .[4] and though his spirit ascended to the celestial spheres and held converse with the holy ones, this did not puff him up with vanity."[5]

A number of Hasidim participated in the formation in 1896 of the *Machzike Shomre Shabbat* which later became known as the *Machzike Ha-Dass*, the Spitalfields Great Synagogue, one of the spiritual fortresses of Anglo-Jewry. In 1896, the Austrian Hasidim established a Dzikover *Stiebel* at 37 Fieldgate Street, in the heart of the East End of London. On March 14, 1908 they even enacted their own bye-laws (*Takkanot*),[6] which consisted of seventeen articles. The Annual General Meeting of members was to be held during the month of *Tishri*. The Executive consisted of a President, (1st *Gabbai*), Vice-President (Second *Gabbai*), six members of the Committee, one Treasurer, two Trustees, a secretary and a collector. Every Sabbath and Festival a prayer was offered in honour of Rabbi Alter Ezekiel Eli Horowitz and for Rabbi Joshua Horowitz, the *Rebbes* of Dzikov. Annually on the eleventh of *Iyar*, the Hasidim commemorated the *Yahrzeit* of Rabbi Naftali of Ropcryce. On May 13, 1914 larger premises were opened at 30 Dunk Street. Among its leaders were Naftali Gerstler, Nahman Israel, Moses Israel and Aaron Feigenbaum.

In 1900, the Hasidim of Rizhyn set up a centre at 13 Buxton Street. Eight years earlier, a *Stiebel Kehal Hasidim* was founded firstly at 18a Old Montagu Street and later in Black Lion Yard to cater for Hasidim on a "non-sectarian basis". On November 6, 1892 it became affiliated to the

Federation of Synagogues.[7] Among prominent members were Asher Weingarten, David Frost (1872–1938), Abraham Phinehas Landau, Barukh Wolkowitch (1833–1953) and Hanina Bluzenstein.[8] Meanwhile, a number of Hasidim were making a name for themselves. For instance, Moses Avigdor Chaikin (1852–1928) wrote *Sepher Kelale Ha-Poskim* ("Rules of the Codifiers"). For thirty years (1890–1920) this fervent Hasid of Habad served Anglo-Jewry as Minister in Sheffield, as Chief Minister of the Federation of Synagogues and as a member of the London *Beth Din*.[9] "His was the joyousness of the true Hasid," declared Chief Rabbi J. H. Hertz, "the optimism, the charity in judgement, the obstinate refusal to despair of his fellow mortals and their destiny, which made him a friend to all, beloved of all, loving God and loving all God's children."[10]

Belgian fugitives from the First World War founded in North-East London such *Stieblech* as the *Schiff Bet Ha-Midrash* (founded by Moses Samuel Schiff), and *Selig Shemiah's Shul* and, in 1916, Galician-born Judah (Leibish) Rickel (d. 1929) opened a *Stiebel* for his countrymen. Among the worshippers here were Hayim David Orlinsky (d. 1941), Hayim Stark (d. 1952), Hayim Rothenberg (1878–1941) and Judah Waller (1871–1953) a devoted Hasid of Bobov.

Among the early pioneers of Hasidism were Rabbi Meshullam Zusya Golditch (1876–1940), father of Dayan I. Golditch of Manchester and popularly known as "Reb Zusya", and Rabbi Alter Noah (Kohen-Zedek) Kaizer (1850–1920), father of the Yiddish writer A. M. Kaizer (1896–1967). Rabbi Noah Kaizer was born in Neshitz, Ukraine, and ministered in a rabbinical capacity to a number of communities in Russia, Austria and Rumania finally emigrating to the Holy Land. He came to England in 1895, where he published a seventy-page Cabbalistic treatise *Nesivot Hen* ("The Paths of Grace")[11] as well as other works.[12] While in England, he studied old Hebrew Cabbalistic manuscripts at Oxford and Cambridge.[13]

The 1920's brought more Hasidic rabbis to London. In 1923 Rabbi Arye Leib Twersky of Turisk, son of Mordecai Zusya, Rabbi of Jassy, Rumania, opened a *Bet Ha-Midrash* in Sidney Square which he later transferred to Cazenove Road. A scion of Rizhyn, his home became a haven of refuge, offering hospitality to many people from the continent. Rabbi Hanoh Heinoh Dov Rubin of Sasov arrived in 1924, but died barely five years later. The scholarly Rabbi Shalom, son of Mordecai Joseph Moskovitz of Shatz (1878–1958), established his court at 67 Chicksand Street. In 1929, Rabbi Zusya Aryeh, son of Ephraim

Zalman Margulies (1885–1957) of Przemyslany, established *Kehillat Yisrael* ("Community of Israel") a *Stiebel* at 45 Umberston Street, in the East End of London. He later moved to the North-West, Cricklewood, and was one of the founders of the North-West London Jewish Day School. Rabbi Yehudah Szenfeld (1892–1967) of Kielce established his *Bet Ha-Midrash Kol Yaakov* ("The Voice of Jacob") first at 17 Fenton Street and then in Golders Green. A gentle and kindly sage, he devoted himself to fostering *Taharat Ha-Mishpacha* ("Jewish family purity"). Both the *Rebbes* of Turisk and Kielce settled in Israel. Another scholarly rabbi of retiring disposition was Rabbi Jacob Joseph Spira (d. 1946), a descendant of Dynov, and Ropcryce. He was the author of a number of works.[14]

Outstanding among the Hasidic pioneers in London was Rabbi Nathan David Rabinowicz. Nathan David was born in Ozarow on May 2, 1899, heir to ancestral traditions that trace back to the Holy Jew of Przysucha. An *illui* (prodigy), he studied in the *Yeshivot* of Ozarow and Radzmyn where his uncle and guardian, the Rabbi of Radzmyn, prophesied a brilliant future for him as a *Gadol B'Yisrael* ("A great one in Israel"). He was eighteen when he married Szaindla Brakha, first and favourite daughter of Alter Yisrael Shimon of Novominsk. Later, he obtained his *Semikhah* from Rabbi Yehiel Meir Ha-Levy Halstock of Ostrowiec and Rabbi Zevi Ezekiel Michelsohn of the Warsaw *Bet Din*.

To his Biala *Stiebel*, first at 6 Osborn Place in London's East End, and then at 10 St. Mark's Rise, in Dalston, streamed people from all walks of life, and of all ages. There were those who had known his grandfather, Rabbi Isaac Jacob, in the old country, and there were others for whom this was the first introduction to Hasidism. His whole life was Torah, and wandering through its fathomless profundities he found challenge and fulfilment. Students enjoyed debating contemporary issues with him and sharpening their young wits against the whetstone of his fiery intellect. They found him approachable and emphatic, articulate and perceptive, equally able to communicate with old time Hasidim and their semi-alienated children.

Londoners who had never heard of Hasidism found a friend in the Rabbi of Biala. He genuinely liked people and his approach was positive. Like Levi Isaac of Berdichev, he looked for a man's good points rather than his failings. Often he would quote the verse: "For the House of Israel is the vineyard of the Lord of Hosts" (Is. v. 7) adding, "Who am I that I should disparage or condemn that which belongs to God himself?" No one was to be thrust out of the fold. Not with "fire and brimstone" but with love were people to be brought back to their Father in heaven. There were no "visiting hours" here. All day long the Rabbi's door was open. All were free to consult him, and most left his presence comforted. Among the Rabbi's supporters were Michael Caplin (1882–1960), Asher Zelig Rubinstein and Leibish Freedman.

The Biala Rabbi's literary output was considerable, and he wrote incisive commentaries on the Pentateuch, the "Ethics of the Fathers" and the Zohar. These writings are as yet unpublished, but one small slim volume has seen the light of day—the *Ethical Will*[15] written in the darkening shadow of illness and death. It is a remarkable document, a loving and luminous message to his children, his wife, his closely-knit Hasidim. Comfortingly, he writes of death as a transition, the changing of one garment for another. With fatherly exhortations he urges his followers to live in fraternal harmony and keep faith with God and man. Steadfastly he voices acceptance of his fate and trust in "The Master of the Universe". So, even as he died, he showed men how to live. His is a glowing testament to Hasidism at its most inspiring level.

There are small groups of Hasidim in the North-West suburbs of London, in Cricklewood under Rabbi B. Finkelstein, and in Golders Green under Rabbi E. Halpern, Berish Hager (d. 1968) and Simha Rubin of Sasov. The largest Hasidic concentration is to be found in North London. In the Stamford Hill area, centring on Cazenove Road, over five thousand Hasidim live. These numerous *Stieblech* include Belzer, Bobover, Gerer and Satmarer. There are many *Bate-Midrash Talmude Torah* and *Yeshivot*, presenting a colourful variety of different Hasidic dynasties. Most of the Hasidic synagogues are affiliated to the Union of Orthodox Hebrew congregations set up in 1928 by Rabbi Victor Schonfeld (1880–1930) and enlarged by his son, Rabbi Dr. Solomon Schonfeld (b. 1912). Today Hasidim and *Mitnagdim* have transcended their one-time rivalries and co-operate harmoniously in Union activities relating to *Shehita, Rabbinate, Mikvaot, Hevra Kaddisha* and *Kashrut*. The Hasidim operate their own educational network, the *Yesodey Hatorah* schools (established in October, 1942 by Wolf Schiff, Getzel Berger and Phinehas Landau), the *Metivta* Talmudical College and a *Bet Jacob* Seminary for girls.

Lubavitch did not arrive in London until 1959, but instantly made its presence felt. A synagogue centre has been built (at a cost of 120,000 dollars) in Stamford Hill, and primary and grammar schools have been set up by dynamic young emissaries of Rabbi Schneerson in New York. Thus Lubavitch helps fill the vacuum left by the departure to Israel of such men as the Rabbi of Trisk who settled in Bnei Brak.

There are also small Hasidic groups in Manchester, among them the *Kehal Hasidim* Synagogue founded in 1902 in Red Bank. A *Nusah Ari Stiebel* was established in Glasgow by Simon Felstein; in 1914 it became known as *Bet Jacob* Synagogue, and in 1938 it amalgamated with the *Poale Zedek* Synagogue. Their spiritual leaders were S. D. Morgenstern, J. D. Luria (d. 1957) and J. D. Siroka. In 1897, the *Hasidishe* Synagogue was established in Leeds, and there is a *Nusah Ari* Synagogue in Liverpool.

United States of America

From 1881 to 1925, over two million five hundred thousand Jews emigrated to the United States of America. The overwhelming number were of East European origin: 1,190,590 from Russia, 281,150 from Austria-Hungary and 95,534 from Rumania.[16] After the First World War, Hasidic Rabbis began to come. Rabbi Yehuda Arye Perlow (1887–1961), a brother of the Rabbi of Novominsk, A. Y. S. Perlow, arrived in New York in 1925. Rabbi Perlow was the author of *Lev Arye* ("The Heart of a Lion"), published in 1939, and *Kol Yehuda* ("The Voice of Judah"). South Ninth Street in Williamsburg, Brooklyn, became one of the first outposts of Hasidism.

Today the dynasty of Novominsk is represented by Rabbi Nahum Mordecai Perlow. A dedicated scholar and an active member of the Aguda, Rabbi Nahum leads a life of study and service to his Hasidim in the tradition of his great father, Rabbi A. Y. S. Perlow of Novominsk. Another early arrival was Rabbi Joshua Heshel Rabinowicz (1860–1938), the Rebbe of Monastyrshshche, one of the founders in 1928 of the Union of the Grand Rabbis of the United States and Canada.

Another Hasidic pioneer was Rabbi Jacob (d. 1946), son of Rabbi Israel of Stolin (d. 1921), who arrived in New York in 1923. He ministered to the four Stolin *Stieblech* in New York and one in Detroit.

When the sun set for Hasidim in Eastern Europe, it rose for them in the New World. With the influx of refugees from Hungary, Czechoslovakia and Rumania, a small part of Hasidic life was transplanted to New York. Many Hasidic families settled in the Williamsburg section of Brooklyn. One of the foremost leaders is Rabbi Joel

Teitelbaum of Satu-Mare (Satmar) in Hungary. Born in 1885, Rabbi Joel is a descendant of Rabbi Moses Teitelbaum (1769–1841), author of *Yismah Moshe* ("Let Moses Rejoice"), a famous homiletical commentary on the Pentateuch, founder of the dynasties of Satmar and Sziget in Carpathian Russia. Rabbi Joel succeeded his father, Hananiah Yom Tov Lippa, author of *Kedushat Yom Tov* ("Sanctity of the Festival"), in 1905. Together with his family, Rabbi Joel was deported to Bergen-Belsen in 1944 and was snatched from the very jaws of death by Dr. Kastner's special intervention with Himmler. After a brief stay in Switzerland, he came to New York in 1946. He is the author of a number of important works.[17]

The Satmar community (*Kehal Yetev Lev Desatmar*) is a self-sufficient and cohesive entity.[18] It issues periodicals, leaflets and circulars, maintains a weekly newspaper, *Der Yid* ("The Jew"), and until recently published *Die Yiddishe Woch* ("The Jewish Weekly"). It has its own welfare organisations, a holiday fund for orphaned children, *Bikkur Holim* ("Visiting the Sick") and a Burial Society. It operates its own butcher's shops selling *glat Kosher* (ultra Kosher) meat, *Mikvaot* (ritual baths), a *Shatness* laboratory, a kindergarten, a *Metivta* (Talmudical College) a *Bet Rachel* School for girls and a bakery where hand-made *Matzot* are prepared. In all, the Satmar *Kehilla* is responsible for the education of over four thousand children. Of these, two thousand two hundred attend the schools in Williamsburg.

The *Rebbe* of Satmar is the spiritual head of the *Natorei Karta* (Lit. "Guardians of the City", a group of orthodox Jewish zealots led by Amram Blau, who oppose political Zionism and do not recognise the State of Israel). Motivated by a passionate commitment to traditional Judaism, Hasidim of Satmar commit acts that most other Jews deplore, such as demonstrating in front of the White House in Washington to protest against alleged "methodical oppression and extermination of religion in Israel."

The district in which most of the Hasidim live is undergoing radical population changes, and the result has been some interesting experiments in Hasidic living. In 1963, a group of Hasidim set up a community in Rockland County, about forty miles from Times Square. Similarly, New Square named after Squir in the Ukraine, was established in Spring Valley, thirty miles from New York, by Rabbi Jacob Joseph Twersky (1900–68) of Squira. The Hasidim inhabit modern Cape Cod cottages scattered over one hundred and thirty acres of grassy wooded slope in Spring Valley. They are mostly artisans and diamond merchants,

235

who commute daily to New York. The son-in-law of the Rabbi of Squira, Rabbi Mordecai (Mottele) Hager of Vishnitz, principal of Yeshiva *Ahavat Yisrael*, leads thirty families in a self-contained community in Monsey.

Whilst Satmar and Squira deliberately live in virtual isolation, Lubavitch has developed a comparatively cosmic orientation. Rabbi Joseph Isaac Schneerson, sixth *Rebbe* of Lubavitch, arrived in New York on March 19, 1940, and devoted the last decade of his life to setting up a framework for Jewish religious education. He founded the *Central Yeshiva Tomchei Tmimim* schools with branches in the United States and Canada. He set up *Machne Yisrael* ("The Camp of Israel") to strengthen orthodoxy, and *Merkaz L'Inyonei Chinuch*, the central organisation for Jewish education (established in 1947). He established girls' schools, *Bet Sarah* ("House of Sarah") and *Bet Rivkah* ("House of Rebecca"), in Canada, the Holy Land, France and Morocco, as well as the *Kehot* Publication Society, which publishes (in English, French, Russian, Spanish, Yiddish and Hebrew) texts on *Habad* philosophy and a vast assortment of material, ranging from elementary guide books on Jewish religion to books on Hasidic philosophy.

After the war, Rabbi Joseph Isaac established *Ezrat Pletim Vesidurom*, with an office in Paris under Rabbi Benjamin Gorodezki, for the relief and rehabilitation of refugees. To thousands of persons physically and spiritually displaced he brought material assistance and a message of hope.

The present Rabbi of Lubavitch, Menahem Mendel Schneerson, was born on *Nisan* 11, 1902 in Yekatarinoslaw, Russia. In 1929 he married the daughter of Rabbi Joseph Isaac Schneerson. He attended the Universities of Moscow and Berlin and studied electrical engineering at the Sorbonne. In 1942 he was appointed Chairman of the Executive Committee of *Merkaz L'Inyonei Chinuch*, and in 1951 he succeeded his father-in-law.

Ufarazta (Gen. xxviii. 14) "And thou shalt spread", is the theme of a melody popular with Lubavitch Hasidim, and it is also the motto of the present Rabbi. He has expanded the already far-reaching and manifold activities of the movement. To give one instance, he has reached out to North Africa, and now Habad brings the Hasidic teachings to the *Sephardim* of Casablanca, Marrakesh, Sefrou, and Meknes. A network of sixty-seven *Oholei Joseph Itzhak* Lubavitch institutions, evening classes, girls' schools and a teachers' seminary have been established to provide for many pupils throughout the world.

Lubavitch disciples have organised a "Peace Corps", student evangelists who bring Judaism to Jews in many far-flung places at home and abroad. A total of 35,000 children are enrolled in the Lubavitch schools in the United States, North Africa, Argentine, Denmark, Brazil, Italy and Canada. Rabbi Shemariah Gourary, brother-in-law of the rabbi, is the director of the United Lubavitch *Yeshivot*, with fifteen branches throughout the U.S.A., where many youngsters receive a Torah education.

From 770 Eastern Parkway, in Brooklyn, New York, the Rabbi directs his far-reaching spiritual empire. He receives visitors on Sundays and Thursdays, starting at 8 p.m. and often continuing until 8 a.m. At such private audiences he meets over three thousand people. The rest of the day is spent in supervising Habad activities.[19]

Another celebrated Rebbe is Rabbi Shapira, a descendant of Rabbi Elimelekh Shapira of Dinov, author of *Bne Issahar* ("Children of Issachar"). Rabbi Shapira, the Bluzhever *Rebbe*, survived the Nazi Holocaust. His life and the lives of 200 other camp inmates were saved at the eleventh hour by the arrival of the American liberation forces headed by a tank driven by a young Jewish soldier, Pinhas Kohn, of Pittsburgh. Also headquartered in Brooklyn is Rabbi Solomon Halberstamm (b. 1908) of Bobov. There he directs his Yeshiva *Kedushat Zion* and the new Hasidic city *Kiryat Bobov* (Bobov city) which is being built in Queens, New York. Boro Park, Brooklyn is the home of the Hasidim of Stolin.

Until just recently a prominent part in New York Hasidic life was played by Rabbi Abraham Joshua Heschel, *Rebbe* of Kopyczynce (1888–1967), an active member of the Aguda and a strong supporter of the *Hinukh Atzmai* (the Aguda's educational network in Israel). The *Rebbe* visited the Holy Land ten times. "To love a great *Talmid Hakham* is easy," he once remarked. "But to love the ordinary man, the one who is even difficult at times, is true *Ahavat Yisrael* (love of Israel)".

Hasidic dynasties flourishing in New York today include Boyan (Rabbi Mordecai Shlomo Friedmann), Talner (Rabbi Abraham Twersky), Kosienice (Rabbi Israel Eliezer Hopstein 1900–66), Amshinov (Rabbi Yerahmiel Yehuda Meir) and Spinke (Rabbi J. Weiss). There are also Hasidic rabbis in Chicago, in Philadelphia and in other American cities. Ten per cent of American *Yeshivot* in the New World are Hasidic, and 8.1 per cent of the Jewish children in New York attend Hasidic schools.[20] There are between 40,000 and 50,000 Hasidim in New York City.

In Montreal, there is a *Metivta* founded by the Rabbi of Klausenburg under the direction of Rabbi Samuel Undsorfer (a former *Rosh Yeshiva* in England), as well as *Yeshivot* under the auspices of Lubavitch and Satmar. There is also a large Lubavitch day school. Toronto, too, has a *Yesodey Hatorah* School. There are also Hasidic groups in the suburb of St. Kilda in Melbourne.

One eighth of Antwerp's Jewish community are Hasidim. Their spiritual leader is the octogenarian Rabbi Itzikel Gewurtzman, whose home is in a house behind Pelican Street.

The second half of the twentieth century has seen a diminution of Hasidism. There are probably no more than two hundred thousand Hasidim throughout the world, but its significance cannot be estimated on a numerical basis. Today the movement is receiving the careful attention of writers and thinkers of many denominations. In the wake of Martin Buber, a neo-mysticism or neo-Hasidism is evolving. Although he has introduced new elements into Hasidism and has evolved a theory of Hasidism that the Besht might not instantly recognise, Buber is largely responsible for the new interest in this remarkable revival movement. "The flowering period of the Hasidic movement lasted five generations," wrote Buber. "The Zaddikim of these five generations offered us a number of religious personalities of a vitality, a spiritual strength, a manifold originality such as have never, to my knowledge, appeared together in so short a time-span in the history of religion. But the most important thing about these *Zaddikim* is that each of them was surrounded by a community which lived a brotherly life, and who could live in this way because there was a leading person in their midst who brought each one nearer to the other by bringing them all nearer to that in which they believed. In a century which was, apart from this, not very productive religiously, obscure Polish and Ukrainian Jewry produced the greatest phenomenon we know in the history of the spirit . . . a society which lives by its faith."[21]

Hasidism is many things to many people. It is Judaism in its finest, most lively and creative form. Hasidism is the struggle for social justice; concern for the poor and the underprivileged; spiritual democratisation, the hallowing of the everyday.

Hasidism brought new hope and new happiness to hundreds of thousands in the darkest days of Jewish history. It brushed away the cobwebs and revitalised Judaism not by introducing revolutionary doctrines, but simply by leading the people back to the principles preached by the great prophets and teachers of Israel.

Today Hasidism exerts a discernible influence on Israeli writers.[22] Its inspiration can be detected in the poetry of Nobel Prize winner Nelly Sachs, the stories of Shmuel Yoseph Agnon—another Nobel Prize winner—the novels of Isaac Bashevis Singer and Eli Wiesel, and the writings of Abraham Joshua Heschel, even as it can be seen in the works of their predecessors, Isaac Leib Peretz, Sholom Asch and Franz Kafka. Our super-sophisticated and over-organised society may well recall with nostalgia the soaring ecstasy of Hasidism and the radiance that illumined the Jewish world for two hundred years. And, recalling this, they may realise that Hasidism has a relevant and immediate message for this generation, and the next.

NOTES FOR CHAPTER 1

1. Wichnitzer, Mark: *A History of Jewish Crafts and Guilds*, New York, 1965, p. 209; Isaac Lewin: "The Protection of Jewish Religious Rights by Royal Edicts in Ancient Poland" in *Quarterly Bulletin of the Polish Institute of Arts and Sciences in America*, April, 1943.
2. Isserles, Moses: *Responsa*, Amsterdam, 1711, Nos. 63 and 64.
3. *Yeven Mezula* (A Chronicle of the Massacres in 1648), Venice, 1562.
4. Dubnow, Simon M. *Pinkas Ha-medinah* (The Minutes of the Lithuanian Council of Provinces), Berlin, 1925. Halpern, Israel, *Pinkas Vaad Arba Arazot* (Acta Congressus Judaeorum Regni Polaniae, 1580–1764), Jerusalem, 1945; "The Council of Four Lands and the Hebrew Book" in *Kirjath Sepher* IX (Jerusalem, October 1932–33), pp. 367–94; Weinryb, Bernard, *Texts and Studies in the Communal History of Polish Jewry*, New York, 1950, p. 14.
5. Dubnow, *History of the Jews in Russia and Poland*, Vol. 1, p. 112.
6. *Ibid.*, pp. 116–18.
7. Lew, Meyer S., *The Jews of Poland*, London, 1944, pp. 90–92.
8. Dubnow, *op. cit.*, pp. 145–6.
9. *Ibid.*, pp. 166–7.
10. Wolf, L., *Menasseh Ben Israel's Mission to Oliver Cromwell*, London, 1901, p. 87.
11. Halpern, Israel, "Al sakanat Gerush liklal Yisrael be Poilen veLite be-mahatzit ha-sheminah shel mea hashvaesra" (Threatened Expulsion of Polish and Lithuanian Jewry in the Latter Half of the Seventeenth Century) *Zion* XVII (Jerusalem, 1952), pp. 65–74.
12. Balaban, Majer, *Die Juden Stadt von Lublin*, Berlin, 1919, pp. 50, 106.
13. Dubnow, *op. cit.*, p. 179.

NOTES FOR CHAPTER 2

1. iii. 21.
2. *Hagigah*, 11b.
3. *Ibid.*, 14b.
4. *Sanhedrin*, 65b and 67b.
5. *Yerushalmi, Sanhedrin*, VII.
6. Tractate *Eikhalot* ed. Jellinek, *Bet Ha-Midrash*, Leipzig, 1853, II pp. 40–47.
7. *Shem Olam*, Vienna, 1891, p. 11.
8. Güdermann, Moritz (1835–1918), *Geschichte des Erziehungwesens und der Kultur der abendländischen Juden während des Mittelalters und der neuen Zeit*, Vienna 1880–88, Heb. Tran. Part 1, p. 141; Kramer, Simon G. *God and Man in the Sefer Hasidim*, New York, 1966.

9. *Zohar*, 11, 149b, 152a.
10. Horodezky, S. A. *Hatekuphah*, XXII (Warsaw, 1926), p. 30, note 1.
11. *The Life of Gluckel of Hameln* ed. by Beth Zion Abrahams, London, 1962, pp. 45–46.
12. *Mayan Ganim*, quoted by Dubnow, *op. cit.*, p. 134.
13. *Autobiography of Solomon Maimon*, London, 1954, p. 43.
14. Dubnow, *Nationalism and History*—Essays on old and new Judaism, ed. by Koppel S. Pinson, Philadelphia, 1958, pp. 4–5.
15. Abrahams, Israel, *Jewish Life in the Middle Ages*, London, 1932, p. 187.
16. *Toledot, Vayyeshev*, Lvov, 1863.
17. Maimon, *op. cit.*, pp. 31–32.
18. *Ben Porat Yoseph, Tzav*, ed. Lvov.
19. *Shibhe Ha-Besht*, Tel Aviv, 1947, pp. 16–17.
20. Isserles, *op. cit.*, No. 7.

NOTES FOR CHAPTER 3

1. According to a Lubavitch tradition the date of birth was 18th *Elul*.
2. *Shibhe Ha-Besht*, p. 13.
3. Abrahams, L., *Midrash Ribash Tov*, Kecskement, 1927, p. 45.
4. *Shibhe Ha-Besht*, p. 41.
5. *Ibid.*, pp. 44–45.
6. Eibeschütz, Jonathan *Luhot Edut*, Altona, 1755, p. 57; Heschel, A. J. "Rabbi Gershon Kutover", in *The Hebrew Union College Annual*, XXIII, Cincinnati, 1950–1, p. 18.
7. *Shibhe Ha-Besht*, 2, 4; Heschel, *op. cit.*, p. 24.
8. *Maggid Debarav L'Yaakov*, ed. Solomon of Lutzk, Korzec, 1781.
9. Buber, *Mamre*, London, 1946, p. 106.
10. *Toledot*, 174b, 58c, 86d.
11. Preface to *Toledot*; Dresner, Samuel, H., *The Zaddik*, New York, 1959, p. 51.
12. *Zavaat Ha-Ribash* (Testament of the Besht), Warsaw, 1913, p. 9.
13. *Toledot*, 59b.
14. Buber, *Tales of the Hasidim*, Vol. 1, p. 5.
15. *Ethics of the Fathers*, VI: 1.
16. Lubavitch give the date as 18th *Sivan*.

NOTES FOR CHAPTER 4

1. Maimon, *op. cit.*, pp. 173–4.
2. *Ibid.*, pp. 175–6.
3. *Shibhe Ha-Besht*, p. 64; Dresner, *op. cit.*, p. 50.
4. Preface to *Toledot*.
5. Dresner, *op. cit.*, p. 251.
6. *Toledot, Bo*.
7. *Ben Porat Yoseph, Vayyehi*.
8. *Toledot*, 85b.

9. *Tosephta to Midrash Phinehas*, Bilgoraj, 1929, p. 21; Heschel, A. J. "Rabbi Phinehas Koritzer" in *Yivo Bleter*, Journal of the Yiddish Scientific Institute, Vol. XXXIII, pp. 1–48.
10. Heschel, *op. cit.*, pp. 44–45.

NOTES FOR CHAPTER 5

1. Berger, Israel, *Esser Orot*. Piotrkow, 1907, p. 55; Shapira, David, "Levi Yitzhak (of Berdichev)" in *Men of the Spirit*, ed. Leo Jung, New York, 1964, pp. 403–15.
2. *Keddushat Levi*, Slawuta, 1789, p. 9.

NOTES FOR CHAPTER 6

1. Barukh of Shklow in his introduction to the Hebrew translation of Euclid's *Geometry*, Hague, 1820.
2. Finn, Samuel Joseph, *Kiryah Neemanah*, Vilna, 1871.
3. Katzenellenbogen, Abraham, *Hesped Al Hagru*, Vilna, 1871.
4. Eibeschütz, Jonathan, *op. cit.*, p. 71.
5. Rabbi Hayim of Volozhin, in *Hut Hameshulosh*, No. 9, see Ginzberg, Louis, *Students, Scholars and Saints*, Philadelphia, 1943, p. 140.
6. Cohen, Israel, *Vilna*, Philadelphia, 1943, p. 225.
7. Maimon, *op. cit.*, p. 172.
8. Dubnow, *Toledot Ha-Hasidut*, p. 112.
9. Commentary on *Proverbs* XXIV: 31 and XXV: 4; Ginzberg, *op. cit.*, p. 140.
10. *Zavaat Ha-Ribash*, p. 23.
11. *Toledot*, 105b.
12. Hielman, *Bet Rabbi*, Pt. 1, Chapter XII.
13. Dubnow, *Geschichte des Chasidismus*, Berlin, 1931, Vol. 1, pp. 181–2.
14. Cohen, *op. cit.*, pp. 235–7.
15. *Ibid.*, p. 237.
16. Dubnow, *Toledot*, p. 121.
17. *Ibid.*
18. Hielman, *op. cit.*, p. 40; Teitelbaum, *Ha-Rav M'Liady*, pp. 218–21.
19. Maimon, *op. cit.*, p. 240.
20. Psalms CIX: 126; *Berakhot* 54a: Cohen, *op. cit.*, p. 240.
21. *Ibid.*, Dubnow, *op. cit.*, pp. 141ff.
22. Marcus, Jacob, *The Jew in the Mediaeval World*, Cincinnati, 1938, pp. 276–8.
23. Cohen, *op. cit.*, p. 244.
24. Levin, Joshua Heshel, *Alijot Elijahu*, Stettin, 1856, p. 74.
25. Dubnow, *History*, Vol. 1, pp. 375–6.
26. Klausner, Israel, *Vilna bi-Tekufat ha-Gaon*, Jerusalem, 1942, pp. 20–45.
27. Rabinowitsch, W. Z. *Lithuanian Hasidim*, p. 46: Dubnow, *Yevreyskaya Starina*, Vol. III, p. 84ff, St. Petersburg, 1910: Hessen, J. *Yevreyi v Rosiyi*, p. 142ff, St. Petersburg, 1906.

NOTES FOR CHAPTER 7

1. Steinmann, Eliezer, *Beer Ha-Hasidut, Habad*, Vol. 1, p. 231.
2. *Ibid.*
3. Horodezky, *Leaders of Hasidism*, p. 49.
4. Teitelbaum, *op. cit.*, pp. 48–9.
5. *Ibid.*, p. 147.
6. Hilman, *Iggrot Baal Ha-Tanya*, p. 238.
7. In Yiddish by Uriel Zimmer, New York, 1958 and in England by Raphael Ben Zion, Los Angeles, 1945, and by Nissan Mindel, *Liqqutei Amarim*, New York, 1962.
8. Mindel, N., *Tanya*, p. XVIII.
9. *Ibid.*, p. XXXI, note 17.
10. *Tanya*, Chapter XIII; Jacobs, Louis, *Tract on Ecstasy*, London, 1963; A bibliography of *Habad* is given by Habermann, A. M. in *Jubilee Volume for Zalman Shocken*, Jerusalem, 1952, pp. 293–370.

NOTES FOR CHAPTER 8

1. Buber, *Tales of Rabbi Nachman*, Tran. by Maurice Friedman, New York, 1956, pp. 24–25.
2. *Shibhe Moharan*, Lvov, 1874, p. 49.
3. Newman, Louis, *The Hasidic Anthology*, New York, 1944, p. 299.
4. Rabinowicz, Z. M. "Yahas ha-Cabbalah V'ha-Hasidut el Ha-Rambam" in *Moses ben Maimon*, ed. by J. L. Fishman, Jerusalem, 1935, pp. 279–87.
5. *Shibhe*, p. 164.
6. Horodezky, *Ha-Hasidut*, II, p. 40.
7. *Kitve Rabbi Nahman*, ed. Steinmann, Tel Aviv, 1951, p. 305.
8. *Likute Moharan*, Ostrog, 1821, 2, 5.
9. *Shibhe*, 9b.
10. *Sepher Ha-Midot*, Lvov, 1872.
11. *Sihot V'Sippurim Moharan*, Jerusalem, 1910, 23, 24.
12. *Likute Tephilot*, Zolkiew, 1872.
13. *Likkute Moharan Tanina*, Mogilev, 1811, 2, 8.
14. Gottlober, Abraham, B. *Ha-Boker*, Warsaw, 1876, VI, p. 75.
15. Horodezky, *Ha-Hasidut*, III, p. 29.
16. Nathan of Nemirov, *Haye Moharan*, Lvov, 1872, 8. 9. 12.; 18.
17. *Ibid.*
18. Minkin, Jacob, S. *The Romance of Hasidism*, New York, 1955, pp. 263–4.
19. Buber, *op. cit.*, p. 43.
20. Levin, Meyer, *The Golden Mountain*, New York, 1951, p. XIII.
21. Horodezky, Berlin, 1922; D. Kahana, Warsaw, 1923; Steinmann, Tel Aviv, 1951.
22. New York, 1956.
23. New York, 1932.

NOTES FOR CHAPTER 9

1. *Menorat Zahav*, Warsaw, 1902, p. 7; see Landau, Bezalel, *Rabbi Elimelekh of Lezajsk,* Jerusalem, 1963, p. 196; See also *Sefer Tiferet ha-Ahim,* Warsaw, 1924.
2. *Sanhedrin,* 37b.
3. Michelson, A. S. B., *Ohel Elimelekh,* Przemysl, 1910, p. 177.
4. Shtik, Eliezer, Zeev, *Sihot Yekarim,* Satmar, p. 1b.
5. Bedek, Menahem, Mendel, *Yalkut Menahem,* Vilna, 1903, p. 16.
6. *Ohel Elimelekh,* No. 192.
7. Ehrman, Dov, *Devarim Arevim,* Munkacz, 1903, p. 17b.
8. Rabbi Henoh Wagshal, quoted by Landau, *op. cit.,* p. 320, 326 note 1.

NOTES FOR CHAPTER 10

1. Mahler gives the number as 750,000 (*Yidn in Amoliken Poylen in likht fun Tzeferen,* Warsaw, 1938, pp. pp. 30–37). Thaddeuz Czascki gives the number as 900,000 (*Presprawa O Zydaichi i Kaitaitch,* Cracow, 1810, p. 117).
2. Dubnow, *History,* Vol. 1, p. 277.
3. Roth, Cecil, *History of the Great Synagogue,* London, 1950, p. 108.
4. Rabbi Joshua of Ostrow, *Toledot Adam,* Juzefow, 1874, in *Rumze Hanukkah.*
5. *Avodat Yisrael,* Juzefow, 1842, *Parshat Vayishlah, Abot* II:2; IV:9.
6. Printed by his grandson, Juzefow, 1842.
7. *Bet Yisrael,* Warsaw, 1876.
8. Anna Potocka "Pamietniki" S 35; Leone Dembowski "Pamietnik" *Ateneum* 1882 3.2, See Rabinowitz, *Ha-Magid M'Koziniece.*
9. *The Cambridge History of Poland 1697–1935,* Cambridge, 1951, p. 210.
10. Rabinowitz, *op. cit.,* p. 59, notes 47–51.
11. Walden, Moses Menahem, *Niflaot Ha-Rabbi,* Warsaw, 1911.
12. Berger, Israel, *Esser Orot,* p. 44b.
13. Walden, *op. cit.,* p. 290.
14. Marcus, A., *Der Chassidismus,* Heb. Tran. Tel Aviv, p. 114.
15. Yitzhak Eisig of Komarna, *Eikhal Habrakha,* Lvov, 1872, p. 276b.
16. Berger, *op. cit.,* 84, 96.

NOTES FOR CHAPTER 11

1. *Yoreh Deah,* ccxlii. 15.
2. *Megillah,* 13a.
3. *Likute Ramal,* Piotrkow, 1910.
4. Rashi and *Rabbenu* Tam differed as to the order of the texts of the four paragraphs in the Bible (Exod. xiii. 1; Exod. xiii. 11. Deut. vi. 4–9; Deut. 11. 13–21). Some pious Jews put on two pairs of *Tephillin* according to the two versions. Rabinowicz, H. M. *Rabbi Jacob Yitzhok P'zisha,* Piotrkow, 1932.
5. Rabinowicz, *op. cit.,* p. 108.
6. Not in 1815 as in *Niflaot Ha-Yehudi,* p. 16 or Marcus, *op. cit.,* p. 16.

7. Levinstein, Joseph, Piotrkow, 1909; *Torat Ha-Yehudi*, Bilgoraj, 1911; *Keter Ha-Yehudi*, Jerusalem, 1929, by Aryeh Mordecai Rabinowicz; *Kitve Kodesh*, Warsaw, 1926, by Moses Joshua Leib Taub.
8. Rabbi Nathan Nato of Korbiel, *Rishpe Esh Ha-Shalom*, Piotrkow, 1907, p. 49.
9. *Eretz Zevi*, Warsaw, 1874, see Rabinovitz, H. M. *Rabbi Simha Bunam of Presysucha*, Tel Aviv, 1944, p. 10.
10. Shinover, Samuel, *Ramatayim Zoffim*, Warsaw, 1881, p. 178.
11. Levinstein, J. *Siah Sarfei Kodesh*, Lodz, 1928, Vol. III, p. 14.
12. Shinover, *op. cit.*, p. 163.
13. Shipper, J. *Zydzi . . . w dobie powstania Listopadowego*, Warsaw, 1923, quoted by Rabinowitz, *op. cit.*, p. 36.
14. Kamelhaer, Y. D. *Dor Deah*, New York, 1952, p. 278.
15. Rabbi Samuel of Sochaczew, *Shem Mishmuel*, Piotrkow, 1927, *Toledot*.
16. Levinstein, J. *Simhat Yisrael*, Piotrkow, 1910, p. 56.
17. *Ibid.*, p. 127.

NOTE FOR CHAPTER 12

1. See Fox, Joseph, *Rabbi Menahem Mendel of Kotzk*, Jerusalem, 1967; Urein, Meir. *Sneh Bo'er Be'Kotzk*, Jerusalem, 1962; *Kottzker mayses: 50 vunderlekhe mayses*, ed. Luzer Bergman, Warsaw, 1924; Glikman, P. Z. *Der Kotzker rebbe admor rebb Menachem Mendel*, Piotrkow, 1938–9.

NOTES FOR CHAPTER 13

1. P. 3. A. I. Bromberg, *R. Israel Friedmann of Rizhyn*, Jerusalem, 1955; Josef Fraenkel, "Der Ryzyner Wunderrabbiner fluchtet aus Russland" *Neue Welt* (Vienna), February, 1967, also *Die Stimme* (Vienna), December, 1966: Eliyahu Kitov, *Keter Malchut-Rabbi Israel of Rizhyn*, Jerusalem, 1967.
2. For the dynasty of Belz see M. E. Gutmann (in the series) *Miggbore Ha-Hasidut* Tel Aviv, 1952; A. I. Bromberg, *Belz*, Jerusalem, 1955, Marcus, *op. cit.*, pp. 224–6.

NOTES FOR CHAPTER 14

1. Wright, P. *Report by Sir Stuart Samuel on his mission to Poland*, London, 1920, p. 35, Comd. 674.
2. Abraham Abele, *Bet Abraham*, Sudzilkow, 1837, end of the book; Jacobs, L. *Tract of Ecstasy*, London, 1963, p. 24.
3. Jacobs, L. *Seeker of Unity*, London, 1966.
4. Nothing, however, is known about the third son of Shneur Zalman and the silence has given rise to many rumours, *Bet Rabbi*, part 1, p. 113.
5. Paragraph 16.
6. Greenberg, L. *The Jews in Russia*, Vol. 1, p. 44.

7. *Outlines of the Social and Communal Life of Chabad-Lubavitch*, New York, 1953 p. 19. Hielman, *Bet Rabbi*, part 11, p. 5, note 1.
8. Lestschinsky, J. *Schriften fur Ekonomic un Statistic* I, Berlin, 1921, pp. 30–32.
9. Dubnow, *op. cit.*, Vol. 2, p. 18.
10. Greenberg, *op. cit.*, p. 33.
11. Schneerson, Joseph, I. *The Tzemah Tzedek and the Haskalah Movement*, New York, 1962.
12. Rawidowicz Lucy S. *The Golden Tradition*, pp. 197–8.
13. Gutmann, *Rabbi Dov Milieowe*, Tel Aviv, 1952; Racker, Joshua, *Der Sandzer Zaddik*, New York, 1961; A. I. Bromberg, *Rabbi Hayim Halberstamm of Sanz*, Jerusalem, 1949.
14. Lyck, 1869, No. 25, edited by Eliezer Lipman Zilbermann.

NOTES FOR CHAPTER 15

1. Bromberg, A. I. *Ha-Yehudi Ha-Tov M'Gostyn*, Jerusalem, 1856; *Bet Warka V'Amshinov*, Jerusalem, 1956; *Rabbi Abraham Bornstein of Sochaczew*, Jerusalem, 1955: *Rabbi Zadok Ha-Kohen of Lublin*, Jerusalem, 1950; Sh. Z. Shragai, "Hasidut Ha-Besht B'Tfisat Izbica-Radzyn" in *Sepher Ha-Besht*, ed. Maimon, pp. 153–201.

NOTES FOR CHAPTER 16

1. *Encyclopaedia shel Galuyot*, Warsaw, II, pp. 220–7.
2. Loewe, L., *Diaries of Sir Moses and Lady Montefiore*, London, 1890, Vol. 1, pp. 354–5.
3. Wolf, Lucian, *Sir Moses Montefiore*, London, 1884, p. 152.
4. Loewe, *op. cit.*, Vol. 1, p. 383.
5. Bromberg, A. I. *Sefat Emet*, Jerusalem, 1956.

NOTES FOR CHAPTER 17

1. Elbogen, I. *A Century of Jewish Life*, Philadelphia, 1945, p. 217.
2. Joseph Samuel, *Jewish Immigrants to the United States from 1881–1910*, New York, 1914, p. 93.
3. Kahan, Israel Meir, *Nidhe Yisrael*, Warsaw, 1894, quoted by Lloyd P. Gartner, *The Jewish Immigrant in England, 1870–1914*, London, 1960, p. 30.
4. *Hamelitz*, xxviii, p. 287 (December 30, 1888), Gartner, *op. cit.*, p. 24.
5. Elbogen, *op. cit.*, pp. 499–500.
6. Laski, Neville, *Jewish Rights and Jewish Wrongs*, London, 1939, p. 73.
7. Bromberg, A.I. *Admore Alexander*, Jerusalem, 1954.
8. Bromberg, A.I. *Admore Neshiz, Lekhovits, Kaidanov, Novominsk*, Jerusalem, 1963. Nahum Perlow, *Shufra de-Yaakov*, Jerusalem, 1964. Z. Rabinowitsch, *Lithuanian Hasidism*, p. 197.
9. *The Jews of Czechoslovakia*, Vol. 1 (New York, 1968), pp. 148–9.

10. Greenberg, Leopold, *Tausant Yahr yidish leben in Ungaren*, New York, 1945, p. 97.
11. Tartakover, Aryeh, "Jewish Migratory Movements in Austria in recent Generations" in *The Jews of Austria*, ed. J. Fraenkel, London, 1967, p. 289.

NOTES FOR CHAPTER 18

1. Edited by A. I. Katsh, London, 1965, pp. 194–5.
2. Zeidman, Hillel, *Togbuch fur Varshawer Ghetto*, Buenos Aires, 1947, p. 147.
3. Ringelblum, Emanuel, *Notisn fur Varshawer Ghetto*, Warsaw, 1952, pp. 297–8.
4. Zeidman, *op. cit.*, p. 64.
5. Elfenbein, Israel, "Menahem Ziemba of Praga" in *Guardians of our Heritage*, ed. Leo Jung, New York, 1958, p. 612; *Ele Ezkero* ("These will I remember") Research Institute of Religious Jewry, Inc., New York, 1957, Vol. 11, p. 61; Prager, Moses, "Tenuat Ha-Hasidut" in *Sepher Ha-Besht*, ed. Maimon, pp. 265–274; and Ungar, Menashe, "Zaddikim Shenesfu Bashavah" in *Sepher Ha-Best*, pp. 274–82.
6. Lewin, Isaac, "Religious Judaism in Independent Poland" in *Israel of To-morrow*, ed. Leo Jung, New York, 1946, pp. 389–401: *Late Summer Fruit*, New York, 1960, p. 19.

NOTES FOR CHAPTER 19

1. Spiegel, Shalom, *Hebrew Reborn*, New York, 1962, p. 124.
2. *History of the Jews*, Philadelphia, 1941, Vol. V, pp. 375–6, and p. 381.
3. *Mein Leben*, p. 11, in Pinson, *op. cit.*, p. 6.
4. Also preface to the German edition, Vol. 1, p. 15. The Yiddish edition originally published in Vilna in 1931 was recently reprinted in Argentine.
5. Baron, Salo W., *History and Jewish Historians*, compiled by Arthur Herzberg and Leon A. Feldman, Philadelphia, 1964, p. 285.
6. *Al Proshat Drahim*, Berlin, 1913, Vol. II, p. 29.
7. *Berakhot*, V: 1.
8. *Sotah*, 21b.
9. Jacobs, L. "The Concept of Hasid in Biblical and Rabbinic Literature" in *The Journal of Jewish Studies*, London, 1957, Vol. VIII, pp. 143–54: Buchler, A. *Types of Jewish–Palestinian Piety from 70 B.C.E. to 70 C.E. The Ancient Pious Men*, Jews College Publications, No. 8, Oxford, 1922.
10. *Moed Katan*, 16b.
11. Buber, *op. cit.*, Vol. 1.
12. *Or Torah*, Lvov, 1863, p. 13.
13. *Shabbat*, V: 9.
14. *Rosh Hashanah*, 16b.
15. Wertheim, Aaron, *Halakhot V'Halikhot B'Hasidut*, Jerusalem, 1960, p. 159.
16. *Sanhedrin*, 92a; *Orah Hayyim*, 170: 3.
17. *Moed Katan*, 11. 3.
18. *Shabbat*, 33b.

19. *Maggid Debarav L'Yaakov*, p. 44; Zimmels, H. J. *Ashkenazim and Sephardim*, London, 1958, p. 326.

NOTES FOR CHAPTER 20

1. Judah b. Samuel He-Hasid, *Sepher Hasidim*, ed. by Wistinetzki, Berlin, 1924, 817, p. 207.
2. *Zohar, Beshalah, Vayyehi*, 249b.
3. Aaron ben Zevi of Opatov, *Keter Shem Tov*, Zolkiew, 1794–5, p. 39.
4. Horodezky, *Ha-Hasidut*, p. 296.
5. *Zofnat Paaneah, Toledot*, Dresner, *op. cit.*, p. 82.
6. *Or Torah, Beshalah.*
7. Zeitlin, H. "L'Hasidim Mizmor", ed. M. S. Geshuri, Jerusalem, 1936, p. 52.
8. Teitelbaum, *op. cit.*, p. 283; *Kunteros Haitpaalut*, Warsaw, 1876, p. 5; Idelsohn, *Jewish Music*, p. 416; Newman, *op. cit.*, p. 283.
9. Jacobs, L. *Tract of Ecstasy*, p. 77.

NOTES FOR CHAPTER 21

1. Ashkenazi, Solomon, *Ha-Isha B'Ispaklrit Hayehudit*, Tel Aviv, 1953, pp. 54–6; Horodezky, *Ha-Hasidut*, IV, pp. 67–71.
2. Grunfeld-Rosenbaum, "Sara Schenirer" in *Jewish Leaders*, ed. L. Jung, New York, 1953, pp. 410–11. S. Yarchi, *Sarah Schenirer (Sifriat Netzach)*; Moshe Prager, *Sarah Schenirer Em Be-Israel*(Jerusalem: *Merkatz Beth Jacob*). Z. E. Kurzweil, *Modern Trends in Jewish Education*, New York, 1964, pp. 266–275.
3. S. Yarchi, *Sarah Schenirer*, Sifriat Netzach, p. 10.

NOTES FOR CHAPTER 22

1. *Zohar, Ahre Mot*, 72.
2. *Shibe Ha-Besht*, 29.
3. Eibeschütz, J. *op. cit.*, p. 57.
4. Heschel, A. J. "Rabbi Gershon Kutover" in *Hebrew Union College Annual*, Vol. xxiii, Part 2, Cincinnati, 1950, pp. 20–1.
5. Printed at the end of *Ben Porat Joseph*, Korzec, 1781; Federbush, Simon, *Ha-Hasidut V'Zion*, Jerusalem, 1963, p. 11.
6. *Shibhe Ha-Besht*, 21.
7. *Ben Porat Joseph, Emor.*
8. *Midrash Phinehas*, Bilgorai, 1929, p. 16.
9. Menahem Mendel of Vitebsk.
10. *Likute Tephilot*, Jerusalem, 1953, 84; Halperin, Israel, *Baaliyot Harishonim shel Hasidim L'Eretz Yisrael*, Jerusalem, 1946, p. 20; Shazar, Zalman, "Kisufe Ha-Gehulah V'rayon Haliyah B'Hasidut" in *Sefer Ha-Besht*, Jerusalem, 1960, Mosad Rav Kook, pp. 93–106.
11. Printed in 1859 in the section *Shelah*.

12. Heschel, "Unknown Documents on the History of Hasidism" in *Yivo Bletter*, New York, 1952, pp. 130–1.
13. *Zikhron Ot*, Lublin, 1890, *Shemot*.
14. Morgenstern, Israel, *Shalom Yerushalayim*, Piotrkow, 1925 and Rabinowitz, *Rabbi Simha Bunam*, p. 83. Montefiore stayed in the Holy Land from October 16 to 25, 1827 (*Diaries of Sir Moses*, Vol. I, p. 43) when Simha Bunam was no longer alive. However, Sir Moses left London on May 1 when Simha Bunam was still alive. On Sir Moses and the Hasidim, see Shapira, M. S. "Moses Montefiore Ugdole Ha-Hasidim" in the Jubilee Volume of *Hadoar*, New York, 1927.
15. Federbush, *op. cit.*, p. 48.
16. Bomberg, *Sefat Emet*, p. 109.
17. *The Complete Diaries of Theodor Herzl*, ed. Raphael Patai, New York, 1960, Vol. I, p. 347.
18. *Hazphirah*, 1899; *Jüdische Rundschau*, 1922; Bromberg, *op. cit.*, p. 108; Federbush, *op. cit.*, p. 52.
19. *The Complete Diaries*, Vol. 2, p. 505.
20. *Ibid.*, p. 495.
21. *Ibid.*, Vol. 1, pp. 640–642; Adler, Joseph, "Religion and Herzl" in *Herzl Year Book*, ed. R. Patai, New York, 1961, Vol. V, pp. 271–305.
22. *Responsa Avne Nezer*, sections 453–457.
23. Marcus, *op. cit.*, p. 222; Federbush, *op. cit.*, p. 178.
24. *Ibid.*, p. 179.

NOTES FOR CHAPTER 23

1. *Trial and Error*, London, 1949, p. 398.
2. Bein, Alex, *The Return of the Soil*, Jerusalem, 1953, p. 378.
3. Yehezkali, Moses, *Hazolat Ha-Rabbi M'Belz*, Jerusalem, 1962.
4. *Hamelitz*, 1887.

NOTES FOR CHAPTER 24

1. *Jewish Chronicle*, October 6, 1845, p. 249; July 21, 1854, p. 356; August 22, 1856, p. 698; June 3, 1859, p. 6; March 18, 1870, p. 5; October 22, 1875, p. 484; June 9, 1876, p. 48; March 29, 1878, p. 9.
2. Marx, Alexander, *Essays in Jewish Bibliography*, Philadelphia, 1947, p. 324; Schechter, Solomon, *Studies in Judaism*, New York, 1896.
3. *Children of the Ghetto*, New York, 1919, p. 193.
4. Wohlgelernter, Maurice, *Israel Zangwill*, New York, 1964, pp. 108, 110, 112, 300 and 301.
5. *Dreamers of the Ghetto*, Philadelphia, 1948, p. 280.
6. Copy available from Mr. Leon Gerstler, London.
7. *Minutes of the Federation of Synagogues*, May 17, 1892, London.
8. The *Stiebel* was destroyed in the Nazi blitz in 1940.
9. Hertz, J. H. *Sermons and Addresses*, London, 1938, pp. 108–15.
10. *Ibid.*, p. 113.

11. London, 1899, printed by Elijah Zeev Rabinowicz, 64 High Street, Whitechapel. British Museum shelf Mark, 1967, d. 32.
12. *Darke Hen, Torat Hen.* He died in Jerusalem 8 *Elul*, 1920.
13. *The Jewish Times*, London, August 26, 1920; *The Jewish Chronicle*, September 3, 1920, p. 18.
14. 81 Cazenove Road, N.16. He was the author of *Mile D'Hespeda* printed in London in 1927.
15. Edited by H. Rabinowicz, London, 1948.
16. Rosenstock, Morton, *Louis Marshal, defender of the Jewish Rights*, Wayne State, Detroit, 1965, p. 14.
17. *Va-Joel Moshe, Al Ha-geulah V'al Ha-Temurah, Likute Torah.*
18. Poll, Solomon, *The Jewish Community of Williamsburg*, New York, 1962.
19. "The Lubavitch Movement" in *Commentary*, New York, March–April 1957; *The American Jewish Year Book*, Vol. 66, p. 79.
20. Schiff, Alvin Irwin, *The Jewish Day School in America*, New York, 1966, pp. 66, 77, 209, 87–89.
21. Dresner, *op. cit.*, pp. 121–2.
22. Scholem Gershom, "Martin Buber's Hasidism" in *The Commentary Reader*, ed. by Norman Pordoretz, London, 1968, pp. 451–66; see also "Jewish Messianism and the Idea of Progress" in the April 1958 *Commentary*; Rabinowich, Isaiah, *Major Trends in Modern Hebrew Fiction*, University of Chicago, 1968, pp. 2, 35, 233, 234, 238, 240; Patterson, David, *The Hebrew Novel*, Edinburgh, 1964, pp. 58, 62, 73, 78, 112, 166–7, 190, 207–9.

Glossary

Ab—Fifth month of the Jewish Calendar.

Adar—Twelfth month of the Jewish Calendar.

Additional Prayer—See *Musaph*.

Aggadah pl. *Aggadot*, Lit. "Narration". The non-legal part of Rabbinic literature. The homiletical sections of Rabbinic literature.

Agudas Yisrael—known as the *Aguda*. "Association of Israel"—a right wing ultra religious party.

Aliya—Immigration to Israel, often used to refer to waves of immigrants.

Amidah—Lit. "Standing". The name given to the chief prayer at each of the Statutory services, whether private or public, which is recited in a standing position. It originally contained eighteen benedictions and now contains nineteen.

Amora—pl. *Amoraim*. Lit. "Speaker", "Interpreter". The name given to the Sages quoted in the *Gemara* (q.v.) between the 3rd and 5th centuries.

Ashkenazim—Jews of Central and Eastern Europe.

Baal Shem Tov—Lit. "Master of the Name". A name given to a man who works wonders through his piety and uses the Divine Name in accordance with the concepts of Cabbalah.

Baal Tephillah—Lit. "Master of Prayer". The leader of prayer in public worship. See *Hazan* and *Sheliah Zibbur*.

Badhan—Master of ceremonies and merrymaker at weddings and other celebrations.

Bahur—pl. *Bahurim*. A youth, a name generally applied to a youth attending a Yeshiva (q.v.).

Bat Kol—Lit. "Daughter of a voice". A voice descending from Heaven to offer guidance in human affairs.

Behelfer—An assistant.

Bet Din—Lit. "House of Law" or "Judgement". An assembly of three or more learned men acting as a Jewish Court of Law.

Bet Ha-Midrash—Lit. "House of Study", equipped to serve also as a place of worship.

Bilu—Spearhead group of *Hovevei Zion* ("Lovers of Zion") who were among the first of the pioneers to settle in the Holy Land.

Breaking of the Vessels—Term denoting the idea that the endless divine light that filled all space before creation was broken by the creation of finite beings and forms.

Cabbalah—Jewish mysticism and its literature.

Cheka—Russian abbreviation of the Extraordinary Commission to combat counter-revolutionary sabotage and breach of duty in the U.S.S.R. The name of the Soviet political police (1917–22).

Codes—The systematic compilation of Talmudic law and later decisions composed at various periods.

C.E.—Common Era. The term used by Jews to describe the period of the current Calendar (following the advent of Jesus).

Dayyan—A Judge.

Devekut—Adhesion to God. (From the Hebrew *Davak* "cleave"). *Devekut* involved the practice of Devotion (*Kavannah*) by which man removes the barriers between himself and God and establishes spiritual communion by "divesting himself of his material being" (*hitpashtut ha-gashmiyyut*).

Dibbuk—Lit. "Attachment". The dismembered spirit of a dead person. This theory of metempsychosis was developed by the disciples of Rabbi Isaac Luria.

Divine Chariot—*Maaseh Merkabah*. Lit. "The work of the Chariot". The speculation about the divine chariot "God's pre-existing throne" arising from the description of Ezekiel (Chapter 1) and from other sources of mysticism.

Elijah—Prophet in the Kingdom of Israel. After his ascent to Heaven, the prophet Elijah, according to legend, continued to help his fellow Jews. Elijah is regarded as the precursor of the Messiah.

Elul—Sixth month of the Jewish calendar.

En Soph—"The Endless", "The Infinite".

Eretz Yisrael—"The land of Israel".

Etrog—A citron. One of the "four kinds of plants" used during the Festival. "The fruit of a goodly tree" (Lev. xxiii. 40) was traditionally interpreted as referring to the citron.

G.P.U.—Russian abbreviation of the State Political administration. The Cheka was renamed in 1922 G.P.U. In 1934 it was renamed N.K.V.D.

Galut—Exile, dispersion. The enforced dwelling of Jews outside the Holy Land.

Gaon—pl. *Geonim*. Title of the head of the Babylonian academies (seventh to the eleventh centuries). Also a title given to outstanding Talmudic scholars.

Gelilah—Lit. "Rolling". The ceremony of rolling up the Scroll of the Law after Reading of the Scriptural portions.

Gemara—"Compilation"; the second and supplementary part of the Talmud that interprets the first part, the *Mishnah*.

Gilgul—Transmigration of Souls, or reincarnation.

Glat Kosher—Lit. "Smooth Kosher". It indicates that the meats or the meat products are *Kosher* without any shadow of doubt.

Habad—An acrostic of the initial letters of the Hebrew words *Hokhmah* (Wisdom), *Binah* (Understanding) and *Daat* (Knowledge). The Lubavitch Hasidic movement founded by Shneur Zalman of Liady.

Haggadah—Lit. "Telling". The *Haggadah* is the book which tells the story of the Exodus from Egypt and is ready at the family table on the first two nights of Passover.

Haham—Lit. "Wise Man". The title *Haham* is applied in England to the Rabbi of the Spanish and Portuguese congregation in London.

Hakkafot—Lit. "Circuits". Processions with the Torah around the *Bima* on *Simhat Torah* (q.v.).

Halakhah—pl. *Halakhot*. Lit. "Walking". The legal elements in Jewish teachings embodying the religious philosophy underlying the Jewish religious life.

Haluka—The distribution of funds.

Hanukkah—Lit. "Dedication". The Festival which is celebrated for eight days from the 25th of *Kislev*.

Haskalah—Lit. "Enlightenment". A movement originating in 18th century Germany to break away from the narrow limits of Jewish life and acquire the culture and customs of the outside world.

Hasid—pl. *Hasidim*. An adherent of Hasidism.

Hazan—The Reader who leads the Synagogue Service.

Hebra Kaddisha—Lit. "Holy Society". Society for the performance of the last rites and the supervision of burials.

Heder—Lit. "A room". A private Hebrew school, usually a room in the teacher's house.

Herem—Form of Excommunication.

Hol Ha-Moed—The half festive days or the secular days of Passover and *Succot*.

Hoshana Rabba—Seventh day of the Festival of Booths.

Illui—Talmudical genius.

Immersion—Bathing in a *Mikvah*, q.v.

Iyar—Eighth month of the Jewish calendar.

Judenrat—Council of Jewish elders: a body appointed by the Nazis to administer Jewish affairs under their supervision.

Kaddish—Lit. "Sanctification". A prayer which marks the end of a unit of the service and refers to the doxology recited in the Synagogue. Also a prayer in memory of a dead person.

Kaftan—(Polish), Long coat.

Kapote—(Yiddish), Long black coat, formerly common among Jews of Eastern Europe.

Kavanah—pl. *Kavanot*. Lit. "Aiming", "Concentration". Devotion in Prayer.

Kelipot—Lit. "Shells" or "Husks". The spirits of impurity or the principles of evil. It is frequently used in Cabbalah to denote "Evil" and the source of sensual desires.

Kiddush—The benediction recited to inaugurate Sabbath and festivals, usually over a cup of wine before the meal.

Kislev—The ninth month of the Jewish calendar, usually coinciding with November–December.

Klaus—The prayer room of a private congregation of worship: chapel.

Kohen—pl. *Kohanim*. Male descendants of Aaron, from the tribe of Levi who are subject to certain privileges and restrictions.

Kol Nidre—"All Vows". Opening words of the formula preceding the religious service on the eve of the Day of Atonement (*Yom Kippur*).

Kvitel—(Yiddish), Note of request. A petition written on slips of paper, containing the name of the suppliant, the name of his mother and the request.

Lag B'Omer—The thirty-third day of the *Omer*, corresponding to the eighteenth day of *Iyar*. It is observed as a minor holiday.

Lurian Cabbalah—The mysticism that Rabbi Isaac Luria introduced into the teaching of the Cabbalah in the sixteenth century.

Maggid—pl. *Maggidim*. Popular preachers.

Matzah—Lit. "Unleavened bread".

Matzah Shemurah—Lit. "Guarded *Matzot*". Matzot which have been carefully supervised from the time of the cutting of the wheat to the final baking.

Megillah—Lit. "Scroll". A term commonly applied to the Book of Esther.

Menorah—Seven-branched candelabrum.

Merkabah—See Divine Chariot.

Meshulah—Lit. "Messenger". A person who collects donations for religious or charitable institutions.

Mezuzah—A small parchment inscribed with twenty-two lines of Biblical verses that is attached to the door-post.

Midrash—pl. *Midrashim.* Lit. "Expositions". Books of Talmudic and post-Talmudic times that deal with the homiletical exegesis of the Scripture.

Mikvah—Ritual bath.

Minhag—pl. *Minhagim.* Custom. Local rite or custom in the variant liturgical usages.

Mishnah—Lit. "Repetition". The collection of the statements of the *Tannaim* (q.v.) edited by Rabbi Judah the Patriarch 135–220.

Mitnaged—pl. *Mitnagdim.* Lit. "Opponents". The avowed opponents of Hasidism.

Mitzvah—Lit. "Commandment". A religious act or a deed of piety. There are two kinds of *Mitzvot*, Positive Commandments and Negative Commandments.

Musaph—Lit. "Addition". The additional *Amidah* recited during the morning service on Sabbath and Festivals.

Musar—Ethical literature.

Nasi—Lit. "Prince".

Neila—"Closing". The closing prayers of the Day of Atonement.

Nisan—The first month of the Jewish Calendar.

Nusah—Pattern, the correct text of a prayer, also the traditional melody of a prayer.

Pale of Settlement—Certain districts in Czarist Russia where the Jews were given permission to reside.

Pesah—(Passover)—The Festival commemorating the liberation of the Jews from their bondage in Egypt. The festival is kept for eight days from the 15th of *Nisan* to the 22nd.

Peshat—Plain meaning.

Pidyan—Lit. "Redemption". The money followers give to their *Rebbes.*

Pilpul—An analytical method used in Talmudic study. A form of Talmudic debate consisting in a display of dialectical skill.

Pinkas—From the Greek "Pinaks" which means "board" or "writing tablet". Minute book or register of Jewish communities. The word occurs in the Mishnah *Abot.* iii. 16, "The *Pinkas* is open".

Piyyut—pl. *Piyyutim.*—Poetical compositions of a liturgical character.

Pogrom—Russian "Destruction". Term used to describe an organised massacre applying particularly to attacks on the Jews in Russia.

Purim—Lit. "Lots". The festival which is celebrated on the fourteenth of *Adar* in commemoration of the deliverance of the Jews in Persia from the hands of Haman.

Rabbi—Lit. "Teacher". A qualified rabbinic authority.

Rav—A religious leader who was appointed by religious scholars.

Rebbe—The religious leader of a Hasidic community.

Rebbetzin—The *Rebbe's* wife.

Rejoicing of the Law—see *Simhat Torah.*

Responsa—Written replies to questions on all aspects of Jewish law by qualified authorities from the time of the late *Geonim* to the present day.

Rosh Hashanah—Lit. "The Head of the Year". The Jewish New Year on the first and second of *Tishri.*

Rosh Hodesh—Lit. "The Head of the Month". New Moon.

Sabbetians—Followers of Shabbetai Zevi.

Sanhedrin—A Council of State during the century or more preceding the fall of the Second Temple, 70 C.E. It consisted of seventy-one members and was presided over by the High Priest.

Seder—Lit. "Order". The Order of the festive meal and home service on the first and second nights of Passover.

Selihot—Penitential Prayers.

Semikhah—Conferment of the title of Rabbi.

Sephardim—Term used to denote Jews of Spain and their descendants; it was later applied to all those who adopted the rite of the *Sephardim.*

Sepher Torah—Scroll of the Law.

Seudah—Meal.

Shadchan—Professional marriage broker.

Shalosh Seudot—The Third Sabbath Meal, eaten after the Afternoon Service on Sabbath and accompanied by community singing and discourses.

Shamash—Beadle.

Shavuot—Pentecost or the Feast of Weeks, celebrated on the 6th and 7th of *Sivan.*

Sheital—Wig worn by women after marriage.

Shekhinah—The Divine Presence.

Sheliah Zibbur—Emissary of the congregation. The Reader at a religious service.

Shemini Atzeret—The Feast of the Eighth day or the Eighth day of the Solemn Assembly on Tabernacles.

Shirayim—Lit. "Remains". The remainder of the food eaten by the *Rebbe*.

Shiurim—Discourses.

Shofar—A ram's horn used in the services of New Year and at the conclusion of the Day of Atonement.

Shohet—Ritual slaughterer.

Shtetel—Village.

Shulhan Arukh—Lit. "Set Tables"—The standard Code of Jewish Law compiled by Joseph Caro in the middle of the sixteenth century and first published in 1565. It contains four parts: *Orah Hayim*, dealing with the ritual obligations of daily life and Divine worship; *Yoreh Deah*, dealing with dietary laws and Jewish home life, *Even Ha-Ezer* on personal status, marriage and divorce, *Hoshen Mishpat*, Jewish civil law.

Simhat Torah—Lit. "Rejoicing of the Law". Name given in the Diaspora to the Second day of *Shemini Atzeret* when the reading of the Pentateuch is completed and re-commenced.

Sivan—The third month of the Jewish Calendar.

Sparks—The divine soul in man is a spark of Godliness. In performing the Divine precepts without material objective the "Sparks" are liberated and returned to their source. The sparks of this broken light wander throughout the universe, and only when they return (after the breakdown of the evil forces in man and in the world), to their original source in heaven will man and the universe be redeemed.

Stiebel—pl. *Stieblech*. Lit. a small room used for prayer by Hasidim.

Succot—*Sukkah*, the booth or tabernacle in which the Children of Israel were enjoined to dwell for seven days. The festival commencing on the fifteenth of *Tishri* (see Lev. xxiii, 33ff). The Festival commemorates the wanderings of the children of Israel in the wilderness.

Takkanah—pl. *Takkanot*. Communal ordinances.

Tallit—The prayer shawl used by males during prayers. It is fringed at four corners (Numbers xv. 38).

Talmud—The general sense of the word is study of the law. It is commonly used in the narrow sense of the comments and discussions (*Gemara*) on the text of the Mishnah by the Palestinian and Babylonian scholars from the third to the fifth centuries C.E. which constitute the Palestinian Talmud and the Babylonian Talmud. The Babylonian Talmud (Bavli) contains nearly 3,000 pages and was edited by Rav Ashi (352–427) whereas the Palestinian Talmud (*Yerushalmi*) was finished in the fifth century and is only one-seventh as long as the *Bavli*.

Tammuz—The fourth month of the Jewish Calendar.

Tanna—pl. *Tannaim*—A teacher quoted in the Mishnah.

Tephillin—Phylacteries; small cases containing passages from the Scriptures and affixed to the forehead and arm during the recital of the morning prayers on weekdays (Deut. vi. 8).

Tevet—Tenth month of the Jewish Calendar.

Tikkun Hatzot—Midnight service bewailing the destruction of the Temple.

Tisha B'Ab—The Fast of the ninth of *Ab* commemorating the destruction of both the First and Second Temples (586 B.C.E. and 70 A.C.).

Tishri—The seventh month of the Jewish Calendar.

Torah—Lit. "Teaching". The whole body of Jewish law (Written and Oral), legislation, practice and tradition.

Tosaphot—Critical glosses on the Talmud by French Rabbis of the twelfth and thirteenth centuries.

Vidduy—Confession.

Wars of Gog and Magog—The prophecies of Ezekiel, Ch. xxxix are interpreted as a vision of a great war of nations preceding the coming of the Messiah.

Yahrzeit—Anniversary of death.

Yeshiva—Academy for Jewish studies especially of the Talmud and religious literature.

Yetzer Ha-Ra & Yetzer Ha-Tov—The evil inclination and the good inclination.

Yishuv—The Jewish community in the Holy Land.

Yom Kippur—The Day of Atonement. The most solemn occasion of the Jewish Calendar, falling on *Tishri* 10 (see Leviticus xxiii. 26–32).

Yom Tov—Lit. "A good day". Name given to a festival or holiday.

Zaddakah—Lit. Righteousness, Charity.

Zaddik—pl. *Zaddikim*. A righteous man. Used frequently to describe a Hasidic leader or *Rebbe*.

Zimzum—"Contraction". The self limitation of the Infinite.

Zohar—Title of the mystical work introduced into Spain by Moses de Leon at the end of the thirteenth century and attributed to Rabbi Simeon Bar Yohai of the Second century.

Bibliography

Abelson, A. *Jewish Mysticism*, London, 1913.

Alfasi, Yitzhak, *Toledot Hahasidut*, Tel Aviv, 1959.

— *Rabbi Nahman Mibraclaw*, Tel Aviv, 1953.

Araten, Israel, *Sepher Emet V'Emunah* (Sayings of Rabbi Mendel of Kotzk) Jerusalem, 1940.

Baron, Salo Wittmayer, *A Social and Religious History of the Jews*, New York, 1965, Vol. X, pp. 31–51, 316–24.

— "Steinschneider's Contribution to Historiography" in *Alexander Marx Jubilee Volume*, New York, 1950.

Ben Yeheskel, M. "Le Mahut ha-hasidut" *Hashiloah*, Vol. XVII, XX, XXII, XXV.

Ben Zion, Raphael, *The Way of the Faithful*, Los Angeles, 1945.

Berger, Israel, *Esser Atarot*, Piotrkow, 1910.

— *Esser Kedushot*, Warsaw, 1925.

Bloch, Chaim, *Die Gemeinde der Chassidim ihr Werden und ihre Lehre, ihr Leben und ihr Treiben*, Berlin-Vienna, 1920.

Bromberg, Abraham Yitzhak, *Rabbi Moses Teitelbaum M'Ohel*, Jerusalem, 1954.

— *Rabbi Abraham Mordecai Alter M'Ger*, Jerusalem, 1966.

Buber, Martin, *Die Chassidischen Bücher*, Hellerau, 1928.

— *The Origin and Meaning of Hasidism*, translated by M. Friedmann, New York, 1960.

— *Hasidism*, New York, 1948.

— *Tales of the Hasidim, The Early Masters*, trans. by Olga Marx, New York, 1947.

— *Tales of the Hasidim, The Later Masters*, trans. by Olga Marx, New York, 1961.

— *Jewish Mysticism and the Legends of the Baal Shem*, London, 1931.

— *For the Sake of Heaven*, trans. by Ludwig Lewisohn, Philadelphia, 1958.

Buber, Martin, *Or Ha-Ganuz*, Tel Aviv, 1957.
— *The Tales of Rabbi Nachman*, trans. by Maurice Friedman, New York, 1956.
— *The Legends of the Baal Shem*, trans. by M. Friedman, London, 1956.
Bunim, H. I., "Ha-Hasidut Ha-Habadit" *Hashiloah*, Vol. xxviii (1913), pp. 250–8, 348–58; xxix (1913), pp. 217–27; xxi (1914–15), pp. 242–52.
— *Mishneh Habad*, Warsaw, 1936.
Chavel, B. "Shneur Zalman of Liady" in *Jewish Leaders*, ed. L. Jung, New York, 1953, pp. 25–51.
Dawidowicz, Lucy S., *The Golden Tradition*, London, 1967.
Dinaburg, Ben Zion, "Reisaht shel ha-hasidut V'yesodateha ha-Socialism V'amshishim" in *Zion*, Vol. viii (1934), pp. 107–15, 117–34, 179–200; ix, pp. 39–45, 89–108, 186–97; x (1945), pp. 67–77, 149–96.
Dubnow, Simon M. *History of the Jews in Russia and Poland*, trans. by I. Friedlaender, 3 vols. Philadelphia, 1916–20.
— *Pinkas Ha-Medinah* (The Minutes of the Lithuanian Council of Provinces), Berlin, 1925.
— "The Council of Four Lands in Poland and its attitude towards the Communities" in *Sefer ha-Yobel* (Jubilee volume in honour of *Nahum Sokolow*, Warsaw, 1904, pp. 250–61.
Dubnow, Simon M. *Toledot Ha-Hasidut*, Tel Aviv, 1960.
Ele Ezkero "These will I remember", Biographies of leaders of religious Jewry in Europe who perished during the years 1939–45, published by the Research Institute of Religious Jewry, Vol. 1, New York, 1956; Vol. 2, 1957, Vol. 3, 1959, Vol. 4, 1961, Vol. 5, 1963, Vol. 6, 1965.
Encyclopaedia of the Jewish Diaspora (Heb.)
  Lublin, ed. N. M. Gelber, Jerusalem, Tel Aviv, 1956.
  Warsaw, Vol. I, ed. Itzhak Gruenbaum, Tel Aviv, 1953.
    Vol. II, ed. Itzhak Gruenbaum, Tel Aviv, 1958.
Finkel, Joshua, "Menahem Morgenstern of Kotzk" in *Jewish Leaders*, ed. L. Jung, New York, 1953, pp. 138–61.
Fishman, Judah Loeb, editor *Sepher ha-Besht* ("Book of the Besht"), Jerusalem, 1960.
Frank, Jacob. *L'Toledot Ha-Tenuah Ha-Frankit*, Tel Aviv, 1934.
Frankel, Isar, *Rabbi Meir M'Lublin*, Tel Aviv, 1952.
Friedenson, Joseph. "A concise History of the Agudath Israel" in *Yaakov Rosenheim Memorial Anthology*, Orthodox Library, New York, 1969.

Friedmann, Maurice, S. *Martin Buber, Mystic, Existentialist, Social Prophet, A study in the Redemption of Evil*, The University of Chicago Library, Microfilm T. 809.
— *Martin Buber, The Life of Dialogue*, London, 1955.
Gersh, Harry, and Miller, Sam. "Satmar in Brooklyn". *Commentary*, 28 (1959), 389–99.
Geshuri, Meir Shimon, *Neginah V'Hasidut* ("Music and Hasidism in the House of Kuzmir"), Jerusalem, 1952.
— *Hanigun V'Harikud B'Hasidut* (Music and Dance in Hasidism), Tel Aviv, 1953, 5 Vols.
Ginsburg, Ch. D. *The Kabbalah*, London, 1865.
Glicksman, Phinehas Zelig, *Der Kotzker Rebbe*, Piotrkow, 1938.
Glittzenstein, Abraham Hanok, *Rabbenu ha-Zemah Zeddek*, New York, 1957.
Goodman, Walter, "The Hasidim come to Williamsburg" in *Commentary*, 19.3, March 1957.
Gourary, S. "The Story of the United Lubavitcher Yeshivot" in *Jewish Education*, 20:1, New York, 1948.
Greenberg, Louis. *The Jews in Russia: the struggle of Emancipation*. Yale University Press, 1955, Vol. 1.
Guttmann, Mattathiah, Ezekiel, *Belz, Mi-Gibore Ha-Hasidut*, Tel Aviv, 1952.
— *Rabbi Dov Milieowe*, Tel Aviv, 1952.
Hager, Barukh. *Malkhut Ha-hasidut*, Buenos Aires, 1955.
Halpern, Israel, ed. *Beth Yisrael B'Poilyn*, Youth Department of the Zionist Organization, Jerusalem, 1953.
Hielmann, Hayim Meir, *Beth Rabbi*, Berdichev, 1903.
Hillman, D. Z. *Iggrot Baal Ha-Tanya*, Jerusalem, 1953.
Horodetzky, Samuel Aba, *Ha-Hasidut, Veha-Hasidim*, Vol. I–IV, Berlin, 1923. Tel Aviv, 1951.
— *Shibre Ha-Besht*, Berlin, 1922.
— *Torah Ha-Cabbalah shel R. Yithak Luria*, Tel Aviv, 1947.
— *Leaders of Hasidism*, trans. by Maria Horodetsky Magasanik, London, 1928.
Idelsohn, Abraham, Zevi. *Jewish Music*, New York, 1948.
Jacobs, Louis. *Seeker of Unity*—The Life and Works of Aaron of Starosselje, London, 1956.
Kahana, Abraham. *Sepher ha-Hasidut*, Warsaw, 1922.
— *Emunat Zaddikim*, Warsaw, 1924.
Kamelhaar, Y. A. *Dor Deah*, Bilgoraj, 1933; New York, 1952.

Kanzler, George. *Williamsburg, A Jewish Community in Transition*, New York, 1961.

Kleiman, J. A. *Niflaot Bet Levi*, Piotrkow, 1911.

— *Niflaot Elimelekh*, Piotrkow, 1916.

— *Niflaot ha-Yehudi*, Warsaw, 1925.

— *Niflaot ha-Maggid M'Koziniece*, Piotrkow, 1911.

— *Niflaot Rabbi Bunam*, Warsaw, 1926.

Landau, Bezalel, *Ha-Gaon Ha-Hasid M'Vilna*, Jerusalem, 1965.

Liberman, Chaim, "Reb Nakhmen Bratslaver un di Umaner Maskilim" in *Yivo-Bleter*, XXIX, New York (1947), 201–9.

Lipschitz, Max A. *The Faith of a Hassid*, New York, 1967.

Mahler, Raphael, *Der Kampf zwischen Haskalah un Hasidism in Galicia* (The Struggle between Haskalah and Hasidism in Galicia in the first half of the 19th century), New York, 1942.

— "The Austrian Government and the Hasidim during the Period of Reaction 1818–1848" in *Jewish Social Studies*, I (1939), pp. 195–240.

Maimon, J. L. (ed.). *Sepher Ha-Besht, Mosad harav Kook*, Jerusalem, 1960.

Miller, Ernest. *History of Jewish Mysticism*, London, 1946.

Mindel, Nissan. *Liqqutei Amarim (Tanya)*, New York, 1962.

Minkin, Jacob S. *The Romance of Hasidism*, New York, 1955.

Mintz, Jerome, R. *Legends of the Hasidim*, University of Chicago Press, 1968.

Newman, Louis, L. *The Hasidic Anthology*, New York, 1944.

— *Maggidim & Hasidim: Their Wisdom*, New York, 1962.

Rabinovitz, Zevi Meir. *Ha-Maggid M'Kozienice*, Tel Aviv, 1947. "Rabbi Simha Bunam M'Pzizhi", *Sinai*, Vol. VII, pp. 153–7, 280–295; VIII, 86–8, 159–63; IX, 231–7, 311–17, 347–53; X, 50–60, 327–331, XI, 50–3.

Rabinowicz, Harry M. *A Guide to Hasidism*, London, 1960.

— *The Slave Who Saved the City*, New York, 1960.

— *The Legacy of Polish Jewry*, New York, 1965.

Rabinowitsch, Wolf, Zeev. *Der Karliner Chassidismus seiner Geschichte und Lehre*, Tel Aviv, 1935.

— *Yivo Annual Jewish Social Sciences*, V. 1950, 123–51.

— *Lithuanian Hasidism*, London, 1970.

Raddock, Charles. "The Sage of Sattmur, Hassidism and Israel Politics." *The Jewish Forum*, May, 1954.

Raphael, Yitzhak. *Hahasidut V'Eretz Yisrael*, Sinai, 1, 74–82; Vol. 2, 163–72.

— *Sepher Ha-Hasidut*, Tel Aviv, 1955.

Rodkinson, M. L. *Toledot Amude Habad*, Königsberg, 1876.

Schacter, Zalman. "How to become a Modern Hasid". *Jewish Heritage*, 2 (1960), 33–40.

Schechter, Solomon. *Some Aspects of Rabbinic Theology*, 1910 reprinted, New York, 1936.

Schipper, Ignats. "The Composition of the Council of Four Lands" (Yiddish) *Yivo Studies in History*, 1 (1929), 73–82.

Scholem, Gershom G. "Baal Shem" in *Ha-Entsiklopediyah ha-Ivrit* ("Encyclopaedia Hebraica"), Vol. 9, pp. 263–4. Jerusalem and Tel Aviv, 1958.

— "Devekuth, Communion with God in Early Hasidic Doctrine." *The Review of Religion*, 15 (1950), 115–39.

— *Major Trends in Jewish Mysticism*, London, 1955.

— "Martin Buber's Hasidism". *Commentary*, 32 (1961), 218–25.

— *Shabtai Tsevi*, 2 Vols., Tel Aviv, 1956–7.

Steinmann, Eliezer. *The Garden of Hassidism*. Translated by Haim Shachter, Jerusalem: World Zionist Organization, 1961.

— *Beer Ha-Hasidut*, Tel Aviv, 1958.

— *Sepher Mishnat Habad*, Tel Aviv, 1957, 2 Vols.

— *Shaar Ha-Hasidut*, Tel Aviv, 1957.

— *Beer Ha-Hasidut, Sepher al Admore Poilyn*, Tel Aviv, n.d.

— *Kitve Rabbi Nahman*, Tel Aviv, 1956.

Teitelbaum, M. *Ha-Rab Miladi U-Miphleget Habad*, Part I, Warsaw, 1910. Part II, Warsaw, 1913.

Tishby, I. *"Bein Shabtaut le-hasidut"* ("Between Sabbatianism and Hasidism"). *Knesset*, 9 (1945), 268–338.

— and Dann, J. *Hasidut* in *Ha-Entsiklopediyah ha-ivrit*, 17, 756–821, Jerusalem and Tel Aviv, 1965.

Unger, Menashe. *Die hasidische velt* ("The Hasidic World"), New York, 1955.

— *Hasidus un Lebn* ("Hasidism and Life"), New York, 1946.

— *Sepher Kedoshim* ("Book of Martyrs"), New York, 1967.

Weiner, Herbert. "The Lubavitcher Movement I." *Commentary*, 23 (1957), 231–41.

— "The Lubavitcher Movement II." *Commentary*, 23 (1957), 316–27.

Weiss, J. G. "A Circle of Pre-Hassidic Pneumatics". *The Journal of Jewish Studies*, 8 (1957), 199–213.

— "Contemplative Mysticism and 'Faith' in Hasidic Piety". *The Journal of Jewish Studies*, 4 (1953), 19–29.

Weiss, J. G. "The Great Maggid's Theory of Contemplative Magic". *Hebrew Union College Annual*, 31 (1960), 137–48.

— "The Kavanoth Prayer in Early Hasidism". *The Journal of Jewish Studies*, 9 (1958), 163–92.

Werfel, Isaac. *Hasidut V'Erets Yisrael*, Jerusalem, 1940.

— *Sepher Ha-Hasidut*, Tel Aviv, 1947.

Wertheim, Aaron, *Halakhot ve-halikhot ba-hasidut* ("The Rites and Ceremonies"), Jerusalem, 1960.

Ysander, Torsten. *Studien zum Bescht'schen Hasidismus*, Uppsala, 1933.

Zeitlin, Hillel. "Maphteah Le Sepher Ha-Zohar" in *Hatekuphah*, Vol. VI, 1920, pp. 314–34; Vol. VII, 353–68; Vol. IX, Warsaw, 1921, 265–330.

— *B'hapardes Ha-Hasidut V'Ha-Cabbalah*, Tel Aviv, 1965.

Zevin, Solomon Joseph. *Sipure Hasidim*, Tel Aviv, 1956–7.

Index